Software Engineering Made Easy

Marco Gähler

Software Engineering Made Easy

A Comprehensive Reference Guide for Writing Good Code

Apress®

Marco Gähler
Zürich, Zürich, Switzerland

ISBN-13 (pbk): 979-8-8688-1385-6   ISBN-13 (electronic): 979-8-8688-1386-3
https://doi.org/10.1007/979-8-8688-1386-3

Copyright © 2025 by Marco Gähler

This work is subject to copyright. All rights are reserved by the Publisher, whether the whole or part of the material is concerned, specifically the rights of translation, reprinting, reuse of illustrations, recitation, broadcasting, reproduction on microfilms or in any other physical way, and transmission or information storage and retrieval, electronic adaptation, computer software, or by similar or dissimilar methodology now known or hereafter developed.

Trademarked names, logos, and images may appear in this book. Rather than use a trademark symbol with every occurrence of a trademarked name, logo, or image we use the names, logos, and images only in an editorial fashion and to the benefit of the trademark owner, with no intention of infringement of the trademark.

The use in this publication of trade names, trademarks, service marks, and similar terms, even if they are not identified as such, is not to be taken as an expression of opinion as to whether or not they are subject to proprietary rights.

While the advice and information in this book are believed to be true and accurate at the date of publication, neither the authors nor the editors nor the publisher can accept any legal responsibility for any errors or omissions that may be made. The publisher makes no warranty, express or implied, with respect to the material contained herein.

Managing Director, Apress Media LLC: Welmoed Spahr
Acquisitions Editor: Melissa Duffy
Development Editor: Jim Markham
Coordinating Editor: Gryffin Winkler

Cover image designed by Freepik (www.freepik.com)

Distributed to the book trade worldwide by Springer Science+Business Media New York, 1 New York Plaza, New York, NY 10004. Phone 1-800-SPRINGER, fax (201) 348-4505, e-mail orders-ny@springer-sbm.com, or visit www.springeronline.com. Apress Media, LLC is a Delaware LLC and the sole member (owner) is Springer Science + Business Media Finance Inc (SSBM Finance Inc). SSBM Finance Inc is a **Delaware** corporation.

For information on translations, please e-mail booktranslations@springernature.com; for reprint, paperback, or audio rights, please e-mail www.bookpermissions@springernature.com.

Apress titles may be purchased in bulk for academic, corporate, or promotional use. eBook versions and licenses are also available for most titles. For more information, reference our Print and eBook Bulk Sales web page at http://www.apress.com/bulk-sales.

Any source code or other supplementary material referenced by the author in this book can be found here: https://www.apress.com/gp/services/source-code.

If disposing of this product, please recycle the paper

Contents

About the Author... xiii

About the Technical Reviewer xv

Foreword xvii

Acronyms xxi

1 Fundamentals of Software Engineering................................. 1

    The Life of a Software Engineer 1
        Writing Readable Code.. 2
        Writing Correct Code.. 3
        Cleaning Up Code 4
        Writing Code with a Purpose 4
        The Four Rules of Software Engineering.................... 5
    Good Code: Some Rules of Thumb 5
    Understandable Code 8
        How Humans Think 8
        Spaghetti Code.. 9
        Examples 10
        AI Code Generation 13
    Single Responsibility Principle 13
        Do Not Repeat Yourself 14
        Advantages of the SRP 15
        Drawbacks of the SRP... 17
    Levels of Abstraction 17
        Real-World Example 17
        Programming Example 19
        The Abstraction Layers.. 21
        About Levels of Abstraction 21
        Summary 24
    Interfaces 25
        Real-World Interfaces 25
        Code Interfaces 26
        APIs 27

		Orthogonality	29
		AI Code Generation	31
	Naming		32
		The Importance of Names	32
		How to Name Things	34
		Naming Functions	36
		Naming Antipatterns	37
		AI Code Generation	37
	Summary		38
2	**Components of Code**		**39**
	Data Types		39
		Lists	40
		Enums	42
		About Booleans	44
		Strings	47
		Dictionaries	50
		Trees	51
		Pointers	51
	Properties of Variables		51
		Compile-Time Constant	52
		Runtime Constant	52
		Immutable Variables	52
		Mutable Variables	53
		Member Variables	54
		Static Variables	54
		Global Variables	55
		Comparison of Variable Properties	55
	Functions		57
		Do One Thing Only	58
		Number of Arguments	60
		Output Arguments	62
		Return Values	63
	Summary		63
3	**Classes**		**65**
	Data Classes and Structs		66
	Private or Public		66
	Different Kinds of Classes		67
		Data Class	68
		Pure Method Classes	68
		Delegating Class	69
		Worker Class	70
		Special Classes	71
		Abstract Base Class	71
		Implementation Class	72

	Inheritance Classes	72
	General Recommendations	74
	One Step Further	75
	Functions vs. Methods	75
	Constructors and Destructors	76
	Getter and Setter Methods	77
	Data Classes	78
	Worker Classes	79
	Delegating Classes	80
	Coupling and Cohesion	81
	Worker Classes	81
	Other Class Types	82
	Coupling and Inheritance	83
	Static Expression	83
	Drawbacks of Classes	84
	Inheritance	85
	Two Types of Inheritance	85
	Drawbacks of Implementation Inheritance	86
	Conclusions on Inheritance	90
	Summary	90
4	**Testing**	93
	Introduction to Testing	93
	A Short Story About Tests	94
	Test Example	95
	Types of Tests	97
	Unit Tests	98
	Integration Tests	104
	Functional Tests	105
	Other Kinds of Tests	106
	When to Run Tests	107
	Who Should Write Tests?	108
	When to Write Tests	108
	The Testing Pyramid	109
	Properties of Tests	110
	What, When, and How to Test	110
	General Thoughts About Tests	112
	Number of Test Cases	114
	Stages of a Test	116
	Problematic Tests	120
	Exceptions and Tests	122
	Not Automatable Tests	123
	Writing Better Code with Tests	123
	Unit Tests	123
	Integration and Functional Tests	124

	Testing Existing Code	125
	Assertions	125
	Test-Driven Development	126
Fakes, Mocks, and Dependency Injection		131
	Mocking	132
	Faking	133
	Dependency Injection	134
Summary		138

5 Design Principles — 139
- SOLID Principles — 139
  - Single Responsibility Principle — 140
  - Open-Closed Principle — 140
  - Liskov Substitution Principle — 142
  - Interface Segregation Principle — 143
  - Dependency Inversion Principle — 145
- Other Software Engineering Principles — 146
  - Divide and Conquer — 146
  - Increase Cohesion — 147
  - Reduce Coupling — 147
  - Increase Abstraction — 147
  - Increase Reusability — 148
  - Design for Flexibility — 148
  - Anticipate Obsolescence — 149
  - Design for Testability — 149
  - Pay Now or Pay More Later — 149
- Summary — 150

6 Programming — 151
- Programming Paradigms — 151
  - Object-Oriented Programming — 152
  - Procedural Programming — 153
  - Functional Programming — 153
  - Temporal Coupling — 154
  - Conclusions — 156
- Programming Languages — 157
  - Existing Programming Languages — 158
  - Code Examples in This Book — 158
  - Python — 159
  - C++ — 161
  - Learning Low-Level Languages — 163
- Physical Laws of Code — 164
  - Entropy — 164
  - Correlation — 165
  - Quality — 165
- Complexity — 167

Contents   ix

	Complexity of Code	167
	Estimating Complexity	168
	Single-Line Complexity	169
	Black Magic Code	170
	Dependencies	171
	The Early Days	171
	The Dependency Graph	171
	Breaking Up Dependencies	172
	Circular Dependencies	172
	Decoupling	174
	Bugs, Errors, Exceptions	174
	Syntax Errors	175
	Bugs	175
	Exceptions	178
	Summary	181
7	**High-Level Design**	**183**
	Software Architecture	183
	The End of Architecture	184
	Designing Interfaces	184
	Separate Libraries	185
	Design Patterns	185
	Factory	185
	The End of Design Patterns	187
	Domain-Driven Design	188
	Ubiquitous Language	188
	The Domain Model	189
	Domain-Specific Language	192
	Domain Boundaries	193
	Building Blocks of DDD	195
	Third-Party Software	200
	Summary	202
8	**Refactoring**	**203**
	Refactoring Fundamentals	203
	There Will Be Change	203
	Don't Let Your Code Rot	204
	Levels of Refactoring	206
	When to Refactor	208
	What to Refactor	209
	Refactoring Process	209
	Refactoring Techniques	210
	Where to Start	210
	Breaking Classes	211
	Renaming	215
	Scratch Refactoring	218

	Extract Function	219
	Further Reading	220
	AI Code Generation	220
	Changing Legacy Code	222
	Nomenclature	223
	Refactoring Untested Code	225
	Problems of Legacy Code	226
	How Do I Get the Code Under Test?	228
	Refactoring Techniques Without Tests	229
	Summary	232

9 Other Common Topics 235

Performance Optimization.. 235
    No Optimization Needed 235
    Optimization May Be Needed 236
    Optimization Certainly Needed 237
    Manual Optimization 237
Comments 237
    Bad Comments 238
    Useful Comments 242
    Commenting Magic Numbers 244
    Summary 245
    AI Code Generation 245
Logging 245
Data Files 246
    CSV 247
    JSON and Co 247
    HDF5 248
    Databases 249
    Custom File Formats 250
    AI Code Generation 250
Setting Up a Project 250
Summary 251

10 Collaborating 253

Working in Teams 253
    Team Structure 254
    Developers Work 255
    Communication 256
    Working with Customers 257
Code Review 257
    Drawbacks 258
    Conclusions 259
Agile 259
    Problems of Waterfall 260
    Agile Was Born 260

		Work Planning	261
		Quality Assurance	262
		Sprints	262
		Becoming Agile	263
		Drawbacks of Agile	264
	Requirements Engineering		264
		Stakeholders	265
		Goals, Context, and Scope	265
		Requirements Elicitation	266
	DevOps		269
		The Early 2000s	269
		Benefits of DevOps	271
	Mental Health		271
	Hiring and Getting Hired		273
		Hiring	273
		Getting Hired	274
	Summary		274

Glossary 275

Index 277

About the Author

Marco Gähler began his career studying physics at ETH Zurich before transitioning to software engineering. In 2018, he joined Zurich Instruments, where he developed electronic devices used in quantum computing. Marco is currently founding a company called EasyCare providing ERP solutions for home treatment. Throughout his career, Marco has observed the pitfalls in code written by self-taught developers, for example, PhD students, and recognized the need for clear, practical guidance on simple programming practices. This book reflects his preference for clear, short functions and minimal class usage, aiming to make good programming practices accessible to all.

About the Technical Reviewer

Naga Santhosh Reddy Vootukuri is a Senior Software Engineering Manager at Microsoft, working within the cloud computing + AI (C+AI) organization. With over 17 years of experience spanning across three countries (India, China, and the United States), Naga has developed a rich and varied technical background. His expertise lies in cloud computing, artificial intelligence, distributed systems, and microservices.

At Microsoft, Naga leads the Azure SQL Database team, focusing on optimizing SQL deployment processes to enhance the efficiency and scalability of services for millions of databases globally. He is responsible for the entire infrastructure of the Azure SQL deployment space and has been instrumental in the development of Master Data Services, a master data management solution by Microsoft. This project earned him recognition for delivering impactful solutions to complex data challenges.

Naga has authored and published numerous research articles in peer-reviewed and indexed journals. He is a Senior Member of IEEE and contributes technical articles as a Core MVB member at DZone, engaging with millions of active readers. He also serves as an editorial board member for a highly reputed science journal (SCI), where he reviews research articles on cloud computing and AI.

In addition to his professional roles, Naga is deeply involved in the tech community as a speaker, book reviewer for Apress, and contributor to platforms like DZone and the Microsoft Tech Community. He recently served as IEEE AI Summit Committee chair and lightning talk chair and selected some of the best lightning talks. He also delivered AI-related workshops and received an AI innovator award from Washington Senator Lisa Wellman. He also served as a judge for the Globee Awards, Fabric AI hackathon, and Cosmos DB AI hackathon on devpost, which further showcased his expertise and commitment to the advancement of technology.

Foreword

The Short Story Behind This Book

Software development is a journey. Every bug fixed is a lesson learned.
—Unknown

I studied physics at ETH Zurich, Switzerland, and I worked as a teacher for a few years before I decided to switch to software engineering. I worked for a few years as a software engineer at Zurich Instruments, a company that develops electronic devices used in quantum computing. There, I was mostly busy developing software for controlling quantum computers.

At the beginning of my time there, I was still a novice in software engineering, but I quickly picked up a lot of new skills. At the same time, I was in touch with many PhD students and realized how poorly written their code was. This is when I came up with the idea to write a book about software engineering. I wanted to write a book for myself at the end of my studies, when I knew the basics of programming, but nobody told me how to structure my code properly. I wanted to write a book that explains everything I learned about good programming practices during the few years I spent in the industry, so that every person with a little bit of programming knowledge can improve their skills to a reasonable level by reading this book. That being said, reading this book will, of course, not be enough to become a proficient software engineer. It also takes a lot of practice and continuous learning.

I wasn't really sure where this book would take me. In the beginning, I didn't even think this would become a real book. I was just writing down my thoughts and ideas – things that I once thought of but couldn't find any literature about or that were only scattered over many different places. My English is fairly poor, and I was never really good at writing essays in school. But as I was reading other books, I got some more inspiration on what to write. As this text got longer and I received some encouraging feedback from my reviewers, I decided to publish this book.

The two books that inspired me the most are Clean Code by Robert C. Martin and The Pragmatic Programmer by Andrew Hunt and David Thomas. I like how they both give some general advice on how to write better code. However, I didn't want to make a copy of these books. Even though there are some similarities, especially with Clean Code, I tried hard to find out why I liked these books and what could be improved, for instance, the code examples given in these books. On one hand, *The Pragmatic Programmer* has no code at all; meanwhile, *Clean Code* frequently has code that is too long to understand.

Therefore, I tried to write a book that has useful topics and, at the same time, some concrete code examples. I really tried to keep the code examples as short as possible in order to make them easy to understand. Always imagine this little piece of code being inside a huge codebase.

If you like long functions and classes, I have to warn you that I don't like them too much. I prefer to structure code with many short functions and very few, small classes. Classes may be useful tools, but they are frequently abused for writing bad code as they are too long and use the member variables as "mini-globals" (*The Art of Readable Code* by Boswell and Foucher). In my opinion, classes should usually do little more than organize data, as done in C-style structs, also known as "POCO" (Plain Old Class Object).

This book contains a lot of fundamentals about software engineering dedicated to any programmer at an intermediate level. However, not all recommendations hold for all fields of software development equally. I'm currently working on some web development, and some recommendations from this book are hard to apply. For example, lines tend to be much longer than I would like them to be, and most of the code is very hard to write tests for. Still, there are many rules in this book that are very helpful. For example, the code becomes much more readable if the functions are short.

As we'll learn, one of the most important aspects of software engineering is that the code is readable. If you think that you have to violate some of the explanations given in this book, feel free to do so. I try to give you some general guidelines, but there are always exceptions. The most important thing is that you understand why you are violating the rules and that you have a good reason for it.

I would also like to mention that computer science is no accurate science and that there are different opinions on various topics. There are cases where my recommendations do not hold. But unless you know exactly why you break these recommendations, I would recommend following the guidelines given in this book.

Whom This Book Is For

This book is dedicated to my younger self at the end of my studies, when I knew what classes were but had no idea what I had to look out for when writing code. This book intends to give you a good overview of what you should look out for when writing code. It is dedicated to everyone who already knows how to write the fundamental syntax of a programming language, though it might take some more experience to understand all the concepts in this book.

I tried to make the rules here as universally applicable as possible. It doesn't matter what programming language you use. I only used Python and a little bit of C++ because these are the languages I'm most familiar with. Though there is no "one-size-fits-all" solution for software engineering, the field has simply become too broad. If you do, for example, web development, not all rules in this book are equally important. However, I believe that there are still plenty of rules that are very helpful for web development as well.

I hope you'll enjoy reading this book.

Zurich Marco Gähler
January, 2025

Acronyms

ABC	Abstract Base Class
API	Application Programmable Interface
AST	Abstract Syntax Tree
AWS	Amazon Web Services
BDD	Behavior-Driven Development
CD	Continuous Delivery
CI	Continuous Integration
CPU	Central Processing Unit
CV	Curriculum Vitae
DAMP	Descriptive and Meaningful Phrases
DB	Database
DevOps	Development and Operations
DI	Dependency Injection
DSL	Domain-Specific Language
FFT	Fast Fourier Transform
GUI	Graphical User Interface
IDE	Integrated Development Environment
I/O	Input/Output
MR	Merge Request, a.k.a. Pull Request
OO	Object-Oriented
OS	Operating System
PM	Product Manager
POCO	Plain Old Class Object
QA	Quality Assurance
RE	Requirements Engineering
SSD	Solid State Drive
SVN	Subversion
TDD	Test-Driven Development
VCS	Version Control System
WSJF	Weighted Shortest Job First
XP	eXtreme Programming
YAGNI	You Aren't Gonna Need It

Fundamentals of Software Engineering

> *If I had an hour to solve a problem, I'd spend 55 minutes thinking about the problem and 5 minutes about solutions.*
>
> —Albert Einstein

In this chapter, we will explore the components that constitute good code. Good code is neither extravagant nor overly complex; rather, it is straightforward and easy to understand. It requires clearly defined levels of abstraction that enhance our comprehension. Additionally, good code must include well-structured interfaces. It should adhere to the Single Responsibility Principle (SRP), which states that each object should have a single, well-defined task. Conversely, violating this principle can lead to a Big Ball of Mud, where the functionality of specific code segments becomes unclear and difficult to ascertain.

The Life of a Software Engineer

I understand that you want me to begin and provide you with some sophisticated code examples. I'm sorry to inform you that this is not happening. We don't even know yet what this book should be about. Of course, you want to become a great software engineer, get an interesting job, earn a lot of money, and live a happy life. But this is not how it works. We first have to sit down and analyze the situation.

Let me start with a very blunt question: "What do you think a software engineer does?"

"They write code" may be your first response.

"They engineer software" is a very smart one.

Indeed, these answers contain some truth. But writing code only represents a small portion of your future workday. One thing you will do is the same as what we are doing right now: analyzing a problem and trying to figure out what to do next.

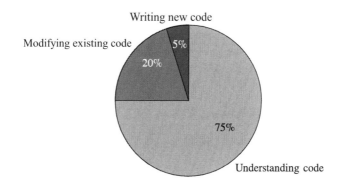

Figure 1-1 Coding activities of a software engineer

You will, of course, spend a fair amount of time with your precious code. But I have to disappoint you once again. It will be like in a marriage: you spend most of your time cleaning up or discussing things. The part that is truly enjoyable only covers a small fraction of it. The plot in Figure 1-1 with highly unscientific numbers that I found somewhere on the Internet sums it up nicely.

You definitely need to take a second look to fully understand the meaning of this plot. You will spend only 5% of your time implementing new features! 5%! Not to mention all the meetings you have to attend as well. Of course, these numbers are only a very rough estimate. They depend on many factors. If you are working on a new project where no refactoring (code cleanup; see p. 203) is required yet, you will have less code to review, allowing you to spend more time coding. In a very large project, it takes more time to implement changes. It can take a year to become fully productive in a large project! But the company has been generating revenue from this code for a long time, so prioritizing the addition of new features is no longer as crucial. Either way, I will continue the discussion with the value from the plot.

The most obvious and undeniable conclusion we can draw from the plot is that software engineering is not merely about writing code. It's about reading code! If you can reduce the time required to read code by half, you will save significantly more time than you spend writing code in total – by a lot.

Writing Readable Code

In accordance with this plot and other fundamental issues in software engineering, I came up with four basic rules that we have to follow. The first one is

> Write code that is easy to understand.

Good code is not fancy; it is not complex, and it is not necessarily short. Good code is simple. It is as simple as it gets. Reading good code should not be like reading Shakespeare; it should rather be like reading Harry Potter, a book series whose vocabulary is comparably limited. This may not be the kind of book you like reading, but it has its merits. Everyone understands it. Even when people are tired, they may enjoy reading it. I sometimes feel embarrassed because of my poor English skills, which had to be improved using some AI tools for writing this book. But writing these lines is really cheering me up. Most people reading this book are not native English speakers either, and, therefore, my somewhat limited language skills may actually be helpful in that regard. It makes this book easier to understand. And I hope I managed to write a good book nevertheless. With code, it's fairly similar. Simple code is good because it is easy to comprehend.

Good code utilizes only the essential syntax provided by a programming language. It is great if you don't know a particular programming language too well. You avoid falling into the trap of using fancy but useless features. Don't learn programming languages; learn programming. Unless you work for a big tech company developing highly specialized software, you will never need all the gimmicks that modern programming languages have to offer.

I'd like to claim that this book covers the most important aspects of writing good code. I barely ever need more than a class and a few functions to explain my point. Therefore, I think that it's possible to write fairly advanced code using only the most basic features of a programming language.

Writing Correct Code

The Second Rule of Software Engineering:

> Write code that can have as few bugs as possible.

Now, it is not only important to ensure that the code works, but we must also verify its correctness. The crashes of two Boeing airplanes in 2018 and 2019 were not the first time that software bugs led to catastrophic damage. Nor will they be the last time, unfortunately.

We don't want to be responsible for people dying or causing other damage. We want to write impeccable code. We want to ensure that there are no bugs to the best of our ability. We constantly check that our code is correct. We test our code. We write automated tests. We're only human, after all. Manual tests are faulty, and no one likes to do them. So we have to write our code accordingly. Test all of your code.

Furthermore, there are some things in software development that are much more prone to errors than others. Most notably, if/else clauses frequently lead to bugs.[1] Try to write code without them. Try to write code that is easy to understand.

Cleaning Up Code

The Third Rule of Software Engineering:

> Constantly clean up your code.

Now, let's return to our lovely plot above. There is one more substantial chunk of work: modifying the current code. As astonishing as it sounds, you have to clean up your code just the same way you have to clean your kitchen. This process is called refactoring, and its importance cannot be understated. It helps you keep the logic of the code under control by sorting things out all the time, over and over again. Without regular refactoring, your code can quickly become a tangled mess, making it difficult to implement any changes. There will be a million places where bugs can hide, though changing code always carries the inherent risk of potentially breaking it. This is one of the reasons why we need good tests. If we have good test coverage, we can change the code with confidence that we won't break it.

Now that you have an idea of what the life of a programmer will look like, you know what to look out for. Now we can do what you wanted me to do half an hour ago: I can explain the fundamental principles of writing good code.

Writing Code with a Purpose

The Fourth Rule of Software Engineering:

> Write code to create value for your customers.

You may already be working in a company, or you will be soon. Your boss is not going to let you write code for a month just because you like it. You will spend a

---

[1] Unfortunately, I didn't find any scientific evidence for this claim. But if you doubt my claim, look at some code with a lot of nested if statements and try to understand what it does. It is very easy to lose track.

considerable amount of time in meetings and engaging in discussions with others to determine precisely what you should do and what your customers want.

If you don't like meetings or customers, you can choose to stay at home and write any code you like. But unless you are a genius, the chances of anyone caring about your code are very low. It is far more rewarding to write mediocre code that is being used than to write brilliant code that no one cares about.

Usually, it is far from obvious what the user really wants. We will go into more detail on this topic in the section "Requirements Engineering" (p. 264).

The Four Rules of Software Engineering

These four rules will accompany us throughout this book, with a strong emphasis on the first one.

> - Write code that is easy to understand.
> - Write code that can have as few bugs as possible.
> - Constantly clean up your code.
> - Write code to create value for your customers.

If you would like to know more about the other rules, I recommend you to read dedicated books on testing, refactoring, requirements engineering, or similar topics. But in this book, we will mainly focus on the first rule. Writing code that is easy to understand.

As software engineering is no accurate science, I can only give you some rough rules of thumb. It is more important to write readable code than following the guidelines given in this book. And if I write "never," you will probably struggle finding a reason why you should violate this rule.

There are different sorts of software engineering. I used to do backend programming using Python and C++. This was the primary target in mind when writing this book. When I was almost finished with writing this book, I started to do some web development, and I realized that some of the things explained in this book are hard to apply. But I can assure you that these four basic rules will always be valid.

Good Code: Some Rules of Thumb

> *Measuring programming progress by lines of code is like measuring aircraft building progress by weight.*
> —Bill Gates

As you probably want to know how to write better code, I will provide you with a list of the most common issues that I have encountered in my career.

First, we have a list of very common issues that I have encountered in my career. I generally use this list to quickly assess the quality of the code.

- Classes and functions are too long.
- The lines of code are too long.
- There are too many levels of indentation.
- There are no unit tests.
- Use of comments instead of good names for variables and functions.
- There are no interfaces recognizable.
- Functions have too many arguments.
- Use of copy-paste code.

For a more detailed assessment, here is a list of rules on how to judge the quality of code. As already mentioned in the foreword, it is not possible to write a conclusive list of rules. These are just some rules of thumb that I have found to be helpful, along with the chapters where you can find more information on the topic.

I'm sorry that there is no inherent order to this list. But it may serve as a lookup table if you have to assess the quality of some code. Furthermore, it may help you find the topics that you may be interested in.

- By definition, good code is easy to understand. Even for new software developers on the team. With good code, even marketing people may comprehend some of your technical discussions as you use the same language. This is explained in the section "Domain-Driven Design" (DDD) (p. 188).
- Good code is well tested (p. 93). It includes unit and functional tests (p. 97). Especially a good coverage with unit tests is essential as it compels you to write high-quality code (p. 123). At the same time, unit tests significantly reduce the number of errors in your code.
- Pretty much all your code follows the SRP (p. 13). Functions, classes, modules. Everything. The build process only requires one command. This makes the code much easier to understand, and naming also becomes simpler.
- Names should be short yet descriptive (p. 32).
- Do not repeat yourself (DRY) (p. 14). Do not copy-paste code around. But also avoid conceptual code duplication. Code duplication is terrible as you can never be sure if making a single change is sufficient, or if it needs to be applied in multiple other locations. This leads to bugs and high maintenance costs very quickly.
- Classes should have high cohesion (p. 65). They should have a strong coupling between the variables (p. 39) and methods (p. 57). On the other hand, they should have weak coupling to other classes. Due to constantly adding functionality, classes tend to lose cohesion. Then, they have to be broken up into several smaller classes (p. 203).
- It feels easy to add features and change code. Thanks to the test coverage (p. 93), you have a safety net, and well-structured code makes it apparent where new features belong (p. 164).

Good Code: Some Rules of Thumb 7

- A function name explains you what the function does (p. 32). There is no surprising behavior. The same holds true for classes and variables. Functions have no side effects (p. 153).
- There are no magic numbers. Assigning the magic number to a variable with a suitable name makes the code much clearer to understand (p. 32).
- Define variables right where they are used. Always assign a value to them immediately.
- Create objects all at once. There are cases where objects are created only partially due to missing information. This is akin to a supply chain issue and should be avoided. Gather all the pieces needed to create an object before doing so. An object should be created completely or not at all. Throw exceptions if objects cannot be created at once.
- Write short functions (<20 lines) and classes (<50 lines) (p. 13). These are very rough estimates and depend on numerous factors, but they shouldn't be longer than these values. Usually, their length is limited by the SRP and the level of abstraction (p. 17). Complicated functions and classes should be kept much shorter than this in order to prevent their complexity (p. 167) from getting out of hand.
- Keep the dependencies between different parts of the code minimal (p. 171). Especially when dealing with third-party libraries (p. 200), it is advisable to create a wrapper (p. 25) around them. This is helpful when you want to replace the library later on.
- Using a debugger (p. 174) frequently is a strong sign that you have lost control of the code. Normally, automated tests (p. 93) should cover all bugs and force you to structure your code that you understand it, rendering the debugger unused.
- YAGNI: You Aren't Gonna Need It. Plan ahead the structure of your code, but refrain from implementing anything you don't need yet (p. 261). Chances are you will never need it. Only architects have to speculate on what will be used in the future (p. 183). Developers implement only features that will definitely be utilized.
- The solution representing the natural logic of the problem is usually the best (p. 188). It has the lowest complexity (p. 167). The complexity of the code is equal to the complexity of the actual problem to be implemented. The sales team can explain the domain logic, and you need to bake it into the code. Don't come up with your own logic on a problem you don't understand well.
- Use the most basic features of your programming language (p. 157). Only use more complex features if you truly benefit from them. Avoid utilizing features of your programming language that resemble black magic.
- Avoid nesting if loops. This violates the SRP and is highly prone to bugs (p. 13). Avoid nested try-catch blocks as well. It is preferable to avoid nested loops entirely. In fact, you shouldn't be having many levels of indentation due to nested logic. These make code hard to understand.
- Avoid using Boolean values (p. 44) and logic as much as possible. Lines dealing with Boolean logic harbor the most errors. Humans are bad in dealing with

Boolean logic. Try to avoid Boolean logic as far as reasonably possible. Ensure that every branch of an if statement is covered by unit tests.
- Avoid passing Booleans as function arguments (p. 57). They are a strong indication of a violated SRP (p. 13). Resolve the consequences immediately and use dependency injection (DI) instead.
- Avoid string comparisons (p. 47). Use enums instead (p. 42). Convert the string into an enum as soon as you have the string object available.
- Write self-explanatory code. Only use comments for aspects that the code cannot explain on its own (p. 237), for example, why something is done. What the code does should be clear from the code itself.

Understandable Code

> Any fool can write code that a computer can understand. A good programmer writes code a human can understand.
> —Martin Fowler

How Humans Think

As we have discussed, good code is easy to understand. But what makes code easy or hard to understand? A computer understands everything. It doesn't care as long as the syntax is correct. And if there is a bug, the computer simply executes it. But we don't care about the computer. This book is written for humans. Code is written for humans. We have to ask ourselves: When does a human understand something? Or what do humans struggle with?

Humans are fundamentally different from computers. We can achieve incredible feats, yet we also have significant weaknesses. Evolution adapted us to our environment. We were made to live in the forest, hunt animals, and socialize with our clan. We needed keen eyes to spot our prey, a vivid imagination to grasp the terrain and wind direction, and familiarity with our hunting companions. These tasks necessitate a great deal of intuition and approximate reasoning. These are challenges that computers or robots struggle with, though they improve thanks to the emergence of artificial intelligence.

One thing is clear: Humans struggle to think logically. We are easily overwhelmed if there is no structure that we can understand. The computer can execute the following line of code without any issues, but I guess only very few readers would be able to determine the result within five minutes.

```
(lambda f, n: f(f, n))(lambda f, n: [
    (not n \% 3 and "fizz" or "") +
    (not n \% 5 and "buzz" or "") or n] +
    f(f, n+1) if n <= 100 else [], 1)
```

The result is the famous "Fizz Buzz" game.[2] Humans struggle with code like this because we struggle to structure it. It is too much code to understand all at once, and most of us can't break it down into smaller pieces.

We are limited by the amount of complexity we can imagine. We are not able to understand this seemingly unordered pile of code. So, there is only one strategy that works: divide and conquer (p. 146). Break up complex problems into many smaller pieces that you can understand. Maybe you will have to repeat this step recursively until you have small enough pieces that you can deal with. This is our area of expertise, where we excel in solving complex problems. Use your imagination!

This is how we are able to create extremely complex objects. We have to break them down into small parts that we understand very well and then build them together like Lego bricks. Every time we assemble a few pieces, we create something new that we give a name to and can explain to other humans what this thing does. It has a higher level of abstraction.

Most people driving a car have a good understanding of how it works. A car consists of various components such as an engine, wheels, brakes, a steering wheel, etc. We can mentally deconstruct a car into smaller parts that we can still comprehend. Now, if the car has a technical problem, we can usually make a fairly accurate guess about which of all these parts broke, even if we are not car mechanics – even though a car consists of many thousands of individual parts.

With code, it should be the same. We should be able to break it down into small parts that we can understand.

Spaghetti Code

I met plenty of programmers who claimed that they were working on really difficult problems. However, the main issue was that they wrote poor code. They all failed to break the problem into small pieces and reassemble them. Or rather, they didn't realize they should do so and wrote spaghetti code instead. You had to take one end of the code and dig your way through the pile of code until you found the actual implementation. The code became so complicated that they were barely able to add any new features. If something is complex, then you absolutely have to break it down. As long as you can explain how something works in words, you can also write it in understandable code.

You should never underestimate the complexity that can arise from poorly written code. If you write a thousand lines of unstructured spaghetti code, it might cost millions to rewrite it. And this is no exaggeration!

This entire book is about writing code with low complexity. The sections on the Single Responsibility Principle, naming, and levels of abstraction are probably the most fundamental ones. It is all about learning how to write human-readable code.

---

[2] https://en.wikipedia.org/wiki/Fizz_buzz

Examples

Structuring Function Arguments

In the following code, one can easily mix up the different arguments, especially when they are all of the same type. This is a very common problem in programming.

```
send_email("google", "new search engine", "it's awesome")
# ...
```

The solution is to use a class object instead of a tuple.

```
from dataclasses import dataclass

@dataclass
class Email:
    to: str
    subject: str
    body: str
email = Email(
    to="google", subject="search engine", body="it's awesome")
def send_email(email):
    #...
```

In Python (and C++ 20), this problem is less prevalent as keyword arguments are supported.

```
def send_email(to: str, subject: str, body: str):
    # ...
    pass

send_email(
    to="google", subject="search engine", body="it's awesome")
```

However, it is still recommendable to use a class instead of named arguments. Classes order the arguments in a logical way. The `email` is of a higher order than the three strings. It organizes these three objects into one logical unit, making it much easier to understand the code.

Some people write functions with 20 arguments. I think this is a really bad coding practice, and using keyword arguments makes it only slightly better. It is clear that they should have structured the arguments using data classes (p. 65). The authors of such code were not able to introduce appropriate levels of abstraction into their code, and now everything has become one big mess.

Complicated Code

Let's review the Fizz Buzz code mentioned on p. 8.

```
(lambda f, n: f(f, n))(lambda f, n: [
    (not n \% 3 and "fizz" or "") +
    (not n \% 5 and "buzz" or "") or n] +
    f(f, n+1) if n <= 100 else [], 1)
```

This example is challenging to comprehend because there is an excessive amount of logic concentrated on a single line. It is very challenging to keep track of all the logic that is happening here. I have to admit that I'm not used to lambdas. Nevertheless, I think it is much easier to understand the code if you break it into smaller pieces, as demonstrated here:

```
output = []
for i in range(1, 101):
    if i % 3 == 0 and i % 5 == 0:
        output.append("fizzbuzz")
    elif i % 3 == 0:
        output.append("fizz")
    elif i % 5 == 0:
        output.append("buzz")
    else:
        output.append(i)
```

This is much easier to understand and therefore the better solution, regardless of it consisting of more code. The amount of code is no merit of quality; only readability is.

Assigning Variables Inside Conditions

Here is an example of how code can become brittle and therefore easy to create bugs: avoid creating assignments within if statements. It is difficult to read and easy to make mistakes. I had to create a C++ example because such code is not possible in Python. Python returns an error message if you make an assignment inside an if statement.

```
if (int t = time_elapsed())
// ...
```

The problem is that you can easily confuse this code with `t == time_elapsed()`. This is a common mistake, and as it's our job to prevent mistakes, we should avoid this kind of code.

In C++ and many other programming languages, it is possible to omit curly braces if there is only one line of code. However, this is error-prone, as people don't pay attention, as has happened before. It's not a big thing, but I recommend always using curly braces. Here is a common bug in C++:

```
if (time_elapsed() > 10)
    cout << "time is up" << endl;
    cout << "this will always be printed!" << endl;
```

If you think that this will never happen to you, think again. We are humans, and we make mistakes. Such code, along with some other deficiencies in the development culture, like lacking test coverage, etc., has already caused a serious security issue in the Apple operating system.[3]

Apparently, in Python, it is impossible to create this kind of bug.

Scope of Variables

It is hard to keep track of variables. One way to mitigate this problem is to use them only in a small scope.

Avoid using `do while` statements if they are supported by your programming language of choice. The issue is that you need to keep track of the conditional variable throughout the entire range of the loop. This is very error-prone because keeping track of a variable over such a long time is challenging. It is much better to use a `while` loop and initialize the variable before the loop.

As `do while` loops are not supported in Python, I provide a C++ example.

```
int i = 0;
do {
    cout << i << "\n";
    i++;
    // lots of code that doesn't use i
}
while (i < 5); // what was i again?
```

The following code using only a `while` loop is easier to understand. `do while` loops are frequently used if you want a loop to be executed at least once. However, this can usually also be achieved by setting the variable of the loop and the condition in the loop accordingly.

```
int i = 0;
while (i < 5) { // you can find out what i is without scrolling
    cout << i << "\n";
    i++;
    // code that doesn't use i
}
```

Though the best solution is, in most cases, to use range-based for loops. This eliminates the need for an index and, therefore, also for index comparisons altogether. Since C++11, range-based for loops have also been available in C++.

```
for(const auto& car: cars) {
    cout << car << "\n";
}
```

---

[3] https://www.codecentric.de/wissens-hub/blog/curly-braces

or in Python:

```
for car in cars:
    print(car)
```

It is generally advisable to minimize the number of variables in use, and they should have only a very small scope. This makes it much easier to keep track of them. If you have to keep track of a variable over a long period, you are very likely to make a mistake. Thus, eliminate intermediate results and make logic as simple as possible. Avoid using control flow variables whenever feasible.

Limit the scope of all variables: avoid globals, keep classes and functions concise, etc. If the scope is larger than necessary, consider making the variable constant if possible. The scope of a variable should never be more than about twenty lines of code, the maximal recommended length of a function.

AI Code Generation

AI code generation tools are generally quite proficient at generating readable code. Frequently, the code is even better than what I write. You can tell that AI tools learned "programming" based on a set of fairly well-written code. It is often beneficial to seek a second opinion from AI code generation as an inexpensive alternative to a code review. I think this is one of the areas where AI tools truly excel. The human-readable version of the Fizz Buzz code on page 11 was written by AI code generation.

Single Responsibility Principle

Every object does exactly one thing. Everything is done by exactly one object.

There are various interpretations of the Single Responsibility Principle (SRP). The original definition was "A class should have only one reason to change,"[4] which, in my opinion, is only a fraction of what the SRP should actually be applied to. The highlighted version above represents my personal interpretation of the SRP. In my opinion, the differences between the various definitions of the SRP don't really matter too much. It is much more important that you understand the general idea behind it.

The SRP is arguably one of the most crucial topics in this book and in all of software development. Every piece of code should have exactly one task. It is the foundation of readable and reusable code.

---

[4] Agile Software Development, Principles, Patterns, and Practices. Agile Software Development, Robert C. Martin

Do Not Repeat Yourself

A direct consequence of the SRP is the "Do not Repeat Yourself" (DRY) principle.[5] You should avoid any kind of duplication in your project. You should not copy and paste your own code (copying from Stack Overflow is fine, though). Instead, you should refactor the code that would be duplicated into a dedicated function. If you have duplicated code, either copy-pasted code or conceptual duplication, it indicates that a task is not being performed by a single object but rather by two or more objects. Instead, write a function and use it from now on. This explanation of DRY covers most cases that violate the SRP.

The DRY principle not only applies to code; it also applies to processes such as constructing your project. If you have to execute many steps by copy-pasting them from some manual to build your project, something is wrong. Instead, you should automate the whole process. Write scripts to build and test your project.[6] The build should run through in one step without any warnings or errors. Warnings are unnecessary mental burdens, even if ignored. Clean them up immediately. The other case involves code that has emerged as duplicated over time. Frequently, the same piece of logic is required in multiple locations, leading to its repeated implementation due to a lack of knowledge. This kind of duplication must be refactored relentlessly. It is very difficult to detect this type of duplication as it accumulates over time. Who knows about every piece of code in a large program? Is it worth the effort to search through the entire codebase for a social security number parser, or would it be more efficient to write a new one from scratch? Writing a new one may be faster; however, this comes at a cost. If the social security number ever changes, it will be nearly impossible to locate all the bits and pieces of code related to it. This could become a significant source of bugs.

As I mentioned, it is difficult to keep track of this type of redundancy. There is no easy way to prevent it. The only way I could think of is keeping the parts of the software small and cohesive so that it is always more or less clear where a certain feature has to be implemented.

One common source of repetition is if statements. They look something like this:

```
if job == "president":
    residency = "White House"
    # ...

if job == "president":
    security_standards = "very high"
```

It is fairly common to have many repeating if statements. Such kinds of `if` statements can be spread around the entire codebase, violating the DRY principle,

---

[5] The Pragmatic Programmer. Thomas and Hunt.

[6] 97-things-every-programmer-should-know, Henney et al.

though it would be quite simple to avoid them, for example, by using polymorphism. Create a `President` class with the appropriate properties.

```
class President:
    def __init__(self):
        self.residency = "White house"
        self.security_standards = "very high"
```

Now you only have to create a `president` object once and pass it around. There is no longer any need for any if statements.

```
president = President()
location = president.residency
```

Another option is to use a dictionary. Dictionaries are great for avoiding switch/match or nested if statements.

```
president = {
    "residency": "White house",
    "security_standards": "very high"
}
location = president["residency"]
```

Exceptions of DRY

The DRY principle does not always have to be strictly followed. It's not always worth trying to find this abstraction with only one repetition of a few lines of code. Also, the overhead of creating a new function might be higher than the benefit gained from refactoring the code. Following the DRY principle increases the abstraction of the code, but at the same time, it also increases coupling. This is a serious issue.

One option is to refactor code only in the case of a threefold repetition, though, generally, I recommend refactoring as soon as you see some repetition that can be refactored out.

Advantages of the SRP

The importance of the SRP cannot be overstated. It alone makes your code an order of magnitude better when applied properly or worse when ignored. It is also fairly simple to learn. There are dozens of reasons why this is the case. Here are the most important ones.

Understanding

A function or class that implements only one thing will always be comparatively easy to understand. It all follows the same logic, and there will be no unexpected behavior. Additionally, the code for a specific problem will be concise as it focuses solely on its core functionality. All other duties are handled elsewhere.

Naming

Assigning names to objects is one of the most challenging tasks for a programmer, and it can be extremely frustrating. Names are always either too long or not expressive enough. This is an indication that you might have violated the SRP. If an object obeys the SRP, it does one thing. Naming an object that serves only one function is typically not that difficult (it's still difficult enough, though). If you choose a name containing an "and," chances are high that you violated the SRP. You are doing two things at once that don't form a new abstraction together.

No Duplication

Any piece of logic should be implemented exactly once. This has the advantage that refactoring becomes comparatively easy since you only have to change the code in one location. Is your payment system in need of an update? Go to the `PaymentSystem` class and make the necessary changes. This is the only thing that has to be done.

You might not be aware of the drawbacks of code duplication, so let me explain it to you. Let's say you are in a US administration and you have to deal with social security numbers. Now you realize that you have to change the parser that checks if the number is valid or not. Sooner or later, you'll have to change your code, either because your code was buggy or because of changing requirements. If you have several (maybe a hundred) places where this parser is implemented, you don't know where you have to change the code, and you'll quite certainly miss one. This may be a huge problem because you are very likely to introduce bugs.

Easy Testing

Writing unit tests becomes fairly simple as well. A class adhering to the SRP is not overly complex. Initializing class instances is likely not a significant issue, nor is comprehending the logic behind it. Understanding the concept of the class makes it easier to identify the key components for testing. Just look at the few public functions. As the class is straightforward, you will immediately be able to determine the expected output of the function.

Less Bugs

Along with easier testing, you will write code containing fewer bugs. As the purpose of each class becomes clearer, it will be easier to structure the logic of your problem. You will only write code that makes sense. You will create fewer bugs, and it's very hard for those bugs to hide. Frequently, you will quickly identify why a bug appeared because it is immediately apparent which part of the code is responsible for the bug's behavior.

Let me provide a real-world example: You are wearing an orange T-shirt, although you should be wearing a white shirt. If the only time you have access to a wardrobe is in the morning after having a shower, you know that it was at that time that you made the mistake. Meanwhile, if you have access to the wardrobe all the time, you never know when you might have incorrectly decided to wear an orange shirt. This example nicely illustrates why it is important to restrict access to objects as much as possible and perform actions in only one location.

Bug Fixing

Tracking down bugs will be much easier. You can understand fairly well what each class should do and, therefore, find unexpected behavior much quicker. Fixing a bug may seem harder at first glance. You are no longer allowed to randomly add an `if` statement in your code. This would violate the SRP and lead to bad code. Instead, you have to find a proper solution. Usually, this turns out to be easier than applying an unsightly hotfix. And especially, it really fixes the bug once and for all. All in all, we can conclude that fixing a bug becomes more challenging, but fixing it correctly becomes much easier if you adhere to the SRP.

Drawbacks of the SRP

There are very few drawbacks to the SRP that I could think of. The SRP is sometimes a bit too strict. It is not always worth obeying it. If a function is very short, it is not necessarily bad to have it duplicated. Adding a function to introduce an additional level of abstraction increases mental workload and may not always be justified, though these are exceptions rather than the norm. When in doubt, it is better to adhere to the SRP and refactor the code.

Levels of Abstraction

You can solve every problem with another level of indirection.

—Andrew Koenig

Except for the problem of too many levels of indirection.

—Unknown

Levels of abstraction are an extremely important concept in software engineering. Yet, it doesn't receive the amount of attention it deserves. It applies to so many things around us, but so few people know about it. It's about taking a few objects and creating a new object with completely different properties. Something completely new emerges.

Real-World Example

You take a CPU, a motherboard, RAM, an SSD, and a power supply – some of the most complex objects humankind has ever created. From some of them, you might have a rough idea of what they do and maybe even how they work. When you assemble these parts, it becomes mind-boggling. So many extremely complex objects. And now we combine them. How is this going to end up? Surprisingly simple. You sit in front of it every day. It's a computer, and all your questions are gone. It represents a higher level of abstraction and is quite simple to use. As I write this book, I only care about the text software that I use. I don't care about the operating system (OS). I don't care about the computer that is standing on the floor. I don't care about the CPU inside. I don't care about the billions of transistors inside the CPU, nor do I care about the quantum mechanical effects that these transistors are based on. My text software relies on all these components, but I don't need to have any knowledge about them. All these things were abstracted away by the next higher level. The text processing program emerged from combining all these immensely complex objects.

One can also look at the problem from the bottom up. Quantum mechanics does not know anything about transistors. Transistors don't know anything about CPUs. CPUs don't know anything about computers; computers don't know anything about the OS, and the OS doesn't know anything about my text software. Some things, like quantum mechanics, just exist. We can't change them, but we can use them to create other objects. Transistors, among other components, are designed to meet the extremely stringent requirements for operating inside a CPU. You could take a CPU, break out a transistor, and use it on its own. It's just a transistor, although it is an extremely small one. You would need an electron microscope to see it. The OS supplies an interface on which the text processing software runs, but the OS does not concern itself with the text processing software. By combining existing objects, you create a level of abstraction. The new object has a higher level of abstraction than the previous ones. It may have completely different properties than the lower levels, also known as emergence. In theory, the higher-level object combines the complexity of all the underlying objects. However, if the higher-level object is well designed, you no longer need to concern yourself with the lower-level objects. Just as it is very challenging to calculate the quantum mechanical properties of a simple molecule, you can still derive accurate predictions about the behavior of a combustion engine or the aerodynamics of an airplane by taking a statistical average of billions of molecules. In the very same way, I can work with my text processing software without having to worry about the quantum mechanical effects in my computer. The properties of the level below are abstracted away.

Creating good levels of abstraction is one of the most important tasks in engineering in general. This is the very core that enables us, as humans, to comprehend and address such exceedingly intricate tasks. You have to break them up into smaller and more manageable blocks that you can understand. One of the main tasks of any software engineer is to find good levels of abstraction that have very simple properties.

Programming Example

C++ is a fairly low-level programming language. Its widespread usage is mostly due to historical reasons. There are many aspects in which newer programming languages outperform older ones. But it's the same as always: the code is working, and it will not be replaced due to some minor inconveniences in the programming language. About a decade ago, some of the most fundamental inconveniences were removed with the release of the C++11 standard.

C++ uses old-school arrays. These commands allocate memory to store objects. If the programmer doesn't know how many objects there will be, they have to use the infamous `new` and `delete` commands to allocate memory on the heap and deallocate it in the end. These commands are extremely error-prone and were extremely difficult to use. If you forgot to use `delete` in a corner case, the software would leak memory. Usually, you had to restart your computer every few days for this reason, as it was leaking memory and became slow.

Here is an example of how to use `new` and `delete`.

```
int * arr = new int[10];
arr[0] = 42;
// ...
delete[] arr;
```

If you use `delete arr` instead of `delete[] arr`, you create a memory leak. Apparently, it is very easy to make mistakes when using `new` and `delete`, so one should avoid using them altogether.

One of the main reasons Java became so popular in the 1990s was the introduction of the garbage collector. It took care of all the deletions. Meanwhile, there are still ways to create memory leaks in Java; however, most issues with memory management were gone. Without a doubt, that was a tremendous improvement at the time.

However, it turns out there is also a solution to the memory allocation problem using only pure C++ code. There is a simple pattern that ensures you always call new and delete in pairs. You create a class that calls `new` inside the constructor and `delete` in the destructor. No matter what you do, every object in C++ is guaranteed to call its constructor when creating and its destructor when deleting the object. The constructor and destructor are each called exactly once. Always. So, if we instantiate `new` inside the constructor and `delete` inside the destructor, they are both guaranteed to be called exactly once. The allocated memory is guaranteed to be freed. Thus, the entire allocation and deallocation process is guaranteed to function correctly.

Here is a very simplified version of what the fundamental idea of the vector class looks like. Our custom `VectorClass` contains an array and manages its size. This requires some logic to understand, but ultimately the user no longer needs to have any knowledge about the array inside the vector class.[7]

```
class Vector {
private:
    int* array;
    int capacity;
    int current;
public:
    Vector()
    {
        // allocate memory inside the constructor
        array = new int[1];
        capacity = 1;
        current = 0;
    }
    ~Vector()
    {
        delete [] array;
    }
    void push(int data)
    {
        // if the array is full, allocate more memory
        if (current == capacity) {
            int* temp = new int[2 * capacity];
            capacity *= 2;
        }
        current++;
    // etc.
    }
}
```

This idea of simplifying the usage of arrays changed C++. One of the biggest problems has been resolved. The user-friendliness has improved significantly. This pattern is used everywhere by everyone and has been called "Resource Acquisition Is Initialization" (RAII) by Scott Meyers.[8]

If there is a code pattern that everyone uses, it becomes part of the programming language. The `Vector` class was created. It is a higher-level object based on the array. It hides all the complex work associated with `new` and `delete` and provides an easy-to-use interface with all the essential functionality one would anticipate. The only price to pay is a slight decrease in performance due to the internal implementation details. This loss of performance is so minimal that you won't be able to measure it using any standard software. This is a perfect example of how

---

[7] https://www.geeksforgeeks.org/how-to-implement-our-own-vector-class-in-c/
[8] Effective Modern C++. Scott Meyers.

Levels of Abstraction

Figure 1-2 The different levels of abstraction in a software project

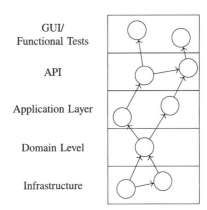

you should let the computer take care of what it can. The loss in performance is minimal, but the gain in usability is very significant.

Vectors are a higher level of abstraction than arrays. They are easier to use and superior to arrays in every aspect. Don't ever bother using old-school arrays. Don't even waste time learning more about arrays. I have told you everything you need to know.

The Abstraction Layers

In your code, you will have different levels of abstraction. Functions and methods of the upper levels always depend on the layers of lower levels. The goal of functions and methods is to increase the level of abstraction. You always want to work at the highest level possible in order to achieve a certain task, as working with high-level code is generally easier.

About Levels of Abstraction

The code can be divided into several different layers of abstraction, each one having its distinct properties. Note that this is what many people understand as a layered architecture. However, in my opinion, layered architecture is just a direct consequence of properly working with levels of abstraction, where each level of abstraction forms a layer. All the properties that people attribute to layered architecture are just a direct consequence of being levels of abstraction. For this reason, I prefer to discuss this topic in terms of levels of abstraction rather than layered architecture.

No matter if you are looking at horizontal layers as shown here, or at onion layers described elsewhere, there is always one rule: dependencies only go in one direction. High levels always depend only on lower levels. This is the essence of the magic: my text processing software relies on the OS, but the OS doesn't need to have any knowledge about the text processing software since the text processing software operates at a higher level.

Furthermore, the dependencies should always be at most one level deep, and they should all rely on the same level of abstraction. Even if some functionality of a high level seems to rely on a very low level, you should still route it through the intermediate level. This is important in order to decouple the levels of abstraction. The text processing software doesn't know anything about the underlying firmware or hardware of the computer. These things got abstracted away by the OS. You should only bypass levels of abstraction if it is absolutely necessary, for example, due to performance reasons. A computer game might have to bypass the OS layer and communicate directly with the graphics card. But these cases are rare and should be the exception rather than the rule.

The code can be divided into several different layers of abstraction, each one having its distinct properties. I like to sort these levels as follows, starting with the lowest level of abstraction:

- Third-party libraries
- Infrastructure code
- Domain level
- Application level
- API
- GUI and functional tests

Of course, there is always a lower level of abstraction. We could also talk about the programming language and assembler code. But for the sake of brevity, I will not go into these details here. On the other hand, we could neglect the third-party libraries or the application level. Defining the layers of architecture is not an exact science and depends on what you are working on exactly.

Third-Party Libraries

The lowest level of abstraction that we look at is the third-party libraries. Modifying code in a third-party library may be feasible in certain situations, but I generally advise against it unless you incorporate the library into your codebase and treat it the same way as all your other code. Doing so is a strong commitment, as it involves a significant amount of work. The only reasonable approach is to contact the authors of the library and offer help to get your suggestions implemented.

As a summary, one can say that third-party libraries do not depend on any of your code. They are the lowest level of abstraction.

Infrastructure Code

One layer above the third-party libraries, we have our own low-level infrastructure code. These are generally all your basic data types and all the input/output (I/O) code. On this level are all the technical details that the user will never see, like the engine parts of your car – parts that the user will not even know about. They can only guess how this stuff could be implemented, but if done properly, they will not have any clue how it's actually implemented, neither in a car nor in your code. Infrastructure code depends only on third-party libraries and nothing else.

The Domain Level

Then there is the domain level; see also the section "Domain-Driven Design" on p. 188. This level is the core of your application. It contains all the business logic of your software. This is where all the complexity of your software lies. It takes an understanding of the business to comprehend this code. The domain model converts the low-level computer language from the infrastructure into human-readable text, although it still adheres to the syntax of a programming language! Every businessperson should be able to comprehend the ultimate outcome of this text.

The domain level is the part that is difficult to develop and cannot be purchased elsewhere. You have to do it yourself. This is what your company will earn money from. It's the core of your business.

The Application Level

The next level is the application-level code. Here, the code follows a logic similar to the problem we are solving. Variables and functions have the same names as those used by the salesperson. It also follows the same logic. If a marketing professional reviews the application-level code, they should be able to comprehend the process and potentially identify any errors.

The application level is not absolutely required. Especially in small projects, you can skip this level. However, in larger projects, I would recommend introducing this level to separate concerns.

API

One level higher is the API. This defines the interface between our code and the user. It is a wrapper around the application-level code. The API provides all the functionality that users would expect in an easy-to-use format. However, the API is not at the highest level; it is still one level below the Graphical User Interface (GUI). It is of utmost importance to decouple the API from the GUI. The API should have no knowledge of the GUI, and the GUI should solely utilize API functions! And the same applies to functional tests.

GUI and Functional Tests

At the highest level are the GUI and the functional tests, both at the same level. If you ever develop a GUI, ensure that its code is entirely decoupled from the rest of the system's code. The only interaction should be through your API. The same principle applies to functional tests (p. 105). The GUI and the functional tests operate at a higher level of abstraction compared to all other code you work with. Already, the programming language for the GUI is completely different. You may write HTML! Due to the SRP, you are not allowed to write any logic in the GUI. Writing tests for the GUI can be challenging. Therefore, the only solution is to write functional tests at the API level and ensure that you never break the GUI by maintaining its simplicity.

Code Example

In the following code snippet, not all lines of code are at the same level of abstraction; therefore, the function does not obey the SRP.

```
def process_email():
    open_email()
    with open('attachment.txt', 'r') as f:
        print(f.read())
    close_email()
```

`open_email` and `close_email` are clearly functions at a higher level of abstraction than `with open ...`. `open_email`, for example, is in the domain level, as it's human-readable code. Meanwhile, `with open ...` is in the infrastructure level of the code, as it deals with low-level details.

In order to ensure that all the code is at the same level of abstraction, we need to relocate the `with open ...` code into a separate function. The code should look like this:

```
def print_attachment():
    with open('attachment.txt', 'r') as f:
        print(f.read())

def process_email():
    open_email()
    print_attachment()
    close_email()
```

Now the code looks much better. All lines of code consist of function calls to higher-level functions. Every line of code within the `process_email` function is at the domain level. They all resemble English expressions rather than typical Python syntax. The cryptic Python code is in our helper function. Note that the overall code has now become a little longer. This is not an issue. The high-level code that you'll have to read more often has become shorter. Meanwhile, the low-level code you don't have to read often if you find an appropriate function name. And always remember: readability counts, not the length of the code.

Summary

As a summary, I want to emphasize once again the tremendous importance of abstraction levels. Different abstraction levels are the key reason we can comprehend highly complex systems. It's your job to define the abstraction levels for your code. Avoid mixing different levels of abstraction.

Interfaces

Make interfaces easy to use correctly and hard to use incorrectly.
—Scott Meyers

An interface is always the boundary between a developer ("upstream") and a user ("downstream"). It is defined by the developer, but it should be designed from a user perspective, as the developer only has to implement it once, while users might have to interact with the interface thousands of times. Therefore, it pays off to design an interface properly, as it was already explained in the chapter on p. 17.

Real-World Interfaces

Functions, classes, libraries, and complete software or smartphone apps all have interfaces. Even technical objects, such as plugs, have an interface. The technical details may vary significantly, but the basic principles are very similar.

"Plugs," you may laugh. Yes, even plugs. Electric plugs in America look different from European ones. It is impossible to plug an American device into a European socket, and vice versa. This is due to historical reasons, but at the same time, it is also a safety measure. It prevents you from connecting an American 110V device to the European 230V grid, potentially causing damage to the device. It's fail-safe. It is a good design that they are not interoperable, even though most devices can now handle both voltages.

An example of poor design is the USB-A port. The USB plug appears symmetric on the outside, but in reality, it is not. Someone once said that you always need three attempts to plug in a device with a USB-A cable. The first time would have been right, but you didn't manage it. The second time was the wrong way around, and the third time you managed to plug it in.

The USB-C port features a much more user-friendly design. You can plug in the cable either way. The lanes can be connected either symmetrically or asymmetrically. The technicians implemented a solution that enabled both types of connections. The two devices involved must negotiate with each other on how to utilize the various lanes of the cable. This was some additional work for the engineers. But once solved, it becomes a very convenient solution for the users.

Another example is water taps for showers, as will be discussed in the section "Orthogonality" (p. 29). There are two tubes for cold and hot water, to which the plumber attached one valve each. This was a pain to use. It took quite a while to set the temperature correctly, and once you changed the amount of water, the whole procedure started again. This was the engineer-friendly solution, not the user-friendly one. This was a bad interface. The new handles allow you to choose the amount of water and the temperature separately. This might be a bit more complicated to implement, but it's much more convenient to use.

Notice how both solutions have two degrees of freedom. A mathematician would refer to this as a coordinate transformation. With the old valve, you and all other users had to perform this transformation yourselves. With the new valve, this issue is resolved permanently through mechanical means.

I hope these simple examples give you an idea of what good interfaces are about. If you design an interface, you should always know your customers. What do they do? How do they think? How will they utilize your product? What are the pitfalls when using your product? This is of utmost importance. A good interface is user-centric. It represents the way the user thinks and conceals all the technical details.

Code Interfaces

Once again, understanding interfaces in general will enable you to write much better code. It's just the same as in the real-world examples above. Try to follow the same principles. Figuring out what the user really wants makes writing a well-designed interface quite easy. Writing some user code examples will help you a lot, as you'll learn in the section "Test-Driven Development" (TDD, p. 126).

Always define an interface from the user's perspective. What does the user want? How do they want to use your code? These are the important questions to ask. Don't just blindly return the values you have at hand.

An interface that is designed from the engineer's point of view is usually poorly designed. It is designed from the wrong perspective. An engineer's interface is easy to implement but not necessarily easy to use, as engineers tend to focus on what they have. They lack the vision of what they could have. Thus, they miss the point of a good interface.

An engineer's interface is like an old Nokia phone. The shape and functionality were mostly determined by the engineers' preferences. The designers had little to say and were only allowed to smooth out the edges. Meanwhile, a good interface is more like an iPhone. Here, it was the other way around. Designers instructed the engineers on the necessary tasks, resulting in a phone with a user-friendly interface. This is how you should design your interfaces. You need someone with a vision for how your code should be utilized, not just an engineer who excels at implementing the code but lacks an understanding of how to use it.

Interfaces are everywhere. Every function (p. 57) or class (p. 65) has an external interface and utilizes multiple interfaces from other functions or classes. This is why understanding good interface design is paramount. Especially with classes, it is challenging to define a good interface that allows the user to perform desired actions without revealing too many internal details of the class. When working with functions, it is important to consider the order in which function arguments should be arranged.

Example

This is a code example for a car. The car has a current `speed` and a `top_speed`. However, the user of this code doesn't know anything about these attributes. They only see the public interface containing the methods `accelerate`, `brake`, and `get_speed`. They don't know anything about the implementation of this class. The variables `_speed` and `_TOP_SPEED` are hidden, and the user doesn't even know they exist.

```
class Car:
    def __init__(self):
        self._speed = 0
        self._TOP_SPEED = 200

    def accelerate(self, amount):
        self._speed = min(self._speed + amount,
                          self._TOP_SPEED)

    def brake(self, amount):
        self._speed = max(self._speed - amount, 0)

    def get_speed(self):
        return self._speed
```

APIs

> With a sufficient number of users of an Application Programmable Interface (API), it does not matter what you promise in the contract; all observable behaviors of your system will be dependent on by somebody.
>
> —Hyrum's Law

If you are expecting a comprehensive chapter that explains all the details of APIs, I'll have to disappoint you. This is a vast topic, and I can only scratch the surface here. I will explain only some of the most important aspects of APIs that I could think of.

An API is an extremely important component of your software. It is the public interface of your software. It is what everyone sees and uses from the outside. Everything we discussed in the interface section applies here as well, but in an API, it is crucial to get everything right. Having a bad API will cost you a lot of money. People won't buy your product if the user experience is bad. They would rather go to the company next door and buy their software: "They even support emojis!" Yes, supporting emojis is important nowadays for business reasons.

That was no joke, by the way. Apple once had an important security fix in one of their updates. They included new emojis in the update as this was a better motivation to install the update than having a security issue fixed.

APIs are an extremely complex subject. Not so much for technical reasons, but rather because you interact with users external to the company. They use your code hidden underneath the API. Every change you make in your code could potentially lead to a bug in your clients' code, even when fixing a small bug in your own code. When maintaining an API, you have exactly one task: never, ever break your clients' code! Now you might think this is doable, but I can promise you will have nightmares.

You are always allowed to add new functionality as long as you do not alter the functionality implemented with the old syntax. The old code is guaranteed to run exactly the same way as it did before, but you can also utilize some new functionality. Conversely, you are never allowed to change or delete existing functionality. This could result in compilation errors or, even worse, bugs in the user code. And that's when customers go on a rampage. "Up to now, the code worked, but all of a sudden, it fails. What the **** did you do?" If you don't understand this harsh reaction, you've never had to work with somebody's API that changed its functionality without notifying you. You would feel exactly the same if your code broke for no apparent reason.

Adding More Functionality

You want to add a new option to one of your API functions, but there is a lot of existing customer code. This code does not currently utilize this new option and won't use it in the future. How can you add this option without breaking this old user code?

The answer is default arguments. The current behavior is set to be the default. After the update, the user can select an alternative option within the function call. This works in all modern programming languages. You don't even need an if statement.

Let's make a brief example. Let's consider the following function:

```
# version 1.0
def my_super_function(arg1):
    return arg1
```

We can easily modify this function with the following code. We added a flag (`arg2`) that alters the functionality. The function now only returns `arg1`, if `arg2` is set to `True`.

```
# version 1.1
def my_super_function(arg1, arg2=True)
    if arg2:
        return arg1
```

However, you can also omit the `arg2`, and the functionality remains the same as it was before the code was changed.

```
my_super_funtion("hello")
```

returns `"hello"`, regardless of the version number.

Removing functionality, on the other hand, is really hard. This inevitably changes the behavior of existing functionality. You are not allowed to do so except under very special circumstances, as explained in the next section.

Semantic Versioning

APIs have version numbers. These are two or three numbers separated by dots. For example, "3.11.2" was the latest Python version at the time of writing. "3" represents the major version, "11" represents the minor version, and "2" represents the trace. The trace is only used in larger projects.

Every time you make a new release, you increase the version number.

- For bug fixes or internal improvements, you increment the trace number. This is for all kinds of changes that the user shouldn't notice or probably doesn't care about. The user should be able to switch to software with a higher or lower trace version without any issues.
- The minor version number is increased for new features. The changes explained so far are still backward compatible as they don't alter any existing functionality.
- The really big disaster begins with major version changes. Sometimes this is required, and it is dreadful. You might think that it's not so much effort for the customers to change some code. "HA!" Think again. Migrating most of the Python 2 code to the major version 3 took 12 years, and support for Python 2 was only discontinued a few years ago. The transition was a nightmare because many available libraries had not been updated yet. Users simply don't have time to update their code to a new major version of your library. So, if you don't want to lose them, you should make sure you don't break the old interface. Only increase the major version of your software if it is absolutely necessary.

Usually, companies support multiple API versions simultaneously. They know that their users need time to adapt to the new version. Some users will never adapt at all. So, the companies are forced to support the old API versions for many more years, even though a better API is available.

Orthogonality

Orthogonality is a mathematical concept. It has been used in software engineering by Thomas and Hunt in their highly recommended book *The Pragmatic Programmer*.[9] Orthogonality states that two objects are at a right angle in the current coordinate system. The first part of this sentence may seem intuitive, but what about the coordinate system? Let me explain code orthogonality by providing a brief example that is familiar to everyone.

On the right-hand side of Figure 1-3, we have old-school water taps. The user has two degrees of freedom (if you're not into math: two function arguments), one for the amount of cold water and one for the amount of warm water. However, this is not what the user typically desires. It turns out that the user wants to be able to control the two degrees of freedom differently. They want to control both the total amount and temperature of the water. The orthogonal solution from the user's perspective is shown on the left-hand side. The solution on the right-hand side is outdated. In the engineer's coordinate system, the solution on the right-hand

---

[9] The Pragmatic Programmer, Hunt and Thomas.

Figure 1-3 Two different water taps

side is orthogonal as it's the easy solution. However, nowadays, users have higher expectations and are no longer satisfied with the engineers' solutions. We expect this coordinate transformation into the user's coordinate system to be performed within the water tap.

In software engineering, we encounter exactly the same phenomenon. We have a downstream person (user) and an upstream person (developer). Both want to work with orthogonal data, but they may be operating in different coordinate systems. Now, it is always the upstream person's job to transform the output to make the data orthogonal in the downstream person's coordinate system. In similar cases, it is always the upstream person's duty to make the downstream person's life as comfortable as possible by converting the data handed over. This also makes sense from an economic standpoint: there is only one developer (upstream person), but many users (downstream persons). So, if the developer handles the coordinate transformation, only one person (or team) needs to do it, as opposed to all users having to do it themselves if the developers don't take on this task. It may not always be obvious how the downstream would like an interface to look. When in doubt, the upstream should return the data in the most general representation. Make sure that no implementation details leak into the interface, even though this is sometimes easier said than done. This general interface has the highest likelihood of being orthogonal from the user's perspective. And try to minimize the interface as much as possible. Less is more.

Frequently, you cannot choose how the data looks when you work with it. For example, if it originates from a third-party library, the data at hand does not align well with the algorithm you intend to use for your specific problem. In this case, you should first orthogonalize the input data before continuing. Separating the orthogonalization and algorithm steps is much simpler than running an algorithm on a data set that is not optimally set up from the beginning. A common example is the coordinate transformation between spherical ($r\phi\theta$) and Cartesian (xyz) coordinates. Some problems are easier to solve in one coordinate system, while others are more easily solved in the other coordinate system. In most cases, it's best to first convert the data into the appropriate coordinate system rather than adapting the algorithm. This keeps the algorithm and the coordinate transformation separate, adhering to the SRP.

Advantages of Orthogonal Systems

Working in an orthogonal system has many advantages:

- Errors propagate directly through the system and are easy to find. They don't spread out.
- Fixing these bugs is easier because the system is less fragile.
- Writing tests for an orthogonal system is easier.
- It decouples the code because the transformation acts as an adapter.

Example of an Adapter

Let's say you have a photodiode (an electric sensor). It measures the amount of light in the room by detecting a voltage. However, this voltage is not the final value you want to work with. Instead, you want to know the density of light. So, you need a function that converts the voltage into the desired units. You do this transformation once, where you get the measured voltage, and this problem is solved once and for all.

```
def light_density_from_voltage(voltage):
    lumen_per_volt = 10.1
    return voltage * lumen_per_volt
```

Now, this function returns the orthogonal data for this specific example. Of course, the transformation required in your code may look completely different. This was just a very simple example. The important point here is that you should do this transformation once and not in every place where you need the light density.

AI Code Generation

AI code generation is generally not very good at writing interfaces. Instead, you should do this yourself and let AI code generation write the code in between. This is generally the better approach compared to writing comments and letting AI code generation define code based on them.

Naming

There are only two hard things in Computer Science: cache invalidation and naming things.
—Phil Karlton

This chapter is a futile attempt to help you find better names. If you are not satisfied with my lousy explanations, I recommend the book *The Art of Readable Code*,[10] which has some more detailed explanations. Though I did my best to distill the most important aspects of naming into this chapter, you probably won't find anything new in that book.

The Importance of Names

How long does a football game last? This is a very innocent question, although people may not agree on an answer. In Europe, most people would say 90 minutes, while in the United States, 60 minutes is the common answer. The reason for these different answers is very simple: names. There are two different sports that share the same name. This can cause some confusion.

The example was cute. Mixing them up may cause amusement, but it does not cause any harm. When it comes to city names, things can get a little trickier. If you miss a job interview because you drove to the wrong city named "Springfield" (there is about one in every state), it can be quite painful. For the healthcare system, it becomes even worse. When there are individuals with identical names present, it can become dangerous. In a hospital, there are issues with using names as an identifier, and so far, there is no unique solution on how to solve it. Using the name combined with the birth date works out quite well, but it is not a perfect solution either. All these things happen for only one reason: name collisions. Various objects share the same name. Names are everything. No matter what you look at, you can name it – a computer, desk, printer, etc. This is the very foundation of our natural language, of every language, including programming languages. In a programming language, we define things by giving them a name. Every variable, function, or class has a name. Every programming construct has a name. You can use this name to search for it on Google or Stack Overflow. But if you don't know the name, you're in trouble.

Choosing good names is paramount in programming. You certainly don't want to encounter name collisions, as explained above. It would cause a lot of confusion and could be the source of many errors. But there is much more to consider when defining the name of an object. We are humans, and we need to be able to read and understand the code. This would not be possible if we used randomly generated names. We need names that provide us with an understanding of an object's purpose and characteristics. This is the only way we can create a mental image of what the

---

[10] The Art of Readable Code, Boswell and Foucher.

code roughly does. It is necessary for everyone involved in the project to understand the meanings of all these expressions. What kind of properties does this object have? Here, we can learn from the law. In the law, every expression has a set of properties. It is well defined what kind of properties, for example, a theft has. "Theft is the act of taking another person's property or services without that person's permission or consent with the intent to deprive the rightful owner of it."[11] We have to do the same when writing software. This is the only way we can prevent misunderstandings and ensure that everyone understands the code.

However, consistency in naming is more important than the actual name. If someone came up with an imperfect name, you either have to change it everywhere or stick to it.

Coming up with your own names is anything but easy. Especially new programmers really struggle to find good names. There are just too many possibilities for naming an object. But there are some rules you can follow, and at least some of the names are quite easy to find. Meanwhile, for other variables, even experienced programmers have to think deeply. In fact, naming consumes a significant portion of our programming time. We do it very often, and there is often no obvious solution; there might be only some vague recommendations. Or, as Michael Feathers stated in his book *Working Effectively with Legacy Code*:

> When naming a class, think about the methods that will eventually reside in. The name should be good, but it doesn't have to be perfect.
>
> —Michael Feathers

If you don't believe me that good names are important, please have a look at the following code:

```python
class A:
    def __init__(self, a):
        self.a = a
        self.b = []

    def c(self, a, b):
        self.b.append(a)
        self.a -= b
        assert self.a >= 0
```

It's just a few lines, but I doubt you have any idea what it does. It's just like reading a foreign language. You might be able to track some of the variables, but you would never know if this was part of a banking software or a weather simulation.

Here is the code with better names. You will understand it in no time. Thanks to the names, you can create a mental image of what the code does.

---

[11] https://en.wikipedia.org/wiki/Theft

```
class Shopping:
    def __init__(self, money):
        self.money = money
        self.items = []

    def buy_item(self, name, price):
        self.items.append(name)
        self.money -= price
        assert self.money >= 0
```

How to Name Things

As I already mentioned, naming is one of the most challenging aspects of programming. I tried to collect and synthesize some rules on the properties of good names. The result is a pretty long list of quite vague recommendations for naming things:

1. Names should be short yet descriptive. Thus, there is a constant trade-off regarding the length of a name. Short names may be unclear, while long names may indicate that the object is difficult to describe. On the other hand, long names are not as detrimental as unclear names. When in doubt, choose a longer name.
2. Should you choose p, price, or price_of_apple? The answer is it depends on the context. In a supermarket, it is clear what the price tag next to the apples refers to, and you don't need to mention that it's a price. However, when you are talking to your friend about the price of apples, you might want to be more specific.
3. Use the same words for creating a name that you would use in a comment. If you use different words, either your abstraction may be bad or your naming is inconsistent.
4. Classes and functions that adhere to the SRP are relatively easy to name because they perform only one task. Vice versa, if it's difficult to find a suitable name, reconsider whether the object adheres to the SRP and rewrite it accordingly.
5. set_color(7): What does 7 mean? Avoid using raw values in your code. Plain values are referred to as magic numbers because their meaning is not immediately apparent. Your code should be understood! Always create a variable instead of using magic numbers. It is better to use set_color(RED), where RED is a constant or, even better, an enum (see section "Enums" on p. 42). Both are much clearer.
6. Well-defined levels of abstraction result in clearly defined and unique properties. This helps with finding names. Maybe you have created a level of abstraction that also exists in real life. At the same time, functions and classes are required to be at a single level of abstraction in order to fulfill the SRP (see section "Levels of Abstraction," p. 17).

7. Name collisions between different libraries are common and nothing to worry about. Use namespaces to distinguish them. Use the `from ... import *` syntax in Python cautiously as this removes this potentially crucial information about where an object is defined.
8. Name collisions within the same library may occur occasionally and need to be resolved. Rename or even refactor one or both variables involved. They might perform very similar functions and should be refactored into a single object. Otherwise, you should be able to find clearly distinguishable names.
9. Use names that are commonly used in real life. Ensure that the object in the code and the actual object have very similar properties. You should be able to communicate with a domain expert (p. 188) about your code, and they should understand at least some of your problems. If they don't understand you, you probably used names or a model that does not exist in reality. You did a great job if a marketer understands your high-level code and can provide you with useful feedback.
10. Use common English words that are familiar to everyone. Avoid abbreviations unless they are commonly used in spoken language, such as "CEO," etc. Whether an abbreviation is "commonly used" depends on the context.
11. You are allowed to adjust the language slightly and sometimes disregard grammar rules. If you have many `fish`, you may call them `fishs` or `fishes` to highlight the plural. Being able to understand the meaning of the code is more important than the usage of proper English. Natural languages have some deficiencies when it comes to explaining things unambiguously. The following code is perfectly viable in Python: `for fish in fishs`.
12. Avoid using "if," "and," or "or" in the names of your variables, functions, and classes. These concise terms may be appealing to employ, but they indicate a breach of the SRP.
13. When a variable is utilized extensively throughout the code, it is important to name it thoughtfully. Consider using a name provided by the marketing team or existing theories and literature. If a variable is used for only about five lines, even i, j, or k is fine.
14. The length of a variable name correlates only lightly with its scope. Variables with small scope may have a short name, while variables with a bigger scope should have long names. However, this is not a strict rule. For example, you may use an `atom` throughout your chemistry simulation, and it is a perfectly fine name.
15. The name of a function should clearly indicate its purpose. There shouldn't be any unexpected behavior hidden in the code. For example, it shouldn't interact with global states, which is generally considered a poor practice.
16. snake_case notation is easier to read than camelCase or PascalCase. This is why I use snake_case notation for variables and functions and PascalCase for class

definitions.[12] Though it is more important to stick to the rules established in an ongoing project than coming up with your own notation.
17. Classes and functions should reveal their purpose through their names. This relieves the developers from reading the internals, thus saving a lot of time. The name should be a part of the domain language (p. 188).
18. Prefer explicit names over implicit names; choose `car` over `steel_frame_with_four_wheels`. Avoid using generic terms such as `data`, `information`, or `manager`. They don't add relevant information and should be omitted. The name `can_buy_food()` is vague compared to `has_enough_money()`.
19. Attach units to a variable name if they exist. For example, `timeout_duration_ms`. Though, once again, consistency is more important. And if you frequently work with units, you should consider using a library that handles units properly.
20. Avoid using negated terms (and preferably avoid Booleans altogether). `is_not_empty` is more difficult to read than `partially_full`.
21. Normal reasoning should be able to help you understand how an algorithm generally scales. A function `size()` should not have a time complexity of O(n). If you want to create a function that calculates the size in O(n) time complexity, you should name it `compute_size()`.
22. At times, it is suggested to use a trailing underscore character for class variables. This is to distinguish them from local variables. However, I think this is a sign of poor code. If you require such a distinction, your methods are likely too lengthy, and your class may be too large.

Naming Functions

Naming of functions becomes less challenging (I would love to write "easier," but it's never easy...) if you follow the rules below:

- The name is a summary of the function content.
- There is no hidden behavior within a function.
- There is no unexpected behavior within a function.
- The entire function body is one level of abstraction lower than the function name.

The following function clearly has a side effect:

```
counter = 0
def log_in(email_address):
    counter +=1
    check(email_address)
```

The function name does not indicate the presence of a hidden counter, making this hidden behavior something that should be avoided. Additionally, side effects

---

[12] https://peps.python.org/pep-0008/#function-and-variable-names

may lead to temporal coupling [see next section] because the order of calling functions with side effects matters.

A more suitable name for this function could be `log_in_and_increase_counter`, but this would reveal that the function performs multiple tasks, contradicting the SRP. A function name should not contain an `and`, as this indicates a violation of the SRP.

Side effects can also become a significant issue when testing code. When calling the function `log_in` twice, the value of `counter` will be different each time. This will make the tests very fragile due to temporal coupling. As we will learn in Chapter 4, brittle tests are a strong indication of poor code quality.

Naming Antipatterns

Useless Words

Sometimes, words within a name can be omitted without losing any information. For instance, instead of using `convert_to_string()`, the name `to_string()` is shorter and does not lose any crucial information. Similarly, instead of using `do_serve_loop()`, the name `serve_loop()` is just as clear. Similar words like `manager` do not add anything to the name of a variable and can, therefore, be omitted.

Generic Names

Another problem is using overly generic names, as shown in the following example:

```
class Airplane {
    def velocity():
        # ...
}
```

What does `velocity()` exactly mean? For an airplane, it can have two different meanings: it can be either the velocity over ground or the velocity through the air. A better name would be `velocity_over_ground()` or `airspeed()`, though, as always, it depends on the context which name is better.

It is quite common for the author of a code to struggle with naming variables and opt for a very generic name. This, however, is really bad practice. Names should be as specific as possible. It is okay to use a generic name temporarily and replace it later when you are smarter. Avoid using generic names in your code; they are a sign of laziness. Even AI tools can help you find better names.

AI Code Generation

Naming is one of the most challenging tasks in programming, and AI code generation is a great aid. One thing you can do is write some code and then let AI code generation find appropriate names for you.

However, at times, you have to write the first letter of the new word in order to get a suggestion. Otherwise, AI code generation simply tends to repeat what you wrote before. Therefore, one can say that AI code generation is a great aid when finding names, but it is not a universal solution to all your naming issues. However, possibly by the time you read this book, AI code generation has improved significantly and can suggest good names for you without any further input.

Summary

In this chapter, we have learned what software engineering is all about: it's about writing human-readable code. This is by no means an easy task and depends on many factors. For example, it is extremely hard to come up with a list of rules how to name things. Yet finding good names is paramount when writing code. If you have bad names, reading your code will feel like reading a text in a foreign language.

Of course, making the code readable is not the only task at hand. The code also has to work. But this is much easier to achieve as you can get precise feedback. You simply run the code, and you'll see whether it works or not. Or even better, write automated tests as we'll learn in Chapter 4 (p. 93).

Components of Code

2

Code essentially consists of data and operations. In this chapter, we will examine data types and functions. Classes will be explained in the next chapter due to their significance.

There are many data types, such as Booleans and strings, that are often misused for storing state. However, high-quality code typically minimizes the use of these types. Strings can be improperly utilized as a primary data type, replacing classes, which constitutes poor coding practice. Good code should contain few strings and even fewer Booleans, as the latter often leads to errors.

Functions have to be short and adhere to the SRP as well. This makes them easy to understand and test.

Data Types

> Primitive obsession[1] is a code smell in which primitive data is used excessively to represent data models.
> —David Sackstein

There are dozens of built-in data types. However, using too many primitive data types is also known as "primitive obsession." Avoid excessive use of built-in data types. Instead, you should use custom types (data classes, structs, and maybe classes) as much as possible. This makes the code more readable and easier to write.

The most common way to structure data is by using nested classes and lists, where one class contains instances of other classes.

---

[1] https://refactoring.guru/smells/primitive-obsession

Using custom types is highly recommended. Utilizing custom types enhances readability and simplifies the writing process of the code. It prevents you from primitive obsession.

Primitive obsession is a very common phenomenon. Integer values are often used to represent time, even though there is typically a dedicated time class in most programming languages. Strings are used to store all kinds of information, as we will see in an example below.

Here is a list of data types that I typically use. They are called differently in most languages. I write the Python name and in brackets the C++ name: floats, ints, lists (vectors), enums, Booleans, strings, dicts (maps), trees, classes, (pointers).

I will provide explanations for all these types except floats, integers, and classes. I don't have much to say about floats and ints, except that I typically avoid using unsigned ints, as advised by the Google Style Guide.[2] Classes are discussed in their own chapter due to their prevalence.

Lists

Lists are the workhorse in programming. Whenever you deal with several values that should all be treated equally, they belong in a list. I would like to emphasize the importance of being treated "equally." When working with a list, you should generally iterate through all elements and perform the same operation on each of them. If you only need one value from a list, it is likely that you should not use a list.

Here is an example of how not to do it:

```
fruits = ['apple', 1.5, 3.1, 'banana', 0.8, 2.1]
print(fruits[4]) # ...?
```

I intentionally made this code so terrible for you to understand. Strings and numbers cannot be equal objects, so they should not be placed side by side in the same list. In C++, this kind of list isn't even possible because C++ vectors and arrays cannot contain objects of different types, at least not without attending a highly advanced course in C++ black magic. In Python, on the other hand, this code is syntactically correct, and it is often tempting to write such a list. Please resist this temptation!

Your code becomes really bad if you store different things in the same list. The print(fruits[4]) in the code example above is extremely error-prone because you have to count the elements in the list. This list does several things at once, and it violates the Single Responsibility Principle (SRP) all by itself. Use data classes instead (p. 65).

---

[2] https://google.github.io/styleguide/cppguide.html#Integer_Types

Apparently, three values inside this list always belong together. A first improvement would be to use a list of lists:

```
fruits = [['apple', 1.5, 3.1], ['banana', 0.8, 2.1]]
```

This provides some structure to the list, making it less likely that this data structure will be used incorrectly. This inner list is still far from optimal. We should use a data class instead.

The code should be rewritten as follows:

```
from dataclasses import dataclass

@dataclass
class ShoppingItem:
    name: str
    weight: float
    price: float

apples = ShoppingItem(name='apple', weight=1.5, price=3.1)
bananas = ShoppingItem(name='banana', weight=0.8, price=2.1)

shopping_list = [apples, bananas]
```

Now the code is much longer, but it is also much better. It is much easier to read and understand. As we learned, this is one of the main quality measures of code. All the elements inside the list are equal. All of them are ShoppingItems. If you can do something, you should iterate over all elements and treat them equally. The data structure is now also pretty safe. Correlated data is all stored together. It is almost impossible to confuse the weight of the apple and the banana. And it's also pretty hard now to make an error when creating the list.

We can summarize: lists are very common. They should always contain objects of equal meaning. If you want to create a list with groups of objects, you should create a data class/struct for these groups and make a list of instances of these classes. If you only need to access a single object from a list, it is likely that your code is bad. You should generally iterate over the entire list and treat all elements equally.

Filtering Lists

Another question: How should you filter lists? The classical way is to use a for loop and an if statement. But there are two alternatives: list comprehensions and lambdas. Both solutions are quite similar (even in performance), so feel free to use the one you prefer.

```
numbers = [i for i in range(1,11)]
odds = [n for n in numbers if n % 2 == 1]
ten_times = [n*10 for n in odds]
plus_five = [n+5 for n in ten_times]
average = sum(plus_five) / len(plus_five)
print(average)
```

Or with lambdas:

```
numbers = [i for i in range(1,11)]
plus_five = map(lambda n: n+5,
            map(lambda n: n*10,
            filter(lambda n: n % 2 == 1, numbers)))
five_list = list(plus_five)
average = sum(five_list)/len(list(five_list))
print(average)
```

I personally prefer the first version of the code, as I am more accustomed to using lists than lambdas. Furthermore, I can read the code top-down, in contrast to the lambda version, where the code has to be read inside out.

Note that the filtering part of both versions could be written in a single line if you insist. However, the line will be pretty long and fairly unreadable. And, of course, one could also use loops. But I'm not showing the loop version of this code as it's too verbose.

Enums

Enums are something that even many experienced software developers don't know about. You don't really need them, but you should know that enums make your code much better. There are several alternative methods to write code without utilizing enums, and they all have some drawbacks.

```
# 1. boolean:
is_blue = True

# 2. string:
favorite_color = "blue"

# 3. integer:
favorite_color = 7

# 4. class instance:
class Blue:
    pass
favorite_color = Blue()

# 5. enum:
from enum import Enum
class Color(Enum):
    BLUE = 1
favorite_color = Color.BLUE
```

The first four options all have some severe drawbacks.

Booleans

The first one is extremely ugly. What does `is_blue = False` mean? Is it red? Invisible? Undefined? There are simply too many different options that can confuse the developer. I advise against using Booleans if possible. Booleans are often used for if-else logic, which is error-prone, and in many cases, enums allow you to write more readable code than using Booleans.

Strings

The second one looks reasonable at first sight. Just write `"red"` and you have a different color. But at the same time, it's easy to introduce bugs. If you write `"blu"` instead of `"blue"`, you might introduce a bug that could result in strange behavior without you noticing either that you have a bug or where the error comes from. The compiler won't be able to help you with this bug. Avoid using string comparisons whenever possible; they are prone to bugs.

There are times when you don't have any other choice than to use strings, for example, if you write or read data from a file. But if you read a file, the first thing you should do is parse it, replacing all the strings with custom data types and enums.

Integers

Third option: 7? A color? No. Please, don't do this to me. This is an example of a magic number and should be avoided. You would always have to look up the number corresponding to one color. This would be very tedious and error-prone, unless it is a well-known international color standard, for example, RGB: `blue = RGB(0,0,255)`.

Classes

Fourth option: Using types is not the best choice in this case. It can be verified using `isinstance(blue, Blue)`, but this process is laborious and not feasible in C++, for instance. Using classes in this case does not offer any advantages, only drawbacks.

Enums

Fifth option: The best solution is certainly using enums, even if it takes getting used to. Enums may seem slightly unusual at first glance due to the `Color::` prefix, and there is no way to alter this. However, this code is really solid and foolproof. If you write `Color::BLU`, you will get an error message because you most likely did not define a color `BLU` inside the enum. This is infinitely better than having a bug (p. 174). Furthermore, most Integrated Development Environments (IDEs) support auto-completion for enums. Gone are the times when you had to look up magic values in the manual. Enums are great. Use them wherever you define a selection from a limited number of options.

Though enums can only be used if you know all possible options when writing the code, if the user can define custom options, string comparison has to be used. Cases where you really have to make string comparisons are rare. It is uncommon to encounter a situation where you receive a random string and then invoke a function based on its content. The only thing you usually have to do with random strings is pass them through your code without altering them.

About Booleans

"Have a seat, my son. There is something very important that I have to tell you. If you hear it for the first time, it may be very shocking. But it has to be said: Booleans are evil."

"What? But... how...? This can't be. Booleans are only a theoretical construct. It's everywhere. The entire binary system consists of Boolean values. What do you mean?"

"Yes, of course, you are right. Let me explain. It's somewhat similar to alcohol. Alcohol does not do any harm if it is inside a bottle. You can drink it and have a great time, maybe the best time of your life. But at the same time, if you drink too much, you can cause a car accident or start a pub brawl. Humans can't handle alcohol. This is why some people say that alcohol is evil. There is a very similar issue with Booleans. Booleans can be used for great things. But at the same time, using Booleans can lead to the creation of bugs. Humans struggle with Booleans. They mix them up too often. And even worse, Booleans lead to if statements. But okay, maybe we should not call them evil, but dangerous."

Of course, I may be exaggerating slightly. But there's no denying that humans struggle with Booleans and if statements. Boolean logic frequently leads to bugs. You will create bugs with if statements if you keep using them. The complexity you have to keep in mind grows exponentially with the number of if statements. Even with two nested if statements, I already struggle to comprehend the whole problem and start guessing instead what they do.

Here are some points to consider when working with if statements:

- Good code design results in fewer if statements.
- Polymorphism can be utilized to avoid using if statements.
- Resolve if statements as early as possible. Use dependency injection (DI, p. 134) instead of Booleans.
- Avoid nesting if statements. Excessive levels of indentation are a sign of poor code quality.
- Avoid passing Booleans as function arguments.
- Consider using enums instead of Booleans; they may make the code more readable.
- Ensure that your unit tests cover all branches of if-else statements.
- Avoid using traditional C++ or Java iterators. Looping over iterators requires comparisons. Range-based loops are much safer and easier to use.

Here is an example how to use DI instead of passing on Booleans:

```
if __name__ == "__main__":
    if "debug" in sys.argv:
        reader = DebugReader()
    else:
        reader = Reader()
    main(reader)
```

Well, yes, we didn't get rid of all `if` statements. This will never be possible. But further down in the code, there are no more Booleans being passed around. Instead, you only have the `reader` object that you can use polymorphically.

Match Case Statements

In case you have a `match case` statement (a Pythonic expression, in other languages called a `switch` statement), you should encapsulate it inside a dedicated function or use a dictionary.

This is not how the code should look:

```
def do_a_lot_of_work():
    # a lot of code here
    # ...
    city_name = "Zurich"
    match city_name:
        case "Zurich":
            return 8000
        case "Bern":
            return 3000
```

This code is flawed for a very simple reason: it violates the SRP, and chances are high that it violates the DRY principle as well. The likelihood is high that this `match case` statement will be repeated multiple times in your codebase. Additionally, it mixes different levels of abstraction. Instead, the `match case` statement should be refactored into its own function.

```
def postal_code(city_name):
    match city_name:
        case "Zurich":
            return 8000
        case "Bern":
            return 3000

print(postal_code("Zurich"))
```

The best solution, in my opinion, is using a dictionary and abandoning `match case` statements altogether. This is shorter and easier to read. If desired, you can still wrap the dictionary in a function.

```
postal_codes = {
    "Zurich": 8000,
    "Bern": 3000,
}
print(postal_codes["Zurich"])
```

For larger dictionaries, this may still appear quite verbose. However, this code will be hidden at a low level of abstraction.

Dictionaries can also be used polymorphically. Depending on the key, it creates an object of a different type. This will prevent some `if` statements in the future, as polymorphism generally does.

```
class Zurich:
    def postcode(self):
        return 8000

class Bern:
    def postcode(self):
        return 3000

cities = {
    "Zurich": Zurich(),
    "Bern": Bern(),
}

zurich = cities["Zurich"]
print(zurich.postcode())
```

However, this is generally an overkill as you now have two locations where you can select the functionality of the object. It is completely sufficient to use *either* a dictionary *or* DI.

In summary, one can say that `match case` statements are not bad at all. Though they could easily be replaced by dictionaries, they should be wrapped inside a function to make them reusable and adhere to the SRP. Additionally, they are a great match with polymorphism in the creation of objects to prevent further `if` statements.

For Loops

A long time ago, for loops required the use of Booleans. Fortunately, these times are long gone. I add this topic here as an example of how to get rid of Boolean comparisons.

There are many ways to implement for loops. If you use them, there are better and worse ways to use them. Let's start with the classical C++ version:

```
#include <vector>
#include <iostream>

std::vector<int> numbers = {1, 2, 3, 4, 5};
for (int i = 0; i < numbers.size(); i++) {
    std::cout << numbers[i] << std::endl;
}
```

Note that I had to use C++ for this example. I wouldn't know how to write such a terrible for loop in Python. There is so much that can go wrong here. You have the < sign, which does a comparison. Comparisons are dangerous because you can always mix up < and <=. These kinds of loops are outdated and should not be used anymore.

One level better is this Python code:

```
numbers = [1, 2, 3, 4, 5]
for i in range(len(numbers)):
    print(numbers[i])
```

Here, we got rid of the comparison. But we still have the index i which can be mixed up. Of course, there are times where you need this index. But generally you can use a range-based for loop instead.

```
for i, number in enumerate(numbers):
    print(i, number)
```

Assuming that you don't need the index i, by far the best code is the following:

```
for number in numbers:
    print(number)
```

Here, you don't need any comparison nor an index. Since C++ 11, you can also use this kind of loop in C++.

Strings

> *You should never use two different languages in a single file. English is also a language.*
> —Adapted from Robert C. Martin

After pointers and Booleans, strings are arguably the third most error-prone data type. Programmers often compare two strings for equality. One of them is written in plain text in the code: a string that is possibly twenty characters long. If a single character is wrong, you have a bug, and there is no way for the computer to know and warn you. Of course, you can make this code work, but it is extremely brittle. You should eliminate such risks whenever possible. String comparison is a potential source of errors, and we should strive to avoid them whenever feasible. Remember, programming is all about avoiding potential sources of errors. As we have already seen, you should always consider using enums if you want to perform comparisons.

Stringly Typed Objects

Some people even start to encode all kinds of logic into strings. This is dreadful. At times, this is also referred to as "stringly typed" to emphasize the importance of using appropriate types instead of strings. See also p. 39.

Here are some examples of strings storing all kinds of information that shouldn't be stored as strings:[3]

```
car.move("3","4")
# Instead of a string you should use integers.
# Or even better: create a Point object.

setattr(light_bulb, "on")
# Better dispatch the function.
# light_bulb.turn_on()

message.push("transaction_started")
# Here you could use an enum
# message.push(MessageType.TRANSACTION_STARTED)
```

I found the following example in the book *Clean Code*,[4] where Robert C. Martin did some refactoring on a unit test. I quite like the book; it served as a model for this book here. However, in this example, he somehow got completely off track. What he explained at first sight all makes sense, but he missed that one should never write code the way he did.

He encoded five Boolean states `heater_state`, `blower_state`, `cooler_state`, `hi_temp_alarm`, and `low_temp_alarm` into a single string ''hbCHl'', where each character encodes whether it was too hot or not, too cold or not, etc. Capital letters represent `true`, while lowercase letters represent `false`. It's such a beautiful example of the kind of logic that can be implemented in strings. But he completely missed the point. Strings should *never* be used to encode logic. To make matters worse, the letter ''h'' is even used twice. Like this, the code becomes even more fragile because the state relies on the order of the characters.

The unit tests written by Robert C. Martin look quite nice at first glance. But it takes some knowledge to understand what these five characters are supposed to mean. Without appropriate background knowledge, it is impossible to understand the meaning of this string. The order of the characters within this string may seem arbitrary, but they must be in the correct sequence. This is not something that should show up in a unit test, nor in your code.

Now let's consider how we could improve things. We have five states that can each be either true or false. Writing a list with five Booleans is probably the first thought, something like `water_state = [False, False, True, True, False]`. This is an improvement over the string logic, but it still requires significant restructuring. As we have learned, all elements in a list should be treated equally and accessed simultaneously. But here, you will probably need only one element at a time: `needs_hot_water != water_state[0]`. Accessing the first element with `[0]` is a clear indication that we should not use a list (p. 40).

---

[3] https://www.hanselman.com/blog/stringly-typed-vs-strongly-typed

[4] Clean Code, Robert C. Martin.

A better solution is to use a data class that stores five different variables, with one Boolean value replacing each character in the string above.

```
from dataclasses import dataclass

@dataclass
class WaterState{
    heater_state: bool
    blower_state: bool
    cooler_state: bool
    high_temp_alert: bool
    low_temp_alert: bool
}
```

Still, this is not optimal yet. What does `heater_state` = `true` or = `false` mean? Let's define an enum instead to make the code more readable.

```
from enum import Enum
from dataclasses import dataclass

class State(Enum):
    on = True
    off = False

@dataclass
class WaterState:
    heater_state: State
    blower_state: State
    cooler_state: State
    high_temp_alert: State
    low_temp_alert: State
```

Now the `heater_state` can be either `on` or `off`. This is much more intuitive to read.

Once you find this solution, it looks so natural. This code is much more readable than the encoded string. It is definitely worth the extra effort required to write this struct and enum. The code has now become significantly longer, but remember: we always write code for readability, not for the fewest lines of code.

The code utilizing this data class, including the unit tests, is very straightforward. Opposite to the string solution, there is no need for logic, usage of indices, or anything similar. It is simply obvious how to use it.

```
if water_state.high_temp_alert == State.on:
    print("Attention: the water is too hot")
```

Natural Language

Many software products are available in many different countries. They have to be available in many languages. But you don't want the translator to write their translations into your code, nor does the translator want to deal with your code. They want to work with only the text visible to the user. They want the text to be placed in a dedicated text file so that they know exactly what to translate. There is no arguing with that. Thus, it is your job to extract all the human-readable text from your code. Upon startup, your software reads this text file and assigns the various strings to the corresponding variables. Selecting a different language is as easy as selecting a different file.

Ultimately, you are left with barely any strings at all. You replaced them with enums, proper logic, and a file containing human-readable text. Only when reading or writing a text file do you briefly have to deal with strings. Then you immediately convert them into data – in theory, at least. For small projects, it is not always worth the effort to convert all strings into objects or dedicated text files.

Dictionaries

When defining your variable, you have two different choices on how to proceed. You may either use normal variables or a dictionary (a map in C++).

```
a = 0
b = 1

vars = {"a" : 0, "b" : 1}
```

These lines do something very similar. They both assign the value 0 to a and the value 1 to b (okay, in the case of the dictionary, it is rather ``a'', but you get my point). Yet, there is a fundamental difference. In the first line, the programmer knows that they need variables a and b as they write the code. In the second case, we have a dynamic data structure. Maybe the programmer knew that there would be ``a'' and ``b'' used as keys. Maybe they didn't, and these dictionary entries were generated by user input that the programmer had no control over.

If the developer knows all the variables that are needed, it is generally advisable to use normal variables. If the data originates from an external source, such as a text file where they don't know the content, they must use a dynamic data structure like a dictionary. At first, this may sound a little confusing. But think about cooking recipes. You might have a few recipes that you define in your code, where the name of the recipe corresponds to the name of the variable. Or, you can write a parser that reads them from a cookbook into a dictionary. Here, you have to use a dynamic data structure because you don't know in advance how the dishes are called and what kind of ingredients will be needed.

Dictionaries are closely related to JSON files and similar (p. 246). They are essentially similar to a nested dictionary serialized into a string. If you ever need to read JSON files, the resulting data structure will be a nested dictionary that you might further convert into nested class instances.

Dictionaries are very helpful. Every time you don't know in advance what kind of data you will be dealing with, you should probably use a dictionary. This is especially true for user input. If you know the data in advance, you should probably use normal variables.

Trees

It is not too often that I've had to create a tree myself, yet I have been working on tree structures for a significant part of my programming career. Trees are an extremely important data structure. When dealing with a recursive data structure, it is highly likely that you should be implementing a tree. This allows you to utilize many standard algorithms that are very efficient, typically with a time complexity of $O(N \cdot \log(N))$. If you implement your own algorithms, ensure that they are recursive and write automated tests that cover the corner cases.

Pointers

Python, like most other modern programming languages, doesn't use pointers. C++, on the other hand, used pointers extensively. Pointers were used to point to a specific location in memory and access the corresponding value. Fortunately, they are barely needed these days. In C++, vectors and smart pointers have completely replaced raw pointers. Vectors and smart pointers both use a pointer, but it is hidden deep inside their implementation (p. 20). However, pointers are still used to implement polymorphism.

Pointers are arguably the most powerful yet potentially risky objects in the programming world. With pointers, pretty much anything can go wrong, and there are many security issues related to them.

The only remnant in C++ where pointers are still needed for technical reasons is interfaces. Use pointers only for interfaces and opt for modern smart pointers (unique pointer or shared pointer), and you will be fine.

Properties of Variables

Once again, things only got started with the introduction to the data types. The hard part is not choosing a data type, but figuring out what properties they should have and how to facilitate interaction between data types. Here, one can easily create a huge mess if things are not considered properly. Even experienced programmers do not always know how to structure them properly. It is challenging, and I'm trying to explain to you at least some very fundamental ideas to look out for.

Variables do not only have a type, but they can also have additional properties that we will explore in this section. They can be compile-time constant, constant, mutable, member, static, dynamic, global, or several of them at once. All these various types of variables have distinct scopes within which they can be accessed and modified. As is often the case in programming, it is very convenient to have access to a variable at all times, similar to a global variable. At the same time, this approach is very likely to result in poor code quality, as this variable is tightly coupling everything together. Therefore, you should always choose a variable type that is just modifiable enough to work with but doesn't grant more accessibility than necessary.

Compile-Time Constant

Compile-time constants are the least powerful variable type. Such variables are known at the time you write the code and will never change their value. In Python, there is no way to enforce const'ness. However, it is generally agreed upon that variables written in all uppercase are constant and may not be changed, such as PI=3.14. In C++, there is the `const` keyword that enforces the const'ness of a variable, for example, `const double pi=3.14`. Now it is no longer possible to change the variable `pi`, or the compiler will return an error. Keep these constants stored separately and avoid cluttering your code. Otherwise, there is nothing you can do wrong with them.

Runtime Constant

Compared to compile-time constants, runtime constants do not know their values at the time of compilation. The values will be assigned at runtime upon the creation of the object.

Once created, you can pass and copy them around as much as you please. You are always guaranteed to deal with the same object. You can even declare a constant global variable and avoid the main issues associated with global variables, though it is still recommended to pass them around as function arguments instead. If it's global, it will be acting as a hidden state, making it much harder to write tests.

Note that in Functional Programming, all variables are runtime constant. The only way to change a variable is to create a new one. This is a severe restriction, but at the same time it makes reading the code easier as there is only one state a variable can be in.

Immutable Variables

Immutable types are safer from bugs, easier to understand, and more ready for change.
—Unknown[5]

Immutable variables are very similar to constant variables. The value of immutable variables cannot be altered. However, immutable variables can be reassigned a completely new value. Immutable variables share many of the advantages of working with constants. For example, they can never be changed when passed as

---

[5] https://web.mit.edu/6.005/www/fa15/classes/09-immutability/

a function argument. This makes the code easier to understand, as there are fewer possible side effects. For this reason, the code is also easier to test.

Note that immutable variables are used in Functional Programming (p. 153). This has its advantages and drawbacks at the same time. I generally encourage you to use immutable variables whenever possible. Though I have to admit that I'm sometimes too lazy and want to change existing variables. Therefore, I use mutable variables as well. Especially if you have one dynamic data structure that you use all the time, it is very convenient to use mutable variables.

Mutable Variables

In many ways, mutable variables can be compared to class instances. They are both very powerful, yet at the same time, they are tricky to deal with as they may change their values. This can easily lead to bugs. On the other hand, writing code without mutable variables (or class instances) is very challenging. If you want to understand the level of difficulty, I can recommend that you try Functional Programming. The problem with mutable variables is, little surprisingly, their mutability. Values may change, even if they are just function arguments. This makes it so hard to keep track of their values.

One option is to work more with immutable objects. For example, you can replace the following code:

```
prime_numbers = [11, 3, 7, 5, 2]
prime_numbers.sort()
```

with something that does not change the list. Instead, it can return a new list.

```
prime_numbers = [11, 3, 7, 5, 2]
sorted_prime_numbers = sorted(prime_numbers)
```

At first sight, the two options look pretty much equal. The first one changes the list instance, while the second one returns a new list. However, there is a quite distinct difference. The first one passes a mutable variable, which is error-prone. Furthermore, it reuses the variable, which is a minor violation of the SRP.[6]

Returning a new variable, as demonstrated in the second code snippet, is a much safer option and is preferred. Furthermore, the second version of the code is much clearer because the variable is not reused. The different names create a clear distinction between the unsorted and the sorted lists.

On the other hand, the second solution may create a performance bottleneck as it requires more memory if the initial value does not go out of scope. This could pose a problem for large lists, particularly within loops. Though this is usually not a significant issue because the `prime_numbers` go out of scope, and the memory will be recycled. Furthermore, the `sort` algorithm anyway requires some memory.

---

[6] https://youtu.be/I8UvQKvOSSw?t=2133

Member Variables

If you write a lot of object-oriented (OO) code, member variables are one of the most common variable types in this list here. Yet, there is a lot that can go wrong as well, as member variables are usually mutable. Most of the information you need to know is explained in Chapter 3 (p. 65). As long as your class design is appropriate (classes should be small!), and the methods are well designed (with no unexpected side effects, as far as this is possible in a class...), you are mostly fine with using member variables, though you have to be careful with them.

If a class becomes too big, the member variables become very similar to global variables, as they can be accessed from almost anywhere in the code. Member variables are a hidden state and thus should be avoided at all costs. For this reason, member variables are also called "mini-globals."[7]

Passing output arguments to functions can make the code less clear. The best solution would be to pass around only immutable variables. However, it would also at times be inconvenient to code in this manner. Functional Programming works this way, but it is not too widespread, even though it has existed longer than OO programming. OO seems to strike a balance between the accessibility and privacy of variables and functions. But you always have to be aware of this and make sure you maintain the balance so that it doesn't tip over to the accessibility side. Keep your classes small and make everything private (or even constant) that can be. If possible, use immutable objects.

Static Variables

Static variables are member variables that share the same value across all class instances. Let's briefly figure out when to use them.

If a static variable is constant, one could also create a constant variable outside the class instead. However, in some programming languages like Java, this is not allowed.

If a static variable is not constant, it is likely intended to modify the value of the variable in all class instances simultaneously. This is a side effect. This is dark magic! This is dreadful! Never use dark magic. Avoid using static variables.

And if you don't believe me, try writing unit tests for a class that contains static variables. With static variables, the tests will contain side effects. For example, you won't be able to change the order of the tests (p. 93) because it might cause them to fail. This is the very definition of brittle. If tests are brittle, it is a clear sign that something is wrong with the underlying code.

---

[7] The Art of Readable Code. Boswell and Foucher.

Global Variables

You might have heard about global variables, that they are bad and you should never use them. This is indeed true. Let me provide an everyday example to illustrate why this is the case.

Let's say you have to give a bag to a friend, but you are not able to meet. Now, your solution is to place it in the middle of a very busy square, and they can pick it up later on. Are you now thinking...? No! NO! Don't even think about it! There is NO WAY this is ever going to work. Everyone around can compromise the integrity of the bag, and they will. Believe me, they certainly will. This is the problem with global variables. Millions have tried this attempt before you, and millions have failed. No one has found a solution on how to safely work with global variables. Do NEVER use global variables. If you believe that using a global variable is the only solution to your problems, you should seek assistance to review your code and address some fundamental issues. Relying on global variables will only exacerbate the situation.

Of course, it's slightly different if the bag weighs 1,000 tons and no one can move it. Not even Superman. This is not a variable anymore; this is a constant. You define it once, and it will never change. But even here, it is considered bad practice to make it global. Pass the variables around as function arguments to make the dependencies apparent.

Now, as you may have already realized, global variables are problematic because any line of code can alter their value – everywhere. You cannot rely on them; you never know if someone compromised their integrity. This also makes the code incredibly hard to understand, as the workflow becomes extremely entangled. All of a sudden, there is temporal coupling between different function calls if they modify this variable. You have to follow every trace where the variable could be changed. This is the very definition of spaghetti code. And once again, if you don't believe me, try writing tests for code containing global variables; they will break all the time.

The opposite of functions using global variables is pure functions. Pure functions are functions that depend solely on their input arguments and do not produce any side effects. You'll always know exactly what they do and can rely on. They will never change any hidden state. Pure functions are great. Write pure functions whenever you can.

Comparison of Variable Properties

The variables we examined vary in terms of how easily they can be changed – starting with a local compile-time constant that cannot be changed and is accessed only locally to a global variable that everyone can access and change. This level of accessibility must be selected carefully for every variable you work with. You can barely write code with only compile-time constants, but if you use only global variables, you'll soon end up with spaghetti code. Generally, it's best to choose variables with the least possible effects that still allow you to implement what you want. Prefer too little accessibility over too much.

Here is a rough list of how variable types are sorted by how easily they can be changed:

Compile-Time Constant < Constant < Immutable Object < Mutable Object < Class Variable < Inherited Variable < Singleton = Global Variable

There is certainly nothing wrong with constants, especially with compile-time constants. It's just that they can't do much. They are just there and do nothing. They store a fixed value, and you are always free to read it. If you enjoy working with constant or immutable objects, I recommend Functional Programming. In Functional Programming, everything is constant or immutable. Immutable (but non-constant) objects can only be used within the current scope. When passed as a function argument, their value cannot be changed. If you use immutable objects, you cannot have output arguments, which, in my opinion, is generally a good thing. Due to the SRP, a function should change the value of only one variable, and in my opinion, this should be the return value because it is more evident what the code does. In general, you should avoid output arguments anyway. Prefer return values, as they are more explicit. The only difference to constant objects is that immutable objects can be reassigned to a different value.

With mutable objects, you have to be careful because it may be unexpected that a function call changes the value of an argument. Make sure your functions modify at most the value of the first argument, as altering other arguments can lead to confusion. This is not a strict law, but rather a convention. Making multiple changes through a single function call is also a violation of the SRP and should be avoided. If possible, create a new object instead of modifying an existing one. The only reason I could think of why one should use mutable objects is performance and possibly the ease of use. Creating new objects all the time may be slow. Though I never measured it, and as we'll learn later on, performance is not the most important thing to consider (p. 235). Only optimize for performance once your code looks good and you have a performance issue.

Dealing with class variables can be quite tricky. There are too many ways they can disrupt the workflow and cause side effects. They may be used, of course, but I provide detailed explanations in Chapter 3 about the considerations that need to be taken into account to avoid causing chaos. Class variables and mutable objects both allow for modifying an object. At the same time, this is also precisely why they are difficult to deal with. Furthermore, class variables are accessible in a significantly broader scope throughout the entire class. This is fine for small classes; however, it is one of the reasons why classes should not be too big. Otherwise, the class has too much hidden state that will confuse the reader.

Inherited variables are even worse than class variables. It is not easy to see where an inherited variable is defined. It's like receiving a couple of tools without knowing their origin or ownership. If you need to exchange a tool, you may be unsure of what to do. Compare this to a composition that provides you with an organized toolbox to work with. Inherited variables make the code more difficult to understand, and there's no apparent reason why one should use inheritance. No, the few words of code saved are not a reason. The number of words used is not a measure of the quality of code; readability is. And readability is certainly better with composition than with inheritance. This is one of the main reasons why it's better not to use inheritance at all; see also p. 85.

A singleton is a class that can have at most one instance. If you create objects of this class in several locations, they all share the same class instance. There are very few cases where singletons are truly useful. This is mostly the case for connections. It allows multiple sections of your code to utilize the same connection to your database, web server, mobile phone, etc. If you have limited communication and only a few relatively large datasets, this is not necessary. You wouldn't gain much from using the singleton pattern. Every class or library can connect to the database to retrieve data when needed and disconnect when finished. For many small database requests, using a singleton may significantly increase performance. However, singletons are commonly abused to act as global variables, and this is really bad. For this reason, it is generally discouraged to use singletons unless you truly understand why you need one.[8] And, once again, you shoud make the code more explicit by passing the connection as a function argument instead of using a singleton.

Functions

Functions should do one thing. They should do it well. And they should do it only.
—Robert C. Martin

Functions (and methods) are, along with classes, the backbone of modern software. People just don't seem to care about functions as much as they do about classes. They are fairly simple to use, and there are only a few things to take care of. Still, there is quite a lot to know about functions as well. We will learn why functions must adhere to the SRP and should not have any side effects.

Throughout this book, we will distinguish between functions and methods, as is common practice among most authors. Even though I would personally like to refer to both of them as functions since they are essentially the same, just in slightly different contexts, most, or even all, of the concepts I write about functions also apply to methods, as they are very similar in many respects. The only difference is that methods have access to member variables. However, you can regard the member variables as additional mutable function arguments, and then methods and functions are equal. Also, if a class doesn't have any member variables, a method is essentially the same as a function. I couldn't find any other differences.

---

[8] 97 Things Every Programmer Should Know, Henney et al.

Do One Thing Only

Due to the SRP, functions should only cover one level of abstraction. Therefore, they have to be short. As a rule of thumb, functions should be at most about 20 lines long, although fewer than 10 lines are certainly preferred because shorter functions are much easier to understand. This is due to the fact that longer functions frequently also contain more variables. And as you have to remember all the variables in every line of code, the complexity of a function scales roughly quadratically with length. And if there are nested if statements, it scales even exponentially!

On the other hand, there is absolutely nothing wrong with functions that cover only one line of code. One-line functions are extremely useful for enhancing code readability, as they elevate all code to a consistent level of abstraction. Furthermore, they are a good replacement for comments (p. 237) as they make the code self-documenting. But this is something that many programmers don't consider.

Here is a very short code snippet:

```
#define enums for Color and Flavor
if fruit.color == Color.yellow and fruit.flavor == Flavor.sour:
    make_lemonade(fruit)
```

This inconspicuously looking piece of code is not optimal. It is implicit. Of course, a fruit that is yellow and sour is a lemon, but it takes thinking, and it is not immediately clear. Let's look at the following code instead:

```
def is_a_lemon(fruit):
    return fruit.color == Color.yellow and
           fruit.flavor == Flavor.sour

if is_a_lemon(fruit):
    make_lemonade(fruit)
```

Here, we refactored the relevant code into a function. It is only one line, but it makes the code so much more readable.

Levels of Indentation

> *If you need more than 3 levels of indentation, you're screwed anyway, and should fix your program.*
> —Linus Torvalds

Assuming that you're not doing something weird, the easiest way to assess the complexity of a function is by counting the number of levels of indentation. Having no or very little indentation in your functions is always a very good sign. This implies that there is hardly any complex logic concealed within a single function. Having many nested `if/else`, `while`, or `for` loops would violate the SRP because the function has two tasks: resolving the logical operator and performing other work. Having only a few levels of indentation in a function automatically makes it easier to name and understand. At the same time, one needs to get used to the formatting of such code. Most code is typically written at the first level of indentation. If you have many levels of indentation, it becomes increasingly difficult to understand the code. This is why you should avoid having more than three levels of indentation.

It is fine though to iterate over the x, y, and z coordinates using three nested for loops, but that should be the exception rather than the rule.

A frequent problem is deeply nested `if/else` clauses.[9]

```
if input() != "":
    if has_disk_space():
        if network_is_connected():
            make_query()
        else:
            print("No connection to the network")
    else:
        print("No disk space left")
```

This code is very hard to understand. It has too many negations. As I mentioned earlier, there are too many levels of indentation. This issue can be resolved by rearranging the `if/else` clauses. Avoid letting them span across the entire codebase. Check if the `input` is empty and return if it is.

```
if input() == "":
    return
if has_disk_space():
    if network_is_connected():
        make_query()
    else:
        print("No connection to the network")
else:
    print("No disk space left")
```

We can apply this technique to the other `if` clauses as well. The resulting code will look like this:

```
if input() == "":
    return
if not has_disk_space():
    print("No disk space left")
    return
if not network_is_connected():
    print("No connection to the network")
    return
make_query()
```

Assuming that this code is written inside a function, we have two levels of indentation, so we are compliant with Linus Torvalds' rule that you should never have more than three levels of indentation.

---

[9] https://youtu.be/rHRbBXWT3Kc

With this technique, the code became much easier to read. Of course, one could also use `if/else` clauses instead of the `if... return` statements. Depending on the complexity of handling the conditions, one could consolidate all conditions within a dedicated function that performs all the necessary checks. Something like this:

```
def can_make_query(button):
    if input() == "":
        return false
    if not has_disk_space():
        print("No disk space left")
        return false
    if not network_is_connected():
        print("No connection to the network")
        return false
    return true
```

We have seen some approaches on how to deal with nested `if/else` clauses. There is usually no perfect solution, but at least we have improved it significantly compared to the initial code.

Break and Continue

As we are already discussing nested logic, let me also briefly explain why one should generally not use the `break` and `continue` statements. If you have to use them, you should reconsider refactoring your code, as they are a sign of too much complexity. They are not always bad, but they are often a sign of poor code quality. Remember that, in general, all elements in a loop should be treated equally, which is obviously violated by using `break` or `continue`. Only use `break` or `continue` if you are certain that it is the best solution.

Number of Arguments

As for the length of the function, the number of arguments should be kept to a minimum as well. This simplifies the function significantly. Having too many variables is always a sign of too little cohesion, while at the same time, the function becomes difficult to understand. Here, I try to provide a rough estimate of the number of variables a function or method may have, but this ultimately depends on the overall complexity of the code, etc.

Note that member variables to methods behave like arguments to functions. Therefore, you have to add up method arguments and member variables to get the total number of variables. We assume there are no global variables, as we learned not to use them.

Now, there are very few functions with zero arguments. These functions are the simplest; they always behave consistently. There's not much to test, but at the same time, there isn't much that such a function can do, especially if it's a pure function (see Functional Programming, p. 153) which doesn't have any side effects.

As a function has more arguments, it can encompass more functionality. Yet, at the same time, it becomes more complex. Functions with one or two arguments are usually fairly easy to handle and should cover most of the code. Functions with three arguments are already quite complex. They are difficult to understand and challenging to test.

Try to avoid functions with more than three arguments. I know what you think now, and I know that this is a very strict requirement. It's just too convenient to simply add another argument to a function, but this is bad design. Instead, we can fit all our arguments into the code equivalent of a toolbox: the data class (Python) or struct (C++) (p. 65). If you are struggling to fit all the variables you require into three struct objects, it may be necessary to rethink your function design. This is a clear sign that you didn't find appropriate levels of abstraction.

When combining method arguments and member variables, it is very easy to exceed the recommended limit of three variables. This is the main reason why I don't recommend using classes. Instead, I generally suggest opting for Procedural or Functional Programming. When dealing with classes containing complex methods, there should be as few member variables as possible. Otherwise, their complexity will quickly go out of hand (see worker classes, p. 70).

A method may access certain class variables. However, one does not know this until one has read all of the methods and sub-methods involved. Furthermore, one must check whether a method modifies the class variables unless it utilizes the C++ `const` expression. It is advisable to minimize the total number of variables in use. This is the only way to keep the code maintainable.

Following the SRP, functions can only be either a query or a command (see command query separation[10]), but never both at the same time. In the best-case scenario, you save one line of code by avoiding an extra check. But at the same time, you make the code more confusing because handling two responsibilities is much harder than dealing with just one. And potentially saving one line of code is not worth violating the SRP. A common antipattern in this regard is returning a Boolean flag with a set command.

```
if set_node("money", 50):
    go_shopping()
```

Here, the `set_node` function performs two actions simultaneously. It sets a value and returns a Boolean. This certainly doesn't help with understanding the code. I would find it better if `set_node` raised an exception if it failed.

AI Code Generation

AI code generation can help reduce the number of arguments by structuring them using data classes, but the suggested code is not always better.

---

[10] https://en.wikipedia.org/wiki/Command%E2%80%93query_separation

Let's say we have the following code:

```
def do_something(a, b):
    return a + b
```

With the command `put a and b into a dataclass`, we receive the following suggestion. Now, as I already mentioned, the suggestions from AI code generation are not always improvements. Whether such kind of refactoring makes the code more readable is a highly specific question and has to be decided by the reader. Furthermore, this change is comparably small and can also be implemented without AI code generation.

```
@dataclass
class Numbers:
    a: int
    b: int

def do_something(numbers: Numbers):
    return numbers.a + numbers.b
```

Output Arguments

One very irritating thing is functions that alter the value of their arguments. This is also a very common source of bugs, as it is something quite unexpected. In C++, one can clarify this by specifying the type of the argument. One can pass the argument by reference to make it modifiable or by const reference to make it non-modifiable. However, in other languages, this clarity has to be inferred from the context of the function.

Changes to function arguments can be challenging to keep track of. For this reason, a function should always modify at most the first argument. Modifying two arguments is a very serious violation of the SRP and makes the code extremely confusing. If you change the value of an argument, it has to be the most important argument. It's a dual-purpose input and output argument, so it has to be special. It has to be first.

Output arguments can be compared to class instance objects. They are essentially both function arguments that may change their values, with the class instance being a very special variable. The function acting on those variables may change the value of the output argument or the class instance, thus potentially causing side effects. This is sometimes necessary, but at the same time, it is undesired behavior as it is difficult to keep track of.

As always, output arguments give you a lot of power when used wisely. But at the same time, they can lead to very confusing code.

Return Values

Return values are, in my opinion, something very normal. Yet many OO programmers tend to dislike them. OO programmers work with class methods that manipulate the existing class instances. However, return values have a distinct advantage as their intention is clearer. It states: "this is a new value", compared to: "this method may alter a variable of the class instance". And once again, keep in mind the SRP. A function should only have either a return value, an output argument, or change a class instance, but never do two of them at the same time.

Return values are central in Functional Programming. In Functional Programming, you are not allowed to alter the values of existing objects. So, you don't have the issue of function arguments changing their values. The only alternative is return values. They have the advantage that it is obviously a new object with new properties. For each state the code is in, there is a different set of variables. You'll never have to track the state of a variable because each variable has a unique state. After every step of your computation, you create a new variable so that you will never store different information inside a single variable. You just create a new one.

There is really nothing wrong with return values. In performance-critical code, creating new objects all the time could be a problem, though compilers are quite good at optimizing such problems away. In most cases, I recommend working with return values rather than mutable objects. Return values are more explicit and easier to understand than mutable objects.

Here is a small Python example. There are two ways to sort elements in a list. You can either use the `sorted` function, which returns a new list, or you can use the `sort` method, which changes the list in place. I generally recommend using the `sorted` function because it makes it clearer that the return value is a new list with different properties than the function argument. When using the `sort` method, the programmer may forget that the elements in the list are now sorted.

```
L = [1, 6, 4, 3, 3]
sorted_L = sorted(L)
print(sorted_L) # [1, 3, 3, 4, 6]

L.sort()
print(L) # [1, 3, 3, 4, 6]
```

Summary

As you might have realized, I am not a big fan of OO programming, and I think that classes are overused. Most of the time, they can be replaced with data classes (structs in C++) and functions. This results in better code, as it decouples it.

It is not that important what kind of object you use, but how you use it. For example, you should always limit the scope of a variable as much as possible in order to decouple your code. Don't use global variables.

I would like to emphasize the importance of considering both the length of a function and the number of arguments. This is especially true for methods and functions that modify the value of a function argument. Changing the values of function arguments is delicate, as it can cause significant confusion.

Return values are completely acceptable, even if some OO programmers tend to dislike them. Use return values every time the object created is not too large to cause performance issues.

Classes 3

I think it's a new feature. Don't tell anyone it was an accident.

—Larry Wall

Classes may be useful at times, but they are also among the most misused constructs in modern software engineering. Classes are frequently too long and, therefore, hard to understand. While it is widely understood that global variables should be avoided, the member variables of a class often behave like mini-globals, accessible throughout the entire class. This practice is only justifiable if the class is very short; otherwise, the member variables serve no better purpose than global variables.

Just like functions, classes should be kept small. Otherwise, they violate the Single Responsibility Principle (SRP). Since classes tend to grow over time, it is essential to refactor them regularly. Generally, it is advisable to maintain classes as small as possible. In many cases, this may mean not having a class at all or using only a data class (a struct in C++).

Classes are undoubtedly one of the cornerstones of modern code and the essence of OO programming. Unless you are one of the few functional programmers, chances are high that you use them every day. Surprisingly, there is very little written about classes in the common literature beyond the fact that they should have high cohesion, be small, etc. Therefore, it is time we had an in-depth discussion about them.

One can distinguish between different types of classes based on the methods and variables they utilize. We will try to understand when a function or variable should be public or private, and I will explain why plain getter and setter methods should generally be avoided.

Data Classes and Structs

The C programming language was specified well before object-oriented programming became mainstream. It doesn't support classes, but it has something similar: structs. It is similar to a data class in Python. A struct is a user-defined object that contains various variables. It is also possible to nest structs within each other. Structs are extremely useful because they allow us to store various data together inside a single object. It's like a toolbox. In theory, you may also store functions within a struct, though this is generally not done, at least not in C++. For storing variables and methods simultaneously, we use classes.

In Python, the equivalent of a struct is a data class. Here is an example of a data class:

```
from dataclasses import dataclass

@dataclass
class Person:
    name: str
    age: int
    city: str

p = Person('John', 30, 'New York')
```

Nowadays, structs (or data classes) are not as commonly used. Especially, the Java community was avoiding such kinds of objects at all costs until they introduced record classes with Java 14,[1] though there is absolutely nothing wrong with structs. In fact, structs are really helpful. Code without structs is like a plumber without a toolbox. It's quite unstructured.

Classes are very similar to structs. Besides some technical details, the only real difference is the encapsulation of variables and functions (methods) by making them private, as well as the introduction of inheritance and some other gimmicks. The additional possibility to add functions to classes makes them strictly more powerful than structs.

But more powerful is not always better. A gun is more powerful than a knife, but simultaneously it is also more dangerous. You can shoot yourself in the foot. So, actually, it might not be the best idea to own a gun because the dangers may outweigh the advantages. With great power comes great responsibility!

Private or Public

If you are not accustomed to working with classes, this may be very confusing. Why would you like to keep anything private at all? Isn't it easier to make everything public?

---

[1] https://docs.oracle.com/en/java/javase/17/language/records.html

Indeed, this is a very important question. Once you are able to create a class and immediately decide which members should be private or public, you are already a fairly good programmer. To put it briefly, it has to do with power once again. Making a variable private reduces the control available to the user. Never give users more power than necessary.

Let's explore the reasons for having private variables and functions. We need something where you only interact with the surface and have very limited ways to engage with it. It's not hard to find an example. This description applies to almost everything around you. Once again, we can take a look at a car. A car is a highly complex object. It contains an engine, brakes, and many other parts. You don't even want to know about them. You only want to drive it. You need the gas pedal, the brake pedal, and the steering wheel.

You have this absolutely massive object, and essentially you can only do three things with it: increase the speed, reduce the speed, and change the direction. And miraculously, that's all you need. As long as your car is running, you don't care about anything else. Or rather, you don't want to know about anything else. Everything else works automatically as it should. It's like magic. You don't want to adjust the fuel pump, modify engine settings, or tamper with the servo control of the steering wheel. It works, and it's fine. You don't want to deal with the internal workings of the car. You don't even want to be able to take care of these parts. These are the private parts of the car and should not be touched by you. Only a mechanic should maintain them.

There is one very simple rule of thumb for determining which parts of a class should be public or private. If a class has no functions, it is a struct, and all variables should be public. Otherwise, as few functions as possible should be public, and all variables should be private. But we will look at this rule in more detail in the next sections.

Different Kinds of Classes

I like to categorize classes by the number of variables and the complexity of the functions they contain. Ensuring that your classes fit into one of these categories is helpful for fulfilling the SRP.

Some of the following class names, namely, the worker class and the delegating class, are not commonly used. I defined them myself because I believe it is crucial to differentiate between various types of classes based on the number of variables and functions they contain, as well as their complexity.

Note that all classes explained here can also be rewritten as a data class and a set of functions instead of methods.

Classes tend to grow too much, and using only functions forces you to write more cohesive code. This is a typical example of where some feature (classes) makes your life easier, but at the same time allows you to write worse code. The simple question is now when should you write a class or replace it with a set of functions? This is a very difficult question to answer. My answer is: I don't know. I just have a preference for functions. I guess it's a matter of taste.

The only case I know of where you need a class other than a data class is when you need a constructor and destructor to manage memory, for example, with `new` and `delete` as done in C++ vectors (p. 20).

Data Class

We have already briefly mentioned the data class (a.k.a. struct) before. It has no member functions, and, therefore, all variables are public. It wouldn't make sense to have private variables if there are no functions because the variables wouldn't be accessible at all. The data class has no functionality by itself, other than a constructor, but it is great for storing data. As mentioned before, it's like a toolbox, and the variables are the tools inside. If a data class has more than about eight variables, it is high time to split up the data class into subclasses, but preferably you do so much earlier. This enhances the general overview.

```
from dataclasses import dataclass

@dataclass
class InventoryItem:
    name: str
    unit_price: float
    quantity_on_hand: int = 0

item = InventoryItem("Widget", 3.0, 100)
```

Pure Method Classes

A pure method class may have no member variables at all. It consists only of static public methods. In programming languages such as Java and C#, writing such classes is necessary because every function must be implemented within a class. I regard this as an OO obsession of these programming languages. In other programming languages, however, there is not much need for pure method classes. In C++ and Python, you can define the corresponding functions as freestanding functions instead. In fact, I prefer a set of freestanding functions over classes with only static public methods, but I guess that's to some degree a matter of taste.

Here is an example of a pure method class:

```
class MyMath:
    @staticmethod
    def add(a, b):
        return a + b

    @staticmethod
    def subtract(a, b):
        return a - b
```

I would rewrite this code to

```
# inside MyMath.py
def add(a, b):
    return a + b

def subtract(a, b):
    return a - b
```

Delegating Class

The delegating class is a combination of a data class and a pure method class. All variables are private, and all methods are public, though they are not static as they use the private variables. Calls to one of these methods are all delegated to one of the member variables. Thus, most methods are fairly simple, usually containing only one or two lines of code. If the methods are longer, consider using some helper functions.

Once again, we can use a car as an example. A car consists of many complex parts, and all of them are controlled by a single interface. When using this interface, you don't care about all these parts. For example, you don't care about the air conditioner (AC). The only thing you really care about is the temperature inside the car. So, you set the temperature, and the AC will take care of the rest. In a car, you have many other parts that are controlled over the very same interface. Therefore, the class has to be a delegating class. If you implemented the functionality of the AC inside the car class, it would become too complex and violate the SRP.

Note that in this example, it was not necessary to write a helper function. I just did so as I saw fit.

```
# This helper function could also be written as a method of the
# Car class. But as I've already mentioned before, I prefer
# free-standing functions.
def _set_temperature(AC, temperature):
    AC.turn_on()
    AC.set_temperature(temperature)
    # ...

class Car:
    def __init__(self, AC, engine):
        self._AC = AC
        self._engine = engine
        # ...

    def set_temperature(self, temperature):
        _set_temperature(self._AC, temperature)

    def increase_velocity(self, speed_increase):
        self._engine.increase_rpm(speed_increase)

    # ...
```

Worker Class

Worker classes implement complex algorithms in your code. Some people may argue that these are the only real classes. The most common design rules for classes apply specifically to worker classes. Worker classes consist of very few public methods, some private methods, and only private variables. The idea is to encapsulate all of the complex implementations and only give public access to a small interface. Worker classes are the only type of classes with private methods. Other classes do not have complicated methods to hide; they only hide variables.

This implies that worker classes are the only classes that perform complex tasks that should be hidden from other programmers. At the same time, worker classes are extremely dangerous. Excessive complexity can be easily concealed within a single worker class, making it incomprehensible to anyone. You have to ensure that your worker classes are small and well tested. In fact, a worker class isn't that different from a function, where the function arguments correspond to the member variables. Therefore, a worker class should never have more than around three member variables and about 50 lines of code, depending on the general complexity of the class – preferably less. An alternative to a worker class is a set of functions. Functions have to explicitly pass around the variables, which might make the code easier to understand and test, even if the code overall becomes slightly longer. Passing the variables around explicitly makes it more apparent if the code has become too complicated.

As a general rule of thumb, one can say that a worker class has become too complex if you struggle to write tests for it. This is a clear indication that it's time to break up the class into smaller pieces. For more details, refer to Chapter 4 (p. 93).

It is challenging to create a good example for a worker class that is not overly complicated for this book. So, I tried to create a somewhat artificial one. Instead of this simple recursion, imagine a highly complex algorithm that is difficult to understand.

```
class Worker:
    def __init__(self):
        self._data = [1, 2, 3]

    def add_entry(self, number):
        # some complicated logic
        self._data.sort()
        self.read_out_entry()

    def read_out_entry(self):
        if(len(self._data) == 0):
            print("No data available")
            return
        entry = self._data.pop()
        print(self._data)
        self.add_entry(entry)
```

Just for completeness, this class could be rewritten using only functions as follows. We pass the `data` around as a function argument instead of using a class variable.

```
def add_entry(number, data):
    # some complicated logic
    data.sort()
    read_out_entry(data)

def read_out_entry(data):
    if(len(self._data) == 0):
            print("No data available")
            return
    entry = data.pop()
    print(data)
    add_entry(entry, data)
```

Special Classes

One type of class that I don't know to which group they belong is classes implementing memory management in C++, for example, the vector class or smart pointers; see also p. 20. These classes are somewhat special as they rely on the constructor and destructor to take care of memory management. Contrary to most other classes, I don't know how to replace such a class using only functions and data classes, as the constructor and destructor are special functions of the class.

Abstract Base Class

The abstract base class (ABC in Python) has a different name in every programming language. In Java, it's called an interface. This class type defines only the interface (shape) of a class. It does not contain an actual implementation or variables. It contains only public method declarations. Variables are a hidden detail that should not be defined in an interface. One must write classes that inherit from this abstract base class in order to implement it. In Python and other dynamically typed languages, you don't need interfaces, but they can make the code easier to understand. In C++ and Java, it is crucial to use interfaces to split up the code into smaller components, minimize compilation time, and enable runtime polymorphism. We'll go into more details in the section "Inheritance" (p. 85).

In Python, a class has to inherit from `ABC` to be an abstract base class. The methods are all `abstractmethod`, and they do not have any implementation. The ABC defines an interface that several programmers can implement with their own classes. This is especially useful if you collaborate with other programmers, as everyone knows what they have to implement. On the other hand, Python uses duck typing, so you don't really need interfaces if you don't like them.

```
from abc import ABC, abstractmethod

class Animal(ABC):
    @abstractmethod
    def feed(self):
        pass
```

An alternative to abstract base classes in Python is protocols. If you want to understand the differences, I recommend watching the following video.[2] I don't have a definitive opinion on whether to use abstract base classes or protocols, and I don't think it's worth bothering about unless you are a really experienced programmer familiar with such details.

Implementation Class

The implementation class inherits from a pure abstract base class defined above and implements it. It contains public functions and may also include member variables. It may be anything: a worker class, a delegating class, or a pure function class, though the pure function class is the most common. This class is implementing an interface, and due to the SRP, it shouldn't do anything else.

```
class Sheep(Animal):
    def feed(self):
        print("Feeding a sheep with grass.")
```

The abstract base class `Animal` serves as the blueprint for the class `Sheep`. `Sheep` must adhere to the pattern specified in `Animal`. `Sheep` must implement all the functions defined in `Animal`. This makes it somewhat foolproof, as you'll get a warning when misspelling a method name or forgetting to implement a method.

Inheritance Classes

Let's discuss implementation inheritance (inheritance from classes that are not abstract base classes). This becomes much trickier. As there is quite a lot that can go wrong, I generally advise against using it. For the sake of completeness, however, I still write down my thoughts.

Inheritance classes typically are delegating classes. They can also be worker classes, although this is not recommended as the complexity of the resulting

---

[2] https://youtu.be/EVa5Wdcgl94

class becomes even higher. However, as I mentioned before, I generally do not recommend using inheritance, except for defining interfaces. Anything you can achieve with inheritance can also be accomplished through composition. Avoiding meddling with inheritance can potentially help you avoid a lot of trouble. I have read some books that discuss various refactoring techniques and code snippets that work perfectly well, except when using inheritance in non-abstract base classes (or global variables).[3] The main problem usually arises from overriding base class functions, which can cause all kinds of issues. Furthermore, you don't really gain anything by using this type of inheritance.

Here is one of the issues with using inheritance:

```
class Animal():
    def feed(self):
        print("Feeding meat.")

class Sheep(Animal):
    def feed(self):
        print("Feeding grass.")
```

Writing such code may seem attractive at first glance, as you don't have to redefine the `feed` method for animals that eat meat. It's already implemented. But saving a few lines of code does not merit code quality; stability does. And this code is brittle. A single typo can create a hard-to-track bug. Let's assume you misspell the function name and define a method `fed` inside `Sheep` instead of `feed`. Then the sheep will most likely be fed with meat, and there is no way the computer can warn you.

Inheritance allows you to reuse functions, so you only need to write them once in the base class and not in the derived classes. This, however, has the drawback that you don't have to override it. Therefore, if you misspell the name of a method, the compiler is not able to warn you, as it is perfectly viable code. This is in contrast to abstract base classes, where you are required to override the base class method, and you will receive an error if you make a typo in the method name.

In the case above, when using an abstract base class, this kind of bug is not possible. The code is a little longer, but much more stable. The following code will return an error message before executing it because `Lion` does not implement the `feed` method:

```
from abc import ABC, abstractmethod

class Animal(ABC):
    @abstractmethod
    def feed(self):
        pass

class Lion(Animal):
    def fed(self):
```

---

[3] Working Effectively with Legacy Code.

```
        # oops... here we'll get an error message
        print("Feeding meat.")

if __name__ == "__main__":
    lion = Lion()
```

This error prevents you from creating a bug that might be very hard to track down, costing you a lot of time. Instead, you immediately receive a message indicating that there is something wrong with your code: `TypeError: Can't instantiate abstract class Lion with abstract method feed`.

In C++ and Java, there is the `override` keyword, whereas in Python, it is not an official language feature. But this only partially fixes the problem. You may forget to specify that a function is `override`, or you may redefine a function entirely. Remember: We're humans; we make mistakes. These problems cannot occur when using composition rather than implementation inheritance.

General Recommendations

It may be convenient to add a method to a data class or a variable to a pure function class. However, this will quite certainly make the code worse, as it violates the SRP.

The most common error is mixing up the worker class and the delegating class. You can easily end up with a fairly complex function within a delegation class that utilizes numerous member variables. This design is flawed because the delegation class operates at a high level of abstraction, while the worker class is intended to be a low-level object. Mixing different levels of abstraction is detrimental. Refactor the complex part into a separate class or function and call it from the delegating class. This should do the job.

```
class Delegating:
    def __init__(self):
        self._worker = Worker()

    def do_something(self):
        # some complicated logic
        self._worker.do_something()
```

Here, we refactor out the `some complicated logic` into a separate function. The entire code will look like this:

```
def some_complicated_logic():
    # some complicated logic

class Delegating:
    def __init__(self):
        self._worker = Worker()

    def do_something(self):
        some_complicated_logic()
        self._worker.do_something()
```

Like this, we have reduced the fairly complex function to a two-liner.

One Step Further

As you have seen, I like to have my classes as small as possible. You can always break down classes into a set of data classes and functions, completely eliminating the need for any "normal" classes. This may seem like a very strict approach, but it is done so in the C programming language, which is still in use for the Linux kernel. If programming in this way were really such a big issue, they would have changed the programming language a long time ago. (At the time of writing, the Linux kernel is written in C, but new code is also written in Rust.)

The only thing that I know of that requires classes is the C++ vectors and smart pointers. This is due to their construction using the constructor and destructor of the class. Furthermore, I don't know how to implement some of the design patterns[4] without classes. Though in many cases, you don't need design patterns if you don't have classes (p. 185).

Functions vs. Methods

There are two ways to modify the value of an existing object using a function or method. Either pass a mutable object as an output argument or use a class instance where the function is a method acting on it. The two cases look like this:

```
a.b() # method
b(a)  # function
```

There are only minor differences between these two lines of code. Let's compare them:

- In both lines, the variable a can be modified, which is not necessarily a good thing, though.
- The function has only access to the public variables of a, while the method can also access its private variables.
- In C++, const can be applied to a in both cases.

In summary, there are no significant differences. The freestanding function b(a) offers slightly better decoupling and should therefore be preferred. But ultimately,

---

[4] Design Patterns. Gamma et al.

it all comes down to readability. Which version is easier to understand: the function or the method? Let's look at the following code:

```
# Function:
if contains(names, "Elton John"):
    print("A candle in the wind")
# Or method:
if names.contains("Mick Jagger"):
    print("I can't get no satisfaction")
```

In this case, I certainly prefer the second option, using a method, due to the readability point of view. It's so much clearer. It reads like an English sentence. From a coding perspective, I prefer the first option utilizing the function. This is one of the cases where the principles explained in this book will not provide a definitive answer on how to address this problem. It can only provide arguments for one solution or the other. You will eventually have to make a judgment call on your own. If you can identify strong arguments for and against both solutions, you are a good programmer. Once you manage to make the right decision, you are a great programmer.

One thing that helps is Test-Driven Development (TDD, p. 126); in TDD, you first write the test. This is akin to the user code of the function/method. This allows you to figure out which version of the code results in better user code.

In software engineering, there are always numerous factors to consider. This was just another example. Probably, there are more arguments for one solution or the other that I may have missed. This might render the entire discussion obsolete.

Constructors and Destructors

Constructors and destructors are very special methods. The constructor is called once every time an object is created. This has severe consequences that many software developers are not aware of. Most notably, writing tests can become nearly impossible if the constructor contains too much logic or has side effects. The author of some code may have assumed that there would be only one class instance and planned accordingly. This might be true in the particular part of the code they wrote. However, their assumption might break down when writing unit tests (p. 93). When creating objects, it is important to ensure that they can exist independently without any interactions between them. Otherwise, your tests will become very fragile.

Therefore, always ensure that the usage of a constructor is foolproof. A constructor should be as simple as possible. Every action performed by a constructor, such as allocating memory or opening a file, must be reversed by the destructor. This constructor/destructor pair is the only way to guarantee that all effects of the constructor are undone. This also means that you should not define a counter in the constructor unless the effect is undone in the destructor. Preferably, your code follows the "rule of zero C++":[5] do not define any custom constructors or destructors. Leave this to the compiler. It will make your code much easier.[6] In data classes, Python automatically generates a constructor.

The only real functionality that has to be implemented inside a constructor and destructor that I know of is memory management. In C++, you have to use the `new` and `delete` operators to allocate and deallocate memory, and the best way to do this is inside the constructor and destructor.

The following code creates a counter for the class instances. It looks neat, and it might be useful to have such a counter at times. However, it will be challenging to test this counter. Every time you add a new test case or change the order of the tests, the counter values will change. When you change the order of test execution, your tests will break.

```
from itertools import count

class Obj(object):
    _ids = count(0)

    def __init__(self):
        self.id = next(self._ids)

obj0 = Obj()
print(obj0.id) # prints 0
obj1 = Obj()
print(obj1.id) # prints 1
```

You will witness what I said here once you write a complex constructor and attempt to write unit tests for it. It is already apparent that in a random test case, you will need to define a variable `obj` with a somewhat arbitrary value 24. This is a clear indication that something is wrong.

```
# Somewhere in your tests. This looks wrong!
assert obj.id == 24
```

Now, if you add one more class instance before this line, the counter will change, and the test will break. If you have a good intuition for code, you might have also realized that this 24 is a very strange number showing up out of the blue. There has to be something wrong with it.

Getter and Setter Methods

There are very few getters and setters that make any kind of sense.
                                                                —@ThePrimeTimeagen[7]

---

[5] Effective Modern C++. Scott Meyers.
[6] https://youtu.be/9BM5LAvNtus?t=2438
[7] https://youtu.be/VRlIGV4gl5Q?t=1778

In Java, it is common practice to define a class and make all its variables private. Then the developer clicks a button in the IDE, and public getter and setter methods are automatically generated – one for each variable. This is extremely widespread and, in my opinion, an absolutely terrible habit. There is also a point in the C++ core guidelines that supports my claim. You should "Avoid trivial getter and setter functions."[8] This quote means that we shouldn't just avoid classes that have trivial getter and setter functions for all variables, but that they should generally be avoided.

In order to understand my claim, let me provide a few examples, distinguishing between the different types of classes.

Data Classes

In data classes, all variables are public. Everyone can work directly with the variables. There is no need for setter or getter functions; just access the variables directly.

The Java community may argue that this approach is unfavorable because you should decouple everything. They were decoupling the implementation of the class (the variable) from the interface (the getter and setter). Yes, they do decouple them. But they might have never really thought about the outcome. They decouple in a significantly inferior manner compared to simply providing direct access to the class variables.

Let me provide an example. We have the class `Bottle`. We look only at the private variable `_size` (the leading underscore indicates private variables in Python). For this discussion, we don't need more than one variable. Now, first of all, it's worth mentioning that in the normal data class, `size` is a public variable, while in the version with getters and setters, it becomes a private variable `_size`. Accessing it should only be done through the getter and setter functions; that's the whole idea behind it.

```
class Bottle
    def get_size(self):
        return self._size
    def set_size(self, size):
        self._size = size
```

It is claimed that writing getters and setters has the following advantages[9] and my response:

- Better control of class attributes and methods: I don't see why getters and setters provide better control.

---

[8] C++ Core Guidelines explained. Rainer Grimm.

[9] https://www.w3schools.com/java/java_encapsulation.asp

- Class attributes can be made read-only (if you only use the get method) or write-only (if you only use the set method): If you want to make a variable read-only, you can make it constant. This prevents changing the variable as well. And it's very uncommon to have write-only variables, so we don't regard this case.
- Flexibility, the programmer can change one part of the code without affecting other parts: This statement is incorrect, as demonstrated below.
- Increased security of data: I don't understand what this means. One advantage is that you can track a variable with the debugger (p. 174). In fact, this is the only advantage I see of writing getters and setters. But having to do this is a clear indication that your code is bad and should be fixed.

Let's have a look at decoupling, probably the most important argument. Let's assume you want to rename `_size` to `_volume` in the code example above. It's easy to do; there are only two places where `_size` is used. Replace them with `_volume`, and you're done. You can even use search and replace. The new code looks as follows:

```
class Bottle
    def get_size(self):
        return self._volume
    def set_size(self, size):
        self._volume = size
```

Do you see the problem? You didn't make any improvements at all. Everyone still uses the `get_size` method, which now returns a `_volume`. This will cause a lot of confusion. You would have to rename the getter and setter functions as well. It decoupled the code only in theory. Writing getters and setters is only useful if the value returned by the getter is the result of a calculation, elevating the code to a higher level of abstraction. But then it's no longer a pure getter function. If you want to properly decouple your code, you should write an adapter instead.

Having accessor methods for class variables only makes sense if they elevate the code to a higher level of abstraction. Then you really gain something, and it is really a form of decoupling. However, this is not possible in data classes, as there is no abstraction that could be decoupled.

Long story short: Avoid using plain getter and setter methods for data classes. They don't improve anything. Avoid using code generation tools that automatically create getters and setters for all variables.

Worker Classes

Member variables of a worker class should be private because they should not be accessed from the outside. They should neither be accessed directly nor through raw setter or getter methods. Member variables in a worker class should be encapsulated within the class and accessed only by the methods of the class. These variables can be considered as intermediate results of internal calculations. They are not intended to be public, neither directly nor via accessor methods. Hence, there is certainly no reason to write setter methods in worker classes, and there is hardly ever a reason to write a pure getter method. Additionally, writing a getter method for testing purposes is just bad programming practice. You should rather break your classes into smaller pieces that you can test.

Delegating Classes

The only class type that has something similar to plain getter and setter methods is the delegating class. However, you should not write them here either. The names of these classes already contradict the concept of getters and setters. Getters and setters are accessor functions, not delegators. Accessors do not increase the level of abstraction; meanwhile, this is exactly the idea of a delegating class.

One example of a delegating class is a car, as we have already seen before. You can adjust the temperature by invoking a `set` function. But this is not a fundamental property that has been established in the car production line. It's simply an environmental parameter regulated by the air conditioning system and a temperature sensor.

There is also no reason to access the `air_conditioning` via a get method. We wanted to abstract it away. It would only make sense to define a get method to measure the current temperature, though one could argue whether it would be the right name for this method. I would rather name it `read_temperature`. Anyway, there is certainly no reason to write trivial getter or setter functions for delegating classes. A function `get_air_conditioning` would not make any sense. Instead, the code should look something like this:

```
class Car:
    def __init__(self, air_conditioning):
        self.air_conditioning = air_conditioning

    def set_temperature(self, temperature):
        self.air_conditioning.turn_on()
        self.air_conditioning.set_temperature(temperature)

    def read_temperature(self):
        return self.air_conditioning.measure_temperature()
```

I hope I managed to convince you not to write bare getter and setter methods in any kind of class. Don't write getters and setters just because someone told you to. Only write them if you have truly found a reason to do so. This should be the exception rather than the norm.

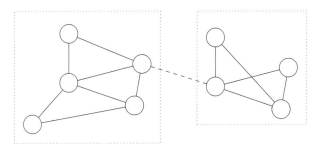

Figure 3-1 Graphical representation of a system with weak coupling and high cohesion

Coupling and Cohesion

Classes should have high cohesion within themselves and low coupling between each other.
—Robert C. Martin

If you don't understand these expressions, we could rewrite it as follows: "There should be significant interaction among methods and variables within classes and minimal interaction between classes." This is indeed a very important rule. However, like most rules in software engineering, it has to be taken with a grain of salt.

As a very simple rule of thumb, you can search the whole class for a variable. If most methods use this variable, it has high cohesion, and the variable should stay in the class. Variables that are only used by very few methods should be removed from the class and passed on as a function argument. These variables have little cohesion.

Worker Classes

The rule cited above by Robert C. Martin was intended for worker classes. Worker classes are a common origin of poor code because they often become overly complex. When breaking worker classes into smaller pieces, this rule is very useful. It gives you a hint on how to break them into pieces. Cluster your methods and variables into small groups. There should be a lot of interaction within the groups and little interaction between the groups. You may also need to rewrite a few methods before dividing the class into smaller parts. It will be worth the effort. If you manage to do this, it will certainly make your code easier to understand, and you will become a much better software engineer.

Two classes have low coupling if the number of interaction points between them is comparatively low. Ideally, every class completes its work and then passes it on to the next one, similar to a relay race. Each class would have an interface consisting of only a few functions. The class takes some data, processes it, and passes it on.

Tight coupling, on the other hand, is like two classes playing ping-pong. The classes all have a comprehensive interface containing numerous functions that call each other several times in a specific order. This quickly becomes terribly complex.

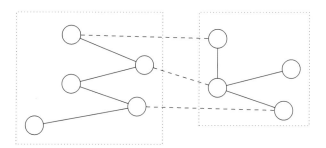

Figure 3-2 Graphical representation of a system with strong coupling and low cohesion

The worst-case scenario is when two classes call each other recursively. I could hardly imagine any worse code than that! This is about the strongest coupling there is (besides inheritance). Neither of the two classes can be changed without also changing the other one. Such code is solid as a rock. You will never be able to change them again.

One way to prevent this problem is to strictly stick to levels of abstraction. Communication goes only in one way. The high-level object communicates with the low-level object, never the other way around.

I hope from this description you already understand that strong coupling makes the code very difficult to understand. Additionally, it becomes increasingly difficult to make any changes without breaking the code. This is called brittle. Implementing new features will take a long time, and fixing bugs is challenging because it is not clear what each class is supposed to do exactly. Having strongly coupled code can become a nightmare.

There always has to be some amount of coupling (p. 174). Code cannot exist without it. It's the glue holding everything together. However, the level of coupling between classes should be minimized because too much glue makes everything sticky. As long as your code works, there is never too little coupling. Furthermore, there are techniques to decouple your code. Creating an adapter between two classes, for instance, can provide more flexibility. This allows you to modify the classes independently, and you will only need to adjust the adapter when necessary.

Anyway, the rule of high cohesion and low coupling is a good rule of thumb when dealing with worker classes. If you stick to it, you can properly structure your classes.

Other Class Types

Maybe you have realized by now why this rule about high cohesion mostly applies to worker classes. A pure data class, for instance, has very little cohesion. The variables are only placed into a data structure because they share some similar properties and are generally used together, like a hammer and a screwdriver both being tools stored in a toolbox. Splitting a data class requires barely any effort at all; you may split it however you like. A delegating class also has very little cohesion. Nevertheless, these classes are extremely valuable as they allow you to structure your code. This rule about cohesion mostly applies to worker classes.

Coupling and Inheritance

Coupling is one of the reasons why I recommend avoiding the use of inheritance. Inheritance is one of the strongest forms of coupling available in software development. The derived class inherits all the implementations of the base class functions. Conversely, the behavior of the base class functions may change if some function calls are overridden by the derived class. Inheritance can obfuscate the code, and removing inheritance at a later stage is extremely challenging.

Static Expression

I discourage the use of static methods. It's not terribly bad, but it's another example of these misguided object-oriented concepts. Let's first look at static methods. Isn't it strange? You write a class with all kinds of member variables, and then there is one static method that doesn't need any of these variables, yet it is still within the class. Didn't we say we wanted to keep classes small? It should have high cohesion. A static method has as little cohesion as a variable in a data class – close to zero.

I fully understand that there are programming languages in which functions must remain within a class, and static functions are the only way to write something akin to a stand-alone function. In all other languages, however, I recommend avoiding the use of static methods, as they do not add any additional functionality or improve the code. In C++, you can mimic a static function using a namespace. The resulting function call will be indistinguishable. At the same time, you can split a namespace over many files, as is done for the `std::` namespace, for example.

As we are discussing static functions, we can also discuss static variables as used, for instance, in languages like C++. Static variables are similar to singletons, and testing classes containing static variables can be challenging. Avoid using singletons and static variables. As soon as you start writing unit tests for static variables, you'll see why I discourage using them. They are like global variables and can be changed everywhere. This can easily end up in a nightmare.

Drawbacks of Classes

> *You wanted a banana, but what you got was a gorilla holding the banana and the entire jungle.*
>
> —Joe Armstrong

Classes are frequently misused for writing poor code without the programmers realizing it. They just think it is normal the way they write them. The most common problem is that classes become too large. It is just too convenient to write everything inside a single class. Having all the member variables readily available makes it easy to work this way. In some cases, I have felt that the authors of some code aimed to write all the code within a single class. This is extremely problematic. If a single class covers the entire code, then the member variables become ... global variables (p. 51)! Member variables are also called "mini-globals"[10] for this reason. This is extremely bad as it violates the separation of concerns. It couples all the code very tightly. With too many member variables, the entire code turns into a Big Ball of Mud.[11]

But also for smaller classes, member variables can be problematic. They represent a hidden state. It is generally preferred to pass variables as function arguments to functions and methods rather than having member variables. This makes the functions easier to test since you don't have to set up a class instance. The desired case is pure functions that only depend on the input variables. These functions are much easier to understand and test.

Be careful with class variables or, even worse, inherited variables. Keep your classes small to limit the scope of your class variables, or replace classes with functions if possible.

If you write a class where all method implementations consist of a single line (delegating class) or you have no methods at all (data class), the number of class variables is not too critical. These classes contain very little complexity. If you have more than about six to eight member variables, you should consider organizing them into subclasses. If the variables don't fit together, you should reorganize these classes even earlier. However, as soon as you have to write complex methods, you have to be extremely careful, as things might otherwise get out of hand. The combination of complex methods and numerous member variables causes the complexity to skyrocket. When dealing with complex methods, it is recommended to keep the number of variables to one or two, as advised in the section "Worker Class" (p. 70). Or even better, replace the class with a few functions if you can find a reasonable way to eliminate all member variables. Writing tests for pure functions is much easier than for class methods.

It's a good rule of thumb to say that the class design is probably okay as long as writing unit tests works out fine and you don't feel the urge to test private functions

---

[10] The Art of Readable Code. Boswell and Foucher.

[11] https://en.wikipedia.org/wiki/Big_Ball_of_Mud

because the class implementation is too complex. Make classes as small as possible while remaining convenient to work with.

Inheritance

Inheritance is the base class of evil.

—Paulo Portela[12]

Inheritance is considered to be one of the integral parts of OO programming and certainly one of the most widely used. Inheritance is often described as an "is a" relationship. A sheep is an animal; therefore, the sheep class has to inherit from the animal class. But, as always, there is more to it.

Two Types of Inheritance

There are two types of inheritance: implementation inheritance and interface inheritance. Interface inheritance is used to define and implement interfaces. In C++, these base classes consist of only pure virtual functions that will be implemented in the derived classes. This type of inheritance is perfectly acceptable. Actually, it is needed for many different purposes, such as runtime polymorphism.

In Python, the same behavior can be implemented using abstract base classes. Even though you don't need inheritance in Python for polymorphism, it is sufficient that two classes implement the same interface, and then you can exchange them.

```
import abc
# abc stands for Abstract Base Class, a Python thing

class Base(abc.ABC):
    @abc.abstractmethod
    def print_a(self):
        pass

class Derived(Base):
    def print_a(self):
        print("derived")
```

There is not much more to say about interface inheritance. It is a good thing, and you should use it whenever more than one class will implement this interface. Interface inheritance is a method to define interfaces and implement them; though in Python, this is not necessary. If you don't like it, you may simply ignore it.

Implementation inheritance inherits the implementation of the base class. Here, all kinds of different problems may occur that we will look at in this section.

---

[12] https://youtu.be/bIhUE5uUFOA

Drawbacks of Implementation Inheritance

Implementation inheritance comes with several issues and should be avoided.[13] In the C++ Core Guidelines, there are at least a dozen points to consider when working with implementation inheritance.[14] Go, for example, doesn't even support implementation inheritance.[15]

Tight Coupling

The most obvious problem with implementation inheritance is that we may create very long inheritance chains. I once read an article about a piece of code that had ten levels of inheritance. It turned out to be absolutely disastrous. There is hardly any stronger coupling between code than in inheritance. It was impossible to apply any changes or to remove all the inheritance. The inheritance structure resembled a tree, with its roots entangling all the surrounding code. The code lost all its fluffiness and became solid as a rock.

I consider the widespread use of implementation inheritance an outdated dogma. It is your responsibility to write code that is easy to understand. Don't let yourself be bothered by someone saying that a `sheep` is an `animal` and you should, therefore, use inheritance. It will almost certainly not improve the code, so you can conclude the discussion. You are probably developing a model of a `sheep` that doesn't need to know about `animals`. You have to be pragmatic. If a `sheep` does not need to be aware of the `Animal` class, there is no justification for inheriting from it.

Inheritance Is Error-Prone

There are several other issues with implementation inheritance. This is already evident from Michael Feathers' book *Working Effectively with Legacy Code*,[16] where he provides numerous examples that he aimed to refactor. In about half of the cases, there were issues with inheritance or global variables because these things can come out of nowhere. It's just too easy to create bugs with these things. One misspelled function will not override the base class function as intended. Even if you delete a function from a derived class, the code will still compile because of the presence of the base class function. Meanwhile, without inheritance, you would get a compiler error for pretty much any kind of typo.

Of course, with the `override` keyword or attribute, this problem has been resolved in some programming languages like C++ and Java. Still, I would recommend avoiding the use of inheritance and always using `override` when necessary to prevent nasty bugs. Working with implementation inheritance remains error-prone.

---

[13] https://youtu.be/da_Rvn0au-g

[14] C++ Core Guidelines explained. Rainer Grimm.

[15] https://golangbot.com/inheritance/

[16] Working Effectively with Legacy Code. Michael Feathers.

Figure 3-3 The diamond structure of multiple inheritance

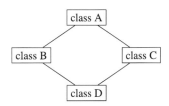

Obscure Code

Additionally, there is a problem with variables inherited from the base class. These are nearly as detrimental as global variables. One doesn't know where they come from and who has access to them. Imagine a variable obtained from ten levels of inheritance, and there are dozens of methods that can modify it. This is absolutely terrifying.

With composition, on the other hand, you would know exactly where a variable comes from, at the expense of some more code. This may seem like a drawback at first sight, but it turns out to be a distinct advantage as you always know exactly where you are in the class instance chain. For this reason, it is generally recommended to use composition instead of inheritance. Honestly, I don't see why inheritance should be used at all, except for defining interfaces. Code reuse can be better implemented using composition or simple functions.

Implementation

The implementation of inheritance can be a complex task, especially for some of the early OO programming languages like C++. In the early days, compilers struggled to handle many tasks. The danger was very high that compilers created very subtle bugs when making some programming mistakes. Even today, it is still challenging to use inheritance correctly in some programming languages. For example, implementing inheritance in C++ requires a considerable amount of knowledge and care to prevent bugs. It is fragile. Avoid fragile code.

When using multiple inheritance, there is an additional issue known as the diamond problem. Let's say we have a base class called A. B and C inherit from A. So far, so good. Now there is a class D inheriting from classes B and C. Classes A, B, and C all have a function f implemented. Which function f should D use? The one from B or the one from C?

This leads to all kinds of nasty ambiguities regarding which functions should be used. For this reason, some languages, like Java, do not support multiple inheritance. While I consider single inheritance to be a bad practice, multiple inheritance should definitely be avoided.

Overriden Base Class Functions

Implementing inheritance properly can be challenging, especially when dealing with constructors and overridden functions. There is quite a bit you have to know about v-tables and other technical aspects. The chances of making errors are significant.

This issue can be avoided by refraining from using inheritance. Implementation inheritance is simply too error-prone in old languages like C++.

Sometimes implementation inheritance can lead to very confusing code. Let's consider the following example:

```
class Animal():
    def feed(self):
        print(f"eating {self.get_food()}")

    def get_food(self):
        return "grass"

class Lion(Animal):
    def get_food(self):
        return "meat"

if __name__ == "__main__":
    lion = Lion()
    lion.feed()
```

Is the lion now eating grass or meat? Of course, it's eating meat. Using overridden functions in the base class can quickly become confusing. This is the simplest version of the Yo-yo problem[17] where the programmer has to switch between reading the code of the base class and the derived class in order to understand the code. The derived class not only depends on the base class; it can also be the other way around. By breaking the encapsulation of the base class, we introduce a mutual dependency. This is so confusing; it is dreadful. Please refrain from writing such code.

This behavior can be avoided by using the `final` keyword in some programming languages. However, it is just another example of why, in my opinion, inheritance should be avoided. It's just another fix for something that is inherently wrong. As I mentioned, in my opinion, there is simply too much that can go wrong with inheritance. Inheritance from a class should only be possible if it is explicitly allowed. The `final` keyword used in C++ and Java to prevent inheritance from an object should be the default value. You should only be able to inherit from a class if it is explicitly allowed.

In inheritance, the derived class inherits all the functions defined in the base class. This might be more than what is actually required. The interface of the derived class is larger than necessary. This violates the Interface Segregation Principle (p. 139). Having to write tests for unused functions in the interface is only the most obvious problem.

Advantages of Inheritance

There are quite a few advantages to implementation inheritance, but none of them outweigh its drawbacks. The only thing that I can think of is code reuse. However,

---

[17] https://en.wikipedia.org/wiki/Yo-yo_problem

it is not worth the drawbacks that come along with implementation inheritance, as mentioned above.

The only real use case of inheritance, in my opinion, is the definition of interfaces using interface inheritance.

Inheritance and Composition

To conclude this chapter, let me provide a brief example to illustrate the distinctions between inheritance and composition. In the class `Lion`, the `lion` can directly access the `food` object from the base class.

```
class Animal():
    def __init__(self, food):
        self.food = food

class Lion(Animal):
    def __init__(self):
        super().__init__(food="meat")

lion = Lion()
print(lion.food) # <-- access of food
```

In the class `Car`, the `taxi` has to access the `power` object through the `engine` object.

```
class Engine():
    def __init__(self, power):
        self.power = power

class Car():
    def __init__(self):
        self.engine = Engine(power=322)

taxi = Car()
print(taxi.engine.power) # <-- access of power
```

Now, there may be many programmers who prefer the code used for the `lion`, for example, because it is shorter. But in my opinion, this is a bad habit. The `lion` code is implicit, and implicit code should generally be avoided because it is not as clear as explicit code. As the Zen of Python states, "Explicit is better than implicit." With that respect, the code used with the `taxi` is clearly preferred, as it is more explicit. Write a little bit (one word!) more code inside the print statement, but the clarity really makes up for it. The code using the `taxi` is much clearer because it indicates the origin of the `power` variable. It is a variable within the `engine`. This is the primary reason why I recommend using composition instead of inheritance; it makes the code much clearer.

If `power` is used frequently, you can also write a method for it.

```
class Car:
    # ...
    def power(self):
        return self.engine.power
```

Conclusions on Inheritance

You don't gain much by using inheritance. Using composition is generally the better solution. If your code looks messy when you start using composition instead of inheritance, you probably wrote messy code all along. You just didn't see it because the inheritance was hiding it. This is another negative aspect. Composition generally makes the code more readable and easier to understand. It is also less error-prone, and it is much easier to test. Implementation inheritance is a common source of poor code quality, and it should generally be avoided.

There are also some more esoteric concepts, such as friend classes. At first sight, friend classes seem like a good idea because they make writing code easier. However, in the long term, this has similar issues to making private variables public. In most cases, it results in poorly written code that lacks proper encapsulation. There are very few cases where friend classes are truly beneficial.[18] Just ignore friend classes and similar concepts and never look back. Write your code using the most common language features, and only consider using fancy language features if they genuinely enhance your code.

Summary

I believe we can agree on the fact that OO programming is important, and it is essential for everyone to know about it. But while classes have advantages, they are also a common source of bad code. Classes have a tendency to grow and become a Big Ball of Mud. Many people are simply unaware that this is an issue. As a rule of thumb, we can say that your class design is acceptable as long as writing tests is not problematic.

Follow the rule of "use composition, not inheritance." Avoid using friend classes and other complex OO constructs unless necessary in your programming language. Unless you absolutely need them for your code design, inheritance introduces very strong coupling, which should be avoided at all costs. The same can be said for friend classes, albeit to a somewhat lesser extent. Numerous guidelines are written only for worker classes. For example, the rule that classes should have high cohesion. It seems like most people overlooked the other types of classes. A data class has only litte cohesion, but it is still a very important object.

---

[18] https://google.github.io/styleguide/cppguide.html#Friends

Avoid writing plain getter and setter functions for your classes. They don't improve anything over using plain data classes. If needed, make variables constant and give the user direct access to them.

Furthermore, you should generally prefer functions over methods. Though sometimes methods may make the code read more like English syntax and are thus preferred. As always, life as a software engineer is not easy. There are so many things to consider...

Testing

4

Testing is a highly important yet frequently neglected topic. Thoroughly testing your code offers several advantages, and, surprisingly, identifying bugs is not the primary benefit.

The most important reason to write automated tests for your code is that they compel you to write high-quality code. Particularly with Test-Driven Development (TDD, p. 126) and writing unit tests (p. 98), you will produce significantly better code. The tests will motivate you to enhance the quality of your code because writing tests for bad code is a real pain. In fact, if I were allowed to give you only one recommendation in this book, it would be to write unit tests, as this will have the largest impact on your code quality.

Another reason why tests are so important is that they provide a form of automated documentation. This documentation is unlikely to change over time, while the underlying code is very likely to evolve. As long as the tests pass, you can modify and improve the underlying code as needed. This is also known as refactoring (p. 203). Once you have good test coverage, you will really enjoy refactoring your code because it's fun if you're not living in constant fear of breaking something.

Introduction to Testing

Software = Algorithms + Data Structures

—Adapted from Niklaus Wirth

Engineering = Abstractions + Testing

—Me

$\Rightarrow$ *Software Engineering = Algorithms + Data Structures + Abstractions + Testing*

It may sound surprising to you, but proper testing is an absolutely essential step toward writing better code. It *forces* you to write better code. In fact, this was the first chapter that I wrote for this book, precisely for this reason. In the following sections, we will learn why tests are crucial, how to write them effectively, and what to consider when creating tests.

A Short Story About Tests

In the early days of software engineering, people wrote code and packaged it into the software they were selling. Before the release, the entire company had to pause all its work for two weeks in order to manually verify that all the features were implemented correctly. The software developers had to work night shifts to fix the bugs as soon as possible; otherwise, the release of the software would be delayed.

But that's not the end of it. Of course, the company wants to make more money. They added some minor features to this extensive software and resold it. But here comes the problem: before they could release the software and make a lot of money, they had to redo the quality assurance process all over again. All the code that has been changed since the last check needs to be tested. *All code* has to be tested because developers also changed the code used by old features. Once again, the entire company will be on a two-week freeze testing the entire software.

Obviously, this is highly frustrating. Before every release, you have to test a feature that didn't change at all, yet the team could have introduced some bugs. Before every release, you waste two weeks of your time on the same boring and repetitive task. Before every release, the company spends millions to test things that have already been tested several times before. And even worse, as the software grows, the number of bugs increases. Some of them even slip through the expensive testing. As the bugs become more challenging to fix, the release gets delayed. It's a nightmare.

During another terrible release, the company is on the verge of collapsing. The CEO comes to meet the development team. His tie is hanging loose, and he looks really tired. Apparently, it has been days since he last slept. He says, "Guys, it cannot go on like this. These tests are killing us. We need the following: Here is a screen. At any time during the development process, I want to have a list of all the features that are currently not working according to the specifications. If everything works, it should be green. If you make this work, I'll pay you one hundred million dollars."

Silence filled the room. One hundred million?? You may laugh, but there are a lot of companies that would actually pay this amount for such a feature. It's an enormous amount, but at the same time, the efforts required for such a feature are incredible. There are millions of lines of code and tens of thousands of features. It's hard to find anyone in the company who knows what the specifications are. It will take years to get these automated tests working, and there is a possibility that the company will go bankrupt before completing all the tests.

On the other hand, the benefits for the company would justify this expenditure. At first, you might think, "Ah, spend one hundred million to save two weeks of testing??" But there is so much more to it.

1. You can release anytime the screen is green. If the team works well, you can release every day (known as a "nightly build").
2. If a customer needs a feature urgently, you can quickly implement it and send them the nightly build.
3. There are fewer bugs because automated tests are more reliable than manual testing.

And that's only the marketing side of it. Equally important is the developers' perspective on this screen. So far, you have always been afraid that you would break some feature when changing code. A feature was working fine, but suddenly it broke down. Nobody realized when it happened. Everyone will be afraid that it will happen again. You'll spend the rest of your life in constant fear. This situation is worse than a zombie apocalypse because you know it will never end. There is nothing that can make you feel safe again. You may never want to touch a single line of code again unless absolutely necessary, as you fear breaking something.

But now, all of a sudden... magic! If you accidentally break a feature, you will know immediately. The screen indicates that everything is alright! Your paranoia starts to fade. You regain confidence in your code, in your abilities, in yourself! You can start replacing all this old, ugly code that has been patched together like a Frankenstein monster. Things were welded together by force because the author was hesitant to rewrite the existing code to create a cleaner solution. Suddenly, things look fine again.

You go to your CEO, give him a hug, and a box of chocolates. You thank him for saving your career, and you repay him the hundred million dollars.

Did I exaggerate a little to make my point? Maybe. But the exaggeration is smaller than you may think. The importance of writing automated tests cannot be overestimated. Tests are no guarantee of making your software project a success. But I can tell you that projects without automated tests are doomed and will fail sooner rather than later.

I hope this serves as sufficient motivation for you to read through this chapter and genuinely attempt to write tests on your own. As always, it's not easy at the beginning; it takes getting used to writing tests. However, the syntax is fairly easy to learn. Ask the Internet and others for advice, and you'll get a fairly good idea of how to write them.

Test Example

Here is a small real-world example of how a test works.

1. Ensure that the coffee machine is clean and equipped with coffee, water, and electricity. Press the coffee button. Wait until the coffee has finished brewing.
2. Taste the coffee. If you like it, the test passes. Otherwise, it fails.
3. Discard the cup and the leftover coffee.

This is it. Tests always consist of a few instructions that should be easy to understand. The result of the test can only take on two values: it passed (you liked the coffee) or it failed (you didn't like it). If it failed, you should call a technician to fix it. Or, even better, you could write a script that automatically calls the technician.

Tests consist of three stages that are conducted on a test bench:

1. Setup: Prepare everything for the test.
2. Execution: Check if the requirements are fulfilled.
3. Teardown: Clean up all the objects created for the test.

Structure of a Software Test

In software, we follow the same process as with the coffee machine in the example above. In every programming language, there is a major testing library dedicated to this purpose. They all function similarly, regardless of the programming language you use. The Python testing library is called pytest.

Here is a small example of a class we want to test:

```
# inside vector.py
class Vector:
    def __init__(self, x, y):
        self.x = x
        self.y = y
    def distance_to(self, other):
        return ((self.x-other.x)**2)**0.5
```

The corresponding test looks as follows. Note that we have to use the `is_close` function as we are comparing two floating-point numbers for equality which may contain rounding errors.

```
# inside test_vector.py
from vector import Vector
import math

def test_distance(self):
    v1 = Vector(0,0)
    v2 = Vector(1,1)
    distance_is = v1.distance_to(v2)
    assert math.isclose(distance_is, 2**0.5)
```

We can run the test in the command line with

```
pytest
```

Unfortunately, we cannot stop here because, as always in programming, learning the syntax is only the first step. The real challenge is to write good tests, and this is what we'll have a look at in the following 50 pages.

Fixing the Test

The relevant part of the output is this:

```
E       assert False
E       +  where False = <built-in function isclose>(1.0, (2 **
0.5))
```

Apparently, I made a mistake in the implementation. The values checked in `isclose` are different from the expected value. When checking the implementation of the code, we can see that in my calculation, I forgot to take the y-component into account. The correct implementation of the `distance_to` function would be

```
def distance_to(self, other):
    return ((self.x-other.x)**2 + (self.y-other.y)**2)**0.5
```

Now the test passes.

In case you find the error message returned by the test not informative enough, you can add an error message either separately or directly to the assert.

There are different ways to change the error message of a failing test. The easiest is adding a message to the `assert` as follows:

```
def test_function():
    a = 1
    b = 2
    assert a == b, f"is = {a}, should = {b}"
```

This returns the following error message:

```
AssertionError: is = 1, should = 2
```

As you can see, it's pretty simple to write a test, not only in Python. There are testing libraries available for all major programming languages. From a syntax point of view, you won't need to learn much more than what I have explained here for a considerable period. Just write your code as you would to check the result, check the output using print statements, and replace the print statements with asserts. That's it!

Types of Tests

There are different types of tests, depending on their scope. For the sake of simplicity, I'd like to reduce it to only three different types. Please note that the distinction between the types of tests is not always clear. Some tests are a combination of two different types. However, in general, the following three categories are sufficient. The naming of these tests is not standardized:

1. Unit tests assess the behavior of individual functions, classes, and modules.
2. Integration tests assess the interplay between different units.
3. Functional tests assess the behavior of the entire software system.

As we will see, each of these categories has its own right to exist, as they each cover different parts of the code. They are all important and should be used in combination. There are also other types of tests that we will delve into later, while others we will simply ignore. Additionally, the naming of the different types of tests is not standardized. There are different names for the same type of test. For example, functional tests are also referred to as end-to-end (E2E) or acceptance tests. Some people may argue that there are differences between these tests, but as this book is not about testing, I will not delve into these differences. I will only use the name functional tests.

The small unit tests are the foundation of the testing infrastructure. They can be executed quickly. Meanwhile, as tests become more complex, they may take longer to execute, as they are designed to assess the interaction of components rather than individual components themselves. Thus, larger tests are more likely to find bugs, but at the same time, they are not suitable for pinpointing them.

Functional tests can also be written in a different programming language and by a different person than the underlying code. They depend, for example, on the API that might be written in a different language. I wrote functional tests for some C++ software in Python because it was easier to process the resulting text files.

Unit Tests

Unit tests have three properties:

1. Unit tests give you a definite answer as to whether a unit works.
2. Unit tests are fast.
3. Unit tests are easy to understand.

Let me briefly elaborate on these points.

First, the goal of unit tests is that they *always* show whether a piece of code really works. It should not depend on *anything* else but your code. It doesn't depend on the file system, a network connection, nor on some random number generator. It only depends on your code, and the tests are therefore deterministic. You'll never have to rerun a unit test because if it works once, you know that it will always work.

Second, unit tests have to be fast. And when I say fast, I mean it. Unit tests should take only a few milliseconds to execute. If there is anything computationally demanding within your test, it's not a unit test. You'll have to use dependency injection (p. 134) to replace the computationally demanding part of the code with some mock or fake. Now, this might seem like cheating, but it's not, as you don't want to test the computationally demanding part of the code. This is done elsewhere. Unfortunately, it is very difficult to write fast enough tests in Python. This is one of the main reasons why I recommend using a compiled language for larger projects.

Third, unit tests should be easy to understand. If it takes more than a few simple lines of code to set up a unit test and check the result of the calculation, your code may be too complex.

You should be able to write unit tests for any piece of code you have. If you don't manage to do so, your code is flawed. This means, at the same time, that unit tests are a good indicator of the quality of your code.

Unit Test Example

Now, let's figure out why unit tests are actually needed.

Many programmers follow this workflow: they write a function and then need to determine if it works correctly. To achieve this, they utilize print statements or the debugger. They run the code and check if the results are correct. Let's look at the following example:

```
def square(x):
    return x**2

print(square(1))
print(square(2))
print(square(5))
```

This works. People have worked like this for decades. But it's absolutely terrible. The print statements will be deleted once the code works. The checks will be discarded, and no one knows anymore what the code is actually supposed to do or whether it still works. When modifying the function, you have to test it again – everything, every time, by hand! This is a typical example of a procedural DRY violation that should be optimized away. And the solution is unit tests.

Unit tests cover relatively small sections of code. Usually, they test a public method of a class or a stand-alone function. In the example above, the unit tests would verify everything that is typically verified using print statements. The unit tests for the `square` function would look something like this:

```
def test_square():
    assert square(1) == 1
    assert square(2) == 4
    assert square(5) == 25
```

This code snippet essentially performs the same function as the print statements mentioned earlier, but with some very important differences: this test code will be executed automatically, reducing the chances of errors. This test goes into the test suite and will remain there indefinitely, or at least as long as you still have the `square` function defined. This test will be executed every time you run all the unit tests. You'll know if the code still works, even after changing the underlying implementation. The only drawback is that it takes a millisecond for each test to execute, and these numbers may add up as you keep writing unit tests. Additionally, you will have to modify the test code if you change the implementation, but the last point is actually a good thing. It prevents you from inadvertently changing the behavior of the code. You have to assert that you want the behavior to change. If you change the actual code, you also have to update the corresponding unit tests.

It may sound surprising, but unit tests are the cornerstone of the testing infrastructure. They are even more important than functional tests. This is because unit tests are fast and can provide precise information about which part of your code contains a bug. In contrast, functional tests can only indicate that something is wrong within the entire codebase, and they require a significant amount of time to execute. Covering all your code with unit tests takes much more effort than covering it with functional tests, but it is certainly worth it.

The drawback is that unit tests do not verify whether these building blocks are connected correctly. Unit tests cannot assess the interaction between different code blocks. However, as most errors occur within a single code block, unit tests are still the most important type of test.

Execution Time

Unit tests have two important properties: they may never fail, and they have to be fast. And when I say fast, I mean it. A single unit test should take only about a millisecond. All unit tests combined shouldn't take more than a few seconds so that you can run them all the time. Therefore, unit tests should never perform any laborious computations. Unit tests should not include performance tests. And unit tests should certainly not wait and test the behavior of some timeouts. Unit tests should really just test the smallest unit possible. Otherwise, it might still be a valid test, but it's not a unit test anymore.

In bigger projects, there will be thousands of unit tests. And as running several thousand unit tests always takes more than a few seconds, you'll have to group them. Of course, it would be preferable to always run all the tests, but in a big project, it is justifiable to run only a relevant subgroup of the tests. I wouldn't know of any other way to keep the execution time of all the unit tests combined below a few seconds. The neat solution would be a test suite that checks the code coverage for every test case and reruns only those tests where the code has changed, but as far as I know, this does not exist yet.

Testing Files in Unit Tests

As we have seen, there are three stages in a test: setup, execution, and teardown. Unit tests, however, only require a setup and an execution phase. There is no teardown function required for unit tests since they do not interact with any files or databases that need to be deleted afterward.

"Why...? How? No files? No database?"

Yes, that's a good point. According to the SRP, a function or class should only perform one task. Therefore, it should not read a text file and perform complicated calculations. Reading a text file should be done in a dedicated function. This

Types of Tests

function will not have a unit test, but it is not necessary to test automatically because reading a file and returning it as a string is not a difficult task. The code will be covered by functional testing.

Let's assume we have the following code:

```
def share_values(filename):
    with open(filename,'r') as f:
        file_content = f.read()
    share_values = parse_share_values(file_content)
    # ... and much more code
    return share_values
```

The section of this code that reads the file is very simple. It is not necessary to test it. Instead, it can be easily extracted into a separate function. This method is referred to as the "Wrap Method" by Michael Feathers[1] (p. 203).

```
def get_share_values(file_content):
    share_values = parse_share_values(file_content)
    # ... and much more code
    return share_values

def read_file(filename):
    with open(filename,'r') as f:
        return f.read()

def share_values(filename):
    file_content = read_file(filename)
    return get_share_values(file_content)
```

Here, we wrapped the code for reading the file into a separate function. The rest of the code is written within a dedicated function. For this function, one can easily write a unit test because it does not depend on the file system. A test might look as follows:

```
def test_get_share_values():
    file_content = "Apple, 150.3"
    assert get_share_values(file_content) == {"Apple": 150.3}
```

This is similar to the GUI layer for functional tests. You pack everything you don't want to test into a thin layer that is unlikely to fail, making the remaining test much smoother. In this case, this small layer is the function `read_share_values`, which reads the file into a string. Robert C. Martin refers to this as a "Humble Object."[2] It is a thin layer that is unlikely to fail and therefore does not need testing. It is simply a thin wrapper around the function that reads the file.

The same holds true for database access or retrieving the current time value. You write a small wrapper function that does nothing but call the database or return the

---

[1] Working Effectively with Legacy Code, Michael Feathers.
[2] Software Craftsman, Robert C. Martin.

current time. Separate the remaining code into a distinct function that can be tested independently.

An even better solution is to implement dependency injection (DI)[3] as explained on page 134. But for the moment, we'll leave it with the small wrapper function.

Testing Classes

Writing unit tests for classes is arguably the most crucial aspect of this chapter. This is not only due to the prevalence of classes but also because classes tend to become messy without any unit tests.

First of all, classes tend to become too large. They have too many member variables and complicated methods. Both will make it very hard to write unit tests. Member variables share the same issues as function arguments do (p. 65). Member variables increase the dimensionality of the problem being tested. This leads to many more possible test cases than should be required for good class design, as discussed in the beginning of this chapter (p. 93).

Furthermore, there is the issue of how to handle private methods in large classes. Apparently, the testing framework does not have access to private methods. No one has, except for the class itself and perhaps some friend classes. One initial approach is to change the private methods to public. This, however, is not recommended. It is not advisable to make methods public solely for testing purposes. This will result in convoluted code with an excessive number of public methods, which is the complete opposite of encapsulation. For the same reason, you should resist the temptation to make the test a friend class of the class under test. Therefore, unit tests (and certainly all other tests) should only test the public interface of a class. They should test the class as a whole. If you are tempted to test private methods, you should resist. This is a clear sign that your class is too complex. Consider creating a separate class for these private methods with a public interface that can be tested.

Classes that are difficult to instantiate pose another problem, for example, if an object is difficult to construct or if the constructor has side effects that are not guaranteed to be undone by the destructor, such as opening a file, incrementing a counter, allocating memory, etc. In the actual code, it can be ensured that all necessary conditions are met so that you never encounter any issues, for instance, if you are instantiating a class only once. When running unit tests, however, these guarantees may be broken in some cases, leading to undesired behavior. For these reasons, the constructors should be small and not execute any fancy operations.

In summary, the following points can be made about classes and tests:

- Classes should be small and contain few member variables. This makes them easier to test (and is good class design).
- If you want to test private methods, consider refactoring them into separate classes.

---

[3] https://martinfowler.com/articles/injection.html

- The constructors should be simple and possibly not have any side effects. All effects have to be undone by the destructor.

All these rules are implied by the topics we have covered so far. But now we have a reason why we absolutely have to obey them: the unit tests compel us to do so.

Here is an example of how to refactor a complex private method into a dedicated class:

```python
class Car:
    def __init__(self, engine):
        self.engine = engine
        self.speed = 0

    def push_gas_pedal(self):
        self.speed += 10
        self._increase_rpm()

    def _increase_rpm(self):
        self.engine.rpm += 1000
```

This code is bad because `increase_rpm` should be part of the `engine`. I made this code deliberately bad in order to fix it now. Let's assume we want to test the `_increase_rpm` method. We can refactor it into a separate class.

```python
class Engine:
    def __init__(self):
        self.rpm = 0

    def increase_rpm(self):
        self.rpm += 1000

class Car:
    def __init__(self, engine):
        self.engine = engine
        self.speed = 0

    def push_gas_pedal(self):
        self.speed += 10
        self.engine.increase_rpm()
```

Now the code is much better. By moving the method `increase_rpm` into the `Engine` class and making it public, we can now test it. Furthermore, this method belongs to the `Engine` class, not the `Car` class.

AI Code Generation

AI code generation can be very helpful when writing tests. I have written a function to convert numerical values into Roman numerals and have created a unit test file. AI code generation started implementing the unit tests without any additional instructions.

```
from refactoring import roman_number

def test_roman_number():
    assert roman_number(1) == 'I'
    assert roman_number(2) == 'II'
    assert roman_number(3) == 'III'
    # ... and tests up to number 42
```

However, there are two minor things that I'd like to have improved. First of all, there should preferably be only very few asserts per test. Here, we have 42 of them.

Second, the test is testing things that were not even implemented in the code. The Roman numeral function was only implemented for values up to 3. So, it seems as if AI code generation somehow guessed what kind of tests were needed but did not check what is actually implemented.

The code above can be refactored, for example, using a dict.

```
# refactor this code to use a dictionary
dictionary = {1: 'I', 2: 'II', 3: 'III', 4: 'IV', 5: 'V'}
for key in dictionary.keys():
    assert roman_number(key) == dictionary[key]
```

Even if I desired this change, upon reviewing the code, it is not entirely clear whether this is an enhancement over the original code. We have removed some redundancy and now only use one assertion. On the other hand, the redundancy was not that significant, and the old code was very easy to understand, which may be even more important than removing the repetitive code. This decision requires human judgment, and I am still unsure which solution is better.

Integration Tests

Integration tests are a mixture of unit and functional tests. They test entire components of the software, such as a module. As you want to isolate this module, you have to mock all the other modules that it depends on. This may be a considerable amount of work, as you have to write mocks for every other module. You can pass these mocks using dependency injection (DI) or run, for example, a mock data server, which is very much simplified.

This effort may be worth it, as integration tests are much faster to run than functional tests. Therefore, you can run them more often, and they are a better help in pinpointing bugs. You'll only need integration tests if you are working on "bigger" projects. On small projects, there is no space for anything in between unit and functional tests.

Functional Tests

Functional tests perform tasks that align with most people's intuitive expectations of a test. Some marketing personnel, for example, the product manager (PM), orders a new feature. They tell you, more or less exactly, what this feature should do and provide you with some examples. The feature is considered complete once these examples can be executed using your software. As you don't want to end up in the same situation as in the story at the beginning of this chapter (p. 93) with the desperate manager, you write automated tests that cover the examples. This is a fairly good guarantee that the feature is still working, even if someone were to change the underlying code. So, there is one thing you will always do: write a functional test for every new ticket.

If you publish code examples as part of your API documentation, you should write a functional test for every single one of them. There's nothing more embarrassing than including failing examples in your documentation.

Functional tests are user-centered. The user lacks knowledge about the internal workings of the code. They don't want to know anything about the internals of the code. They only have the interfaces you provide: GUI, API, keyboard, webcam, etc. This is all they care about. They want to watch a YouTube video. They want high image quality and fast response time. They don't care what kind of fancy algorithms the thousands of Google employees developed to run their server farms.

Sounds good. But at the same time, it seems extremely difficult to write these tests. Testing a GUI or webcam input seems quite challenging.

True. But when making a few simplifications, the effort becomes quite reasonable. Most importantly, you need to have well-structured code. As shown in Figure 1-2, the GUI is an abstraction level higher than the API. Don't mix the two! The GUI code consists of HTML and CSS code, images, buttons, and graphs. These things are difficult to test automatically, but they do not contain any logic that is likely to have bugs. As mentioned before, this is called a Humble Object. This layer is difficult to test but unlikely to fail. Every mouse click corresponds to a function call to the underlying API. If the GUI looks fine, it is most likely functioning correctly. It is a thin layer that does not contain any logic and is unable to hide bugs.

Of course, if you neglect the GUI layer, the tests are not real functional tests anymore. Maybe one should rename them. However, I continue referring to them as functional tests since the API remains a public interface to your software.

Writing tests at the GUI level is quite challenging. Though there are tools, such as Selenium,[4] that automate clicks on the GUI and translate them into API calls, it is generally recommended to keep the number of GUI test cases as low as possible. However, there are simply too many programs that are not structured the way I recommend it in this book. They cannot be tested otherwise because they don't have an API that is well separated from the GUI. Meanwhile, there is considerable

---

[4] https://www.selenium.dev/

demand for testing these programs nonetheless. Needless to say, using these testing tools adds significant overhead to the testing efforts required. Testing on the API level is comparatively easy. If you have separated the levels of abstraction and made sure the GUI depends only on a few API calls, you can translate each button click from the GUI examples directly into API function calls. Write a test that makes the API calls, checks the results, and you're done. However, there is one problem with functional tests. In practice, you have to deal with potentially large files, databases, and slow network connections. This may significantly slow down your tests. Additionally, the files or databases must first be created. This task can be accomplished either by using a script or by copying them from another location.

The output of the tests may potentially result in large files as well. Comparing the results of these large files may not be very helpful. One tiny difference in these large files won't provide much insight into what is malfunctioning. One option for improving performance is to compare hash values instead of complete files. It won't provide more information than indicating that the files are different, but at least it is much faster to compute. And remember: functional tests are not there to pinpoint the source of a bug; they are just an indication that something might be wrong.

One solution is to use small files. This makes the tests run faster. However, having only tests with relatively small datasets and files is not representative of the everyday usage of your software. You absolutely have to run performance tests with realistic datasets as well. Otherwise, you might run into all kinds of performance problems at the release.

Functional tests are often highly correlated. A single bug in your infrastructure code can cause many tests to fail. Therefore, it is important to mark functional tests in Python with `@pytest.mark.dependency()` as explained in the section "Dependent Tests" (p. 120).

You should always combine functional tests with unit tests to pinpoint the source of the bug.

Other Kinds of Tests

Unit and functional tests are not the only kinds of tests. As we have seen, there are, among others, also integration and performance tests. Here, we'd like to briefly have a look at what other kinds of tests there are.

Performance Tests
Performance tests are one type of test class that is frequently overlooked. Functional tests are often developed using small databases to minimize execution time. However, this leads to the problem that executing the code with normal-sized databases is not tested, and there is a chance that this would be unacceptably slow. For this reason, entire projects have already come to a standstill. It is important to write performance tests that run with realistic parameters to prevent a poor user experience caused by slow response times. Additionally, they should be written early on.

There are many different types of performance tests. The most common type of testing is load testing, where, for example, the number of users is increased until the system breaks down, or one measures the response time of the system. The goal of these tests is to determine the system's limits.

Explorative Tests

Explorative tests are designed to uncover bugs that the developer may not have considered. They are typically carried out by the testing or quality assurance team. They are not automated and are not part of the test suite. They are executed, and if a bug is found, it is reported to the developer. Otherwise, it is just ignored. Explorative tests are not a substitute for unit or functional tests. They are just an additional tool to find bugs.

Conducting explorative tests requires some experience in anticipating potential issues. What corner cases might have been overlooked by the programmers?

To a certain degree, explorative tests can also be automated by writing randomized tests. With these tests, you generate random input data and check whether the output is as expected. This is a good way to find bugs that you didn't anticipate. However, it is not a substitute for explorative tests, as it is still limited by the imagination of the programmer.

When to Run Tests

It is very important that all tests, excluding explorative tests, are run automatically. This is the only way to ensure that they are always run. When they are run exactly, however, depends on the kind of test.

Unit tests are fast. Each one of them takes only a few milliseconds to run. All together, they shouldn't take more than a few seconds. It is important that unit tests are fast because they are run frequently. You should run them every few lines of code that you write.

Code is only allowed to be merged into the master branch if all unit tests pass. This means that every programmer has to run the unit tests before creating a merge request (MR, p. 257) in the same way as ensuring that the whole project compiles. It is mandatory to fix the code that broke the unit tests; otherwise, it will not be merged.

Now let me reiterate: It is *mandatory* that all unit tests pass before an MR can be merged into the master branch. This is a rule that should be automated. Set up the Continuous Integration (CI, p. 269) accordingly. It should check the unit tests just the same as it checks the formatting and the compilation of the code. This is just another mandatory requirement within the MR, in addition to ensuring that the code compiles. This is the only way to ensure that the unit tests always pass. There is *no* reason why unit tests should not pass. When it comes to functional or performance tests, things get a little trickier. They are slow and cannot be run before every MR. It would slow down the entire development process too much. Therefore, you can't guarantee that all functional and performance tests will be run all the time. Instead, you have to set up the CI to run them overnight ("nightly build"). If a test fails, it should send an email to all the developers who made changes the previous day. The team must then gather and determine the reasons behind this situation. Usually, it is fairly obvious why the tests failed, and it won't take much time to figure out who broke the test and how. But it is important that the problem is resolved as soon as possible.

Integration tests are once again a mixture between the two. They are usually too slow to be run after every code change. But they don't have to be fast. They are only checking complete modules, and not every code change alters their behavior. Integration tests should take only a few minutes, compared to potentially hours of functional tests. This allows them to be run in every MR.

Who Should Write Tests?

With unit tests, it is evident that the responsible developer must write the tests themselves. They know the code best and understand what it is supposed to do, unless you work in the automotive, medical, or aerospace industry, where the tests are written by a dedicated testing team due to high regulations.

When it comes to functional and performance tests, the situation is not that clear. Should the tests be written by someone from the development team, the marketing side, or an independent tester? As always in software engineering, such questions have no easy answer. There are trade-offs to consider when choosing between different solutions.

Having developers write the tests has the advantage that they know the code. They know the difficulties. They can address these challenges by creating specific tests. A developer might also understand what the customers want and where the common issues lie. This also helps to target the most critical areas of the code.

On the other hand, having an independent tester also has some advantages. They don't know about the weaknesses of the code; instead, they write more explorative tests. These tests might uncover bugs that developers did not anticipate, as they are in areas of the code where bugs were not expected. Additionally, developers are usually overconfident about the quality of their code; they think the code is better than it actually is. This is why it is beneficial to have an independent tester who is not influenced by the code. Furthermore, independent testers are typically closer to the customer and create tests that closely resemble the actual use case.

When to Write Tests

Tests should be written as early as possible. This principle applies not only to unit tests but also to functional and performance tests. Writing tests at the end of a project has the drawback that possible issues will be very hard to resolve because the entire software is nearly finished, making changes very difficult and potentially expensive.

Types of Tests

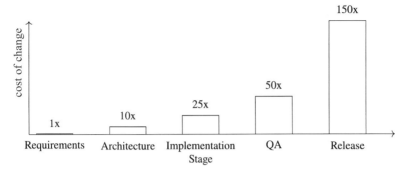

Figure 4-1 The cost of fixing a bug at different stages

Figure 4-2 The testing pyramid

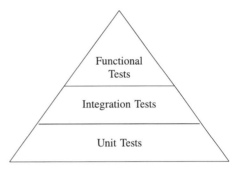

As a general rule of thumb, the cost of fixing a bug increases exponentially over time.

The Testing Pyramid

We have said that we should write mostly unit and functional tests and maybe also integration tests. Additionally, we have performance tests, explorative tests, and a few manual tests. As a rule of thumb, one can say that the testing suite of any program should consist of many fast, fine-grained tests and comparatively few slow, coarse tests.

Unit tests are the foundation of the testing pyramid. They are generally the most useful, as they check each part individually and can provide detailed feedback if something is broken. They are like testing the individual parts of a car radio before assembling it. Unit tests prevent the use of faulty components. Roughly, an estimated 80% of all tests should be unit tests.[5]

Integration tests are the second level of the testing pyramid. They are like testing the assembled radio on a test stand. Integration tests are coarser than unit tests and

---
[5] Software Engineering at Google. Winters et al.

cannot pinpoint errors as precisely. However, they are still useful for checking the functionality of the radio. About 15% of all tests are integration tests.

Functional tests should only verify that the installation of the radio in the car was successful as expected. Turning it on once should be completely sufficient, as there is not much more that can still go wrong.

Functional tests are the least common. They are very valuable for verifying that a program actually works. There are always some things that can go wrong, even if all unit tests pass. However, the feedback you receive from a functional test is very limited. It will mostly indicate that something is wrong, but you will spend a lot of time debugging the cause of this issue. On the other hand, you don't need too many functional tests. If you have good test coverage with your unit and integration tests, the likelihood of experiencing numerous failing functional tests is low.

Once you confirm that the engine, gearbox, and brakes of a car are functioning properly and working in harmony, there is not much more to test on the fully assembled car. If it runs, it's probably fine. Therefore, only about 5% of all tests are functional tests.

Properties of Tests

What, When, and How to Test

Once again, the difficulty lies not in the complexity of the syntax nor the usability of the testing framework. The much harder questions are what, when, and how you should test. Let's have a look at the code and try to understand.

What

A common question is, "What to test?" A very simple answer is: everything. This is certainly a correct answer, although you cannot always test everything equally extensively. You will simply lack the capacity for that, unless you work in the aerospace industry, where you have to test everything very thoroughly. Instead, at Google, they came up with the Beyoncé Rule.[6] She sings in her song, "If you like it, then you should have put a ~~ring~~ **test** on it." Apparently, this applies to most of your code. You do like your code, don't you?

Our class `vector` on p. 96 contains the member function `distance_to`. It is part of the class interface and, therefore, must be tested. This is the price you pay for public functions. Or rather, it's a small fraction of the price you pay for having public functions. Keep functions private whenever possible. Private functions offer greater flexibility since you can modify them freely without the need for testing. For public functions, you have to ensure that the interface remains unchanged. Otherwise, you'd break a customer's code. Avoid altering existing interfaces; it requires a significant amount of work. You'd have to adapt a lot of code, including

---

[6] Software Engineering at Google. Winters et al.

Properties of Tests

your tests. Write tests for public functions to assert that you don't accidentally change their behavior and break your code.

When

Most tests you'll be writing are unit tests (p. 98). Unit tests are fast. And when I say fast, I mean it. Unit tests should only take a few milliseconds each. Even if you have several thousand unit tests, they still take only a few seconds to execute. So you can run them after every few lines of code you write. This way, you will have constant feedback on whether your code is still working.

Note that unit tests are the main reason why I don't like Python. Python is slow. This in itself may not be an issue for production code. But if you write large programs, your unit tests will become unbearably slow. This is the main reason why I recommend writing large-scale software in compiled languages.

How

As this is probably one of the most crucial points of this book, I'd like to go through the very short test we have seen above, line by line. Everyone needs to understand how the test works.

Inside the test_vector.py file, we write the test case. Before you miss it, I'd like to emphasize the very first line. We want to test the Vector class. We have to import the corresponding file (or library).

```
from vector import Vector
```

Next, we will define the test case. Every test case receives a unique name. This name will appear in the test report if this test fails. It is good practice to give the test case a name that explains what the test does. These names may be up to one line long if necessary. You don't use these names anywhere else, so it doesn't hurt much to have very long test names.

```
def test_distance(self):
```

Inside the test, we start with the setup part. In order to test the distance_to function, we need two vector objects v1 and v2.

```
def test_distance(self):
    v1 = Vector(0,0)
    v2 = Vector(1,1)
```

In the following line, we calculate the distance between v1 and v2:

```
distance_is = v1.distance_to(v2)
```

Now comes the execution of the test. We check if the test result is correct. Note that you can calculate the value of distance_is inline if you want. I only calculated the intermediate result for pedagogical purposes.

```
assert math.isclose(distance_is, 2**0.5)
```

Good inputs should thoroughly test the code. But they should also be simple so that they are easy to read. For tests, it is even more important that they are easy to read than for normal code. Tests may *never* contain any complex logic. Just follow the pattern of the example above: set up, check, tear down. Make it as easy as possible.

General Thoughts About Tests

Tests can only prove the existence of bugs, not their absence.

—Edsger Dijkstra

One of the main misunderstandings about tests is that they are supposed to prove that there are no errors present. This corresponds to Dijkstra's fundamental attempt to mathematically prove that a certain algorithm is correct. This approach failed miserably. Programming is way too complex for mathematical proofs to be applied. It is simply impossible to prove that a program is correct. Therefore, it is also impossible to write tests that prove that a program is correct.

Many people believe that the sole purpose of writing tests is to discover or prevent bugs. They couldn't be further from the truth. Of course, this is one of the reasons why we write tests, but another reason is probably even more important: tests enable us to fixate on the behavior of the code.

Double-Entry Bookkeeping

Robert C. Martin compared programming with tests to double-entry bookkeeping.[7] I really like this comparison. In both cases, you have two independent truths (credit and debit or code and tests, respectively) that must produce the same result. Once both propositions yield equal results, it is highly likely that this outcome is correct, especially if one of them is as simple as the test code. It is unlikely that the same mistake was made in both the code and tests when implementing them independently, especially since the test code is supposed to be very simple.

Having two absolute truths allows you to refactor one of them. You still have the other truth to ensure that the final result is correct. This allows you to refactor the code while leaving the tests unchanged. Alternatively, you may change the tests while leaving the code as is. The other, untouched component always serves as a ground truth against which you can compare your changes. This allows you to refactor your code without the fear of breaking it. If your tests fail for an unknown reason, you can simply revert your changes.

Here is a very small example of a function with a test:

```
def add(a, b):
    return a + b
```

---

[7] Clean Craftsmanship. Robert C. Martin.

Properties of Tests

```
# inside test_add.py
def test_add():
    assert add(1, 2) == 3
```

Now you could *either* rewrite the function implementation, for example:

```
def add(a, b):
    return b + a
```

or you could change the test case:

```
def test_add():
    assert add(3, 5) == 8
```

As long as all the tests pass, you are most likely fine, and your change didn't break any functionality.

Now, if you want the function `add` to return a different result, you'll also have to change the test accordingly. Such changes have to be applied in both the code and the test at the same time. Make sure to keep such changes as small as possible, as they are extremely fragile. Fortunately, it doesn't happen often that you have to change the functionality of a public function or method. In our example, it would be very surprising if all of a sudden the function `add` had to return a different result.

Understand What You Do

When writing tests, there are numerous factors to consider. The example above was very simple. In actual code, you have to work with much more complex objects and many more arguments. But all together, it comes down to one point: Do you really understand what you want to test? If not, there is no need to start writing a test nor any production code. It would never work and would be a waste of time. Rewrite your code to simplify it or seek assistance to better understand the problem you need to solve.

A Few Recommendations

Ensure that all the tests pass. Tests that do not pass are worthless. Even worse, they are a nuisance. When you run the tests, failing tests can be confusing. They will confuse your coworkers. Everyone will waste time trying to fix the failing test, or they will start ignoring failing tests. There is only one solution to prevent this: all tests have to pass all the time. Therefore, ensure that your Continuous Integration (CI, p. 250) enforces that all tests pass. Tests that do not pass should be deleted.

In the setup phase, it is very common to have helper functions that create all the necessary objects. These are standard Python functions that generate the required objects. It is common to have some files containing helper functions to set up all the objects required by the tests. Write the tests the same way you write the normal code: make the tests work, and if you realize there is some duplication in the test code, refactor it out.

There are also some aspects to be mindful of during the execution phase of the test. The first mistake that almost everyone makes is checking two floating-point numbers for equality. Due to rounding errors, this will probably fail. There are specific approximate checks you should use instead. One possibility is the `isclose` function, which is used in the example above. Bugs quite frequently occur if your tests miss some branches of if-else statements (p. 44). Ensure that you address all cases, if needed, by utilizing a code coverage tool.

Similarly, you have to make sure your tests cover all the corner cases. This is one of the reasons why tests should be written by the same person who wrote the actual code as well. The developer knows what the corner cases are, unlike some independent testers.

When refactoring code, ensure that you only modify *either* the code *or* the tests. This is the only way you can be sure that the changes are correct. Only change the code and the tests simultaneously if the change is straightforward.

Quality of Test Code

Tests are somewhat special, but ultimately they are still code. In a serious project, the test code is likely longer than the actual production code you work with. In highly regulated areas, such as medicine, automotive industry, military, etc., the tests are usually several times as long. When considering this, it becomes apparent that when writing tests, certain coding guidelines must also be adhered to.

When it comes to tests, it is even more crucial for the code to be easy to understand compared to regular code. It can't be too easy. You are even allowed to repeat yourself, at least a little. Or, as Jay Fields[8] put it: "When writing tests, you should prefer DAMP (Descriptive And Maintainable Procedures) to DRY."

Still, you should value the SRP. The code in tests should be clear to the reader. Refactor it as you would with any other code. Keep the functions short, use appropriate names, and eliminate unnecessary duplication. These aspects are often overlooked when writing tests, even though the requirements for test code are somewhat different from those for production code.

If the test code seems complicated, it may also indicate that the actual code is flawed and difficult to work with.

Number of Test Cases

Probably the most challenging decision is determining the values you want to use in your tests. Writing one test case for a function is much better than having none. But maybe you just got lucky, and your code works exactly for this one number?

For a single-argument function, I recommend testing all possible corner cases and approximately two random values. As you wrote the function, you should know the corner cases: division by zero, passing an empty array as a function argument,

---

[8] Working Effectively with Unit Tests. Michael Feathers.

Properties of Tests

testing for a non-existing file, etc. This is one of the reasons why a person writing the code should also write the unit tests. Only this person knows the corner cases. The functional tests, on the other hand, should be written by an independent person. But we'll come to that later.

When dealing with functions that have many arguments, it can become quite challenging to write tests. If you have 3 arguments and you would like to test 3 values for each, you end up with $3^3 = 27$ test cases. This is quite a lot. Now, you really have to ensure that you understand what you are doing.

Here is an example of a function with three arguments. I have not documented all the test cases, but you can imagine how tedious this process might become.

```
def f(a,b,c):
    return a + b + c

# my_test.py
def test_f():
    assert f(0,0,0) == 0
    assert f(1,0,0) == 1
    assert f(0,1,0) == 1
    # ...
```

In some cases, the variables don't interact with each other. They are independent. You may test them independently. The number of tests reduces to about 3 for each variable, resulting in $3 * 3 = 9$ test cases. This sounds much more reasonable, although it's still quite a lot.

Usually, the function arguments are not independent, or at least it is not clear how they interact. Otherwise, they wouldn't be in the same function. And it's generally not feasible to write 27 test cases; that's just too many. Just do your best instead. Test all corner cases and include a few random values. If the function consists of well-written code that doesn't appear to be intentionally hiding bugs, you should be in good shape. And even more importantly, try to keep the number of arguments and the complexity of the functions low.

I'd like to reiterate the importance of truly understanding the functionality of a function. As I have already mentioned several times, you need to test the corner cases, and you can only identify them if you know the code. Of course, you may get lucky by trying an empty array or passing 0, but generally, corner cases cannot be discovered by chance. Nor can you figure out whether some variables are independent of each other or not. These are just two of the reasons why you have to write tests right along with the actual code. If someone else has to write the tests for your code, they are missing this crucial information and either have to read and understand all the code or just guess what it does. Both cases are suboptimal.

You may also have structured objects as input or output of a function. This can become significantly worse than dealing with three variables by orders of magnitude. Structured objects may contain a multitude of fields, such as elements in a list. Everything we have discussed so far becomes insignificant as you cannot test every element. But we can still achieve reasonable test coverage if we try. First of all, all elements in a list have to be treated equally in your code. Avoid using a single list to store different elements! This is a fundamental rule when dealing with lists; see p. 40. It allows you to write tests for a fairly short list and deal with only one element of it or at least by selecting one element from a long list. All the other elements will behave the same. If the code is well written, you don't even have to care about the case of an empty list.

But also in large structured objects, the complexity is usually manageable. Most of the entries are typically quite independent and can be tested accordingly. Most of the entries from a large structured object are probably not even necessary within a function, as the object is quite generic. If you have a nested struct as a function argument, only pass the sub-structs that are actually used inside the function. Only change the values that truly influence the object under test. By following this approach, you can significantly reduce the number of test cases.

Again, it all comes down to the programmer understanding the relationship between different objects. Which parts of the object are actually utilized within the function? Write a generic test with default values for each component of the object. Then, also write tests for specific values of the object. Though, again, here you'll have to figure out which values are important.

If you have to pass a lot of objects as function arguments, it may be an indication that your code is badly structured. Functions should use similar data as arguments, and similar data in a structured object should be stored nearby (p. 164). Only pass to functions what they really need, and sort your objects properly. Tests will help you find cases where you violated this rule.

As you can see, most of the complexity in tests originates from suboptimal code. If you write good code, the tests will be easy to write. In good code, there are few arguments with a minimal nested structure, and all elements in a list are treated equally. Therefore, the number of test cases is low, and setting up the required data structures is comparatively easy.

Stages of a Test

As we have seen, a test generally consists of three stages:

1. The first stage is the setup. It creates all the necessary objects for the test. Usually, this consists of initializing all variables. For functional tests, however, this may also involve copying or creating files or even databases.
2. The second stage involves executing the test. When testing, execute the function you wish to test and verify that the outcomes align with your expectations.
3. The third stage is the teardown. It cleans up all the files you created during the setup and execution stages of the test.

Setup and Teardown

Dedicated setup and teardown functions are automatically called at the beginning and end of a test, respectively. This is ensured by the testing framework. The setup can also be replaced by a few helper functions. There is absolutely nothing wrong with that. At the end of the test, the interpreter or compiler cleans up all the variables as they go out of scope.

In most cases, especially in unit tests, there is no need for a dedicated teardown function. Unit tests have no lasting effects that have to be cleaned up. However, if you write functional tests that use some persistent state, things become tricky. Your tests may require temporary files, modifications to database values, network connections, etc. It becomes messy. You need a foolproof way to ensure that your file handling always works reliably, regardless of the outcome of a previous test, even if it throws an uncaught exception. This is where setup and teardown really come into play.

For file creation, there is not much that can go wrong. You can create it from code or copy it from another location. This is to be implemented in the setup part of the test or by using a specific function. When copying files or databases, ensure that the original file is write-protected. Otherwise, you might change it accidentally. Or you can also create the file using some code.

The tricky part is deleting the files at the end of the test. And yes, it has to be at the end of the current test rather than the beginning of the next test. Since you will likely rearrange the order of the tests at some point, cleaning up at the beginning of the test would not work anymore. Cleaning up at the beginning of a test is a fairly desperate measure and an obvious sign that something is seriously flawed with your test design. Every test should be able to assume that everything is cleaned up before execution.

It may sound very simple to delete a file at the end of the test, but if the test fails, for example, due to an uncaught exception, it aborts. All the code that follows in the normal control flow will be skipped. A typical function call to delete the file will never be executed. There would be a mess of undeleted files. This might impact future runs of the tests, causing them to become flaky (sometimes they pass, sometimes they don't; see p. 121). Flaky tests are one of the worst scenarios because they confuse everyone, and there is a high risk that errors will pass unnoticed.

This problem can be solved by implementing a teardown function, which is guaranteed to always be executed, regardless of the test result. It is guaranteed to be executed even if there is an error occurring inside the test. Only in very serious cases, such as a segmentation fault, may the teardown not be executed. However, this is only a problem with low-level languages such as C++.

Anyway, try to write tests that do not require files or input/output operations. It makes things much easier. Especially with unit tests, you won't have to deal with setup and teardown functions.

Here is an example of a test with the special setup and teardown functions:[9]

```
class TestClass():
    def setup_class(self):
        print("setup_class called once for the class")
```

---

[9] https://code-maven.com/slides/Python/pytest-class

```
    def setup_method(self):
        print("  setup_method called for every method")

    def teardown_method(self):
        print("  teardown_method called for every method")

    def teardown_class(self):
        print("teardown_class called once for the class")

    def test_one(self):
        print("    before assert")
        assert False
        print("    after assert")
```

The captured output is this:

```
------------------ Captured stdout setup --------------------
setup_class called once for the class
  setup_method called for every method
------------------ Captured stdout call ---------------------
    before assert
------------------ Captured stdout teardown -----------------
  teardown_method called for every method
teardown_class called once for the class
```

This code shows that the teardown functions are called even if the test fails (the teardown print statements are executed), while a normal function like this `print("after assert")` statement is not executed. It is skipped as the `assert` raises an exception.

Whether you use the class or the method functions has to be decided in each case individually. This is a detail, as you're anyway not often writing tests that interact with the file system, and therefore it is rare that you need tests with a teardown function.

Helper Functions

A test is also a programming object. Accordingly, it has to follow the basic rules, for example, the SRP. Though you don't have to follow the SRP as strictly as in regular code, as written above, in tests, DAMP is more important than DRY.

Each test serves a singular purpose. It tests exactly one function or method. Testing multiple functions within a single test is considered bad practice. Some people even say that having more than one assertion in a single test would be bad.

Write helper functions to set up a test, as it makes it easier to add more test cases. You may even use a little bit of copy-paste code in tests if it makes the code more readable! Having many smaller tests forces you to structure them better and improves the overall overview.

Here is an example where we could use a helper function in order to make the code more readable:

```
def test_car_accelerates_if_gas_pedal_is_pushed():
    engine = Engine()
    wheels = [Wheel() for _ in range(4)]
    board_electronics = Samsung_TV()
    initial_speed = 0
    car = Car(engine, wheels, board_electronics, initial_speed)

    car.push_gas_pedal()

    assert car.speed == 1
```

This test has the problem that the setup takes much more than just one line. Of course, we could squeeze the code into a single line, but that's not the point here. The better solution is to create a helper function that takes care of the creation of the car. This helper function can be used in other test cases as well.

```
def create_standing_car():
    engine = Engine()
    wheels = [Wheel() for _ in range(4)]
    board_electronics = Samsung_TV()
    initial_speed = 0
    return Car(engine, wheels, board_electronics,
               initial_speed)

def test_car_accelerates_if_gas_pedal_is_pushed():
    car = create_standing_car()
    car.push_gas_pedal()
    assert car.speed == 1
```

Now the test case looks much better. There is only one line for the setup, one line for the action we want to test, and one line for the assertion. The test case is now much easier to read and understand.

The helper function can probably also be used in other test cases, reducing the total amount of code needed and eliminating duplication.

One open question is where the line `car.push_gas_pedal()` belongs. Here, I prefer to have a fourth stage: setup, *execution*, checks, teardown. I like this explicitness and don't see how this execution stage could be part of the setup or the checks. In my opinion, it does something quite different and therefore deserves its own stage.

One final note regarding this test: If you are not accustomed to writing unit tests, you may find the test name to be quite lengthy. But this is not a problem. The test name is only used in the test report; it is not used anywhere else. Thus, it doesn't hurt to have a long test name. It is actually good practice to have a long test name, as it enhances the readability of the test report. If you read a test report, you should be able to pinpoint the error by reading the name of the test alone. A test name consisting of 50 characters is completely normal.

Problematic Tests

Just as with regular code, there are certain indicators that a test may be problematic.

Dependent Tests

It is common to encounter situations where a functional test can only pass if another test passes as well. They are coupled. For example, you have a function that creates a file and writes a number to it. You should write a functional test that calls this function and checks for the existence of the file (this is not a unit test, as it may fail if there is not enough disk space).

Next, you write a test that reads the contents of this file. In this test, you will first call the function to create the file and then call the function to read it. Now there is a problem: these two tests are dependent. If the code fails to create a file, it will not be possible to read it. If the first test fails, the second test inevitably fails as well. This type of dependency represents poor design and violates the SRP. For one failing feature, only one test should fail. This makes it much clearer where the error originates. Having 50 failing tests at once can be extremely frustrating because you'll have to search for a while until you find the cause of the failing tests.

Unfortunately, having all the tests completely separated is a very difficult, if not an impossible, task. There is always some correlation between the results of tests. However, there is a technical solution that helps to some extent. In Python, you can skip tests if a requirement for the test is not met. Tests can depend on each other using the `@pytest.mark.dependency` attribute. This allows us to skip tests that would fail because another test has already failed.

```
pip install pytest-dependency
```

The corresponding tests look as follows:

```
import pytest

@pytest.mark.dependency()
def test_a():
    assert False

# skip test_b if test_a fails
@pytest.mark.dependency(depends=["test_a"])
def test_b():
    print("This will never be printed.")
    assert False
```

As in this example, `test_a` is always going to fail, so `test_b` will be skipped as it depends on `test_a`.

When running these tests, the output will be `1 failed, 1 skipped`. Only `test_a` was executed (and failed), while `test_b` was skipped. Once `test_a` is fixed, `test_b` will be executed as well.

For unit tests, dependent tests are generally not an issue. Each test covers only one unit, which shouldn't depend on any other units. Thus, unit tests are independent. For integration or functional tests (p. 97), this is a different story, as they cover vast areas of code. They can easily become related if they rely on the same area of the code. This is why it is important to keep track of the dependencies of the different tests.

Flaky Tests

Tests that do not always return the same result are called flaky. Flakiness is probably the worst property a test can have. It's just like a false alarm once in a while. You may become annoyed and start ignoring it. Or maybe even worse, the alarm doesn't go off even though it should. Try to avoid flaky tests at all costs.

It won't take much effort to rerun the tests. But the main problem is that it undermines the team's confidence in the test suite. You will never know if a test is failing due to your changes in the code or because, for example, the network is down. At times, rerunning a test might help, but this is only a superficial fix.

The only real solution is writing fail-safe tests. Write, for example, a test that checks the network connection. All tests that rely on the network connection will be dependent on this test. Structuring the tests in this way can significantly reduce flakiness. It is crucial to design your tests so that they don't become flaky.

Especially, unit tests should never be flaky. A test only becomes flaky if some part of the code under test is flaky, but this should never be the case for unit tests. Unit tests should not depend on things that can fail, change over time, or are random, such as the file system, network connections, time, or random numbers. This is one of the reasons why you should avoid testing input/output (I/O) for unit tests and minimize it as much as possible for all other tests.

The following test is flaky and consistently fails late at night:

```
from datetime import datetime

def test_time():
    assert datetime.now().hour < 23
```

Of course, this is a pretty dumb example, but it's less exotic than you may think. Tests (and code) have probably already failed for similar reasons. This could have been a bad fix for the nightly build. People find plenty of reasons to write such kinds of code. For example, someone wants to exploit the fact that the tests are always run in the middle of the night.

Probably you now wonder how you can test code that uses time or random numbers. The answer is dependency injection (DI, p. 134). You create a fake time or random number object that always returns the same values. In this way, you can write tests that return reliable results.

Brittle Tests

Tests that are overly specified are called brittle. They break when changing the code in seemingly unrelated places. One example is testing a JSON file for formatting, even though the contents of the JSON file (p. 246) do not depend on the formatting. The formatting does not matter; it does not change any of the values in the file.

Testing the formatting of a JSON file is just a waste. Even worse, it is an unnecessary liability because it tests something that should not be tested – something that the result does not depend on. Instead, utilize a JSON library to extract only the real values stored in the file and then compare them. This is what we are really interested in. Avoid using string operations when reading a JSON file. JSON should never be read as a string and parsed by your custom library. This is the very definition of brittle code!

```
import json

def test_json_stable():
    x = '{"a": 1, "b": 2}'
    y = json.loads(x)
    assert y == {'a': 1, 'b': 2}

def test_json_brittle():
    x = '{"a": 1, "b": 2}'
    y = {x[2]: int(x[6]), x[10]: int(x[14])}
    assert y == {'a': 1, 'b': 2}
```

Another example of brittle tests is testing methods that should be private but are made public in order to test them. This prevents you from refactoring this function because it is now part of the public interface. Changing it will break the tests, even if the original public interface remains unchanged. This is why private methods should not be made public for testing purposes. If you truly feel the need to test a private method, you should refactor it into a separate class. You should always just test interfaces; they are more stable than implementations.

Random Numbers

If you ever use random numbers in your code, you might get stuck with your tests. You think, how can you test something that is random? Well, you can. Random numbers generated are typically not truly random. Your computer generates them. It uses an algorithm to generate numbers that seem to be random, but the numbers produced are still in a deterministic sequence. Always use the same random number algorithm and seed (initial value) consistently to ensure reproducible results for each test case. Only use truly random numbers once you have deployed your software.

Exceptions and Tests

One thing people frequently forget to test is exceptions. You should not only test the type of the exception but also the exception message. Both the exception type and the message are important; they are part of the code specification.

Test-Driven Development (TDD) may help to avoid this issue. With TDD, you first write the test, and you'll realize right away that your tests already pass, which is an indication that there is something wrong with your tests.

Here is an example code to check that the `div` function really raises a `ZeroDivisionError` if it gets a 0 as a second argument.

```
import pytest

def div(a,b):
    return a/b

def test_div():
    assert pytest.raises(ZeroDivisionError, div, 1, 0)
```

Not Automatable Tests

As software engineers, we aim to automate everything, including tests. However, this is not always possible. There are still things that we can hardly automate. One example is image processing algorithms. How much can an image be compressed while still maintaining good quality? This is very difficult to determine with an automated test and is better assessed by humans. When running complex simulations, such as analyzing the aerodynamics of an airplane, it is impossible to create a test to verify the accuracy of the simulation results, simply because you don't know the correct result. You can only judge if the result makes sense based on your experience. There are still things that are better tested by humans than computers.

A common attempt to deal with this issue is writing tests for simple cases that can be solved analytically or the result is known at least with some precision. Every software should be able to solve these cases, though it is a very challenging task to find these cases.

Writing Better Code with Tests

> *Quality is a product of a conflict between programmers and testers.*
> —Yegor Bugayenko[10]

Tests are not only important for writing correct code; they are equally important for enhancing the code you write, at least if you embrace them and are not just writing tests for the sake of it.

Unit Tests

Unit tests ensure the correctness of your code at a small-scale level. Thanks to unit tests, you no longer have to manually verify if the results of a function or class are

---

[10] https://www.testim.io/blog/test-automation-benefits/

correct. The unit tests check them automatically. But this is only half the reason why they are so important. The other half might be a little unexpected for you: unit tests compel you to write better code. When writing unit tests, you realize immediately whether your code is good or bad. If writing a unit test is difficult, writing normal code will be difficult as well. It indicates that there are some design issues in your code, and you should consider redesigning it.

During the setup phase of the test, you have to create all the required objects. If this task becomes more tedious than expected, your data may be scattered in inappropriate locations. This is a strong indication that the design of your code is poor and needs to be reworked. When writing a test, you are a user of your own code, and your code should be user-friendly, as we have learned in the section "Interfaces" (p. 25). Thus, if your code is difficult to use, it is considered poor quality.

In good code, all the relevant data is easily accessible, and constructing it manually for a test case is fairly simple. Preferably, you should have one large object with relatively static information that you can reuse in all tests, along with a few small, dynamic objects that vary in each test.

If you write a test, you have to know the expected outcome of the function call. If you struggle with the simplest cases, chances are high that your functions are too complex. They should be simplified. Rewrite the code until you can explain to your colleagues the functionality of the code and until you can write a test case. Otherwise, you'll run into significant problems along a bumpy road.

You will be running the unit tests continuously. After every function you define, after every successful compilation, after every coffee you drink, and certainly every time you pull code from the repository, it provides constant feedback on whether everything is functioning properly or if something has been broken. This is invaluable. The only price you pay is the execution time of the unit tests. Keep the tests small and fast. A single unit test should not take more than a few milliseconds. As you will be running hundreds, if not thousands, of tests all the time, execution time is crucial.

Finally, I would like to emphasize once again the importance of this chapter. Learn how to write effective unit tests. Read this chapter again or, even better, search for more elaborated examples. There are thousands out there. And, most importantly, once again, write tests yourself and discuss the design questions with your colleagues. This is how you will really make progress.

Integration and Functional Tests

At first, it sounds great to write integration or even functional tests. With relatively few tests, you can cover a significant portion of the codebase. But this comes at a price.

Integration tests cover much more code than the sum of many unit tests. This has the advantage that a single test is much more likely to find a bug, but it also has its drawbacks. Integration or functional tests cover a large amount of code, which makes them slower and less precise when it comes to pinpointing an error. Fixing bugs identified through integration or functional tests is much more challenging than addressing bugs discovered through unit tests. At the same time, integration tests are also more brittle than unit tests. The interfaces are much larger, and there is a substantial amount of code underneath that can be altered. Ultimately, these tests are expensive to run; they are huge and slow.

Despite these drawbacks, integration and functional tests have their own right to exist. They help improve your code and also encourage you to write proper interfaces. It is important to write these tests from the beginning of a project to ensure that your components and the API are easy to use and to locate potential bugs early. Functional tests, for example, are important to demonstrate that the user stories are truly functional, to prove that the software really works, and to write a test case if a bug is found.

Testing Existing Code

Having code without tests is a huge issue. First of all, you don't know if the code is correct. Probably, you don't even know what the code is really doing. Secondly, you can't change the code anymore, as you never know if you will break something.

Writing tests for existing code might be extremely difficult, if not impossible. This is because the code may be very convoluted and difficult to understand; therefore, it is very hard to write tests. As already mentioned above, it is very important that the author of the code writes the tests in a timely manner. Everything else is highly ineffective.

As Michael Feathers stated, "To me, legacy code is code without tests." He then wrote an entire book about this topic.[11] Code without tests is indeed a huge topic, and I also dedicated a section to this topic (p. 222) where the issues and solutions will be discussed in more detail. For an in-depth understanding of this topic, I recommend reading Michael Feathers' book.

Assertions

There were times when people thought that using assert commands in production code was a good replacement for writing tests. This is so terribly wrong!

The most obvious reason is that using asserts inside production code is a violation of the SRP. You are writing tests inside production code. I believe that nowadays it is widely accepted that tests and production code should be stored in separate files.

Secondly, your production code is not designed to run automated test cases. Assertions are only executed if you run the software you create. It will highlight any violations of the assertions along the way, but this process cannot be automated.

---

[11] Working Effectively with Legacy Code. Michael Feathers.

It can be used as something akin to an emergency sign. It is advisable to prioritize improving the quality of your tests over relying on asserts in production code.

Don't get me wrong. There is nothing wrong with asserts in general. But using asserts in production code as a substitute for tests is not recommended.

The following two code snippets are perfectly normal and almost identical:

```
def root(x):
    assert x >= 0, "smaller than 0"
    return x**0.5

def root2(x):
    if x < 0:
        raise AssertionError("smaller than 0")
    return x**0.5
```

This is because the `assert` statement raises an `AssertionError` if the required condition is violated. You can even add a message to the `assert` command using the `"smaller than 0"` syntax. The only advantage of the second code snippet is that you can use custom exceptions instead of the `AssertionError`, as we'll learn on p. 174.

Now, as I said, this code is perfectly fine. But it is no replacement for unit tests, as it doesn't test anything. It only checks the precondition of the function.

Test-Driven Development

Write tests until fear is transformed into boredom.

—Kent Beck

So far, we have written tests to verify the correctness of our code. We wrote the tests once we were done with the code, but there is nothing wrong with writing the tests up front. It is called Test-Driven Development (TDD).[12] In fact, I recommend using TDD in general. It forces you to think more about what you want to do. You have to figure out how the interfaces should look before writing the actual code. Once the test is written, you need to think about how to write the actual code between the interfaces defined in the tests. The importance of the test cannot be understated; it helps you understand what you really have to do. The test forces you to structure your code accordingly, which is a really good thing. Before writing the implementation of a class, you must define its interface. With TDD, you decouple the code because your tests compel you to do so.

In software development, it may happen frequently that you have a specific model in mind intended to solve your problem. But it turns out to be too complex, and somehow, you don't manage to get it working. This might be a case of YAGNI (You

---

[12] Test Driven Development: By Example. Kent Beck.

Aren't Gonna Need It).[13] Chances are you will never need this complex structure. YAGNI is a very common issue and can be really expensive. Furthermore, it is a sign that you think you know what you have to do, but actually you don't. YAGNI happens more often than you think.

A very simple remedy against YAGNI is to write test cases for your specific requirements before writing the code. As a next step, you only write enough code to make the tests pass. Everything else can be taken care of later, once you determine that it is truly necessary. If you do not need a piece of code to make the tests pass, simply do not write it. Even if you truly believe that it would be significant, aesthetically pleasing, and perhaps even enjoyable to write some additional piece of code, using TDD, you found out that you don't need this code now, and chances are it will never be needed at all.

Perhaps you do not fully understand yet how TDD really works. Don't worry. You should maybe first gain some experience with standard tests, if you don't immediately see how a test should look, at least. If you are unsure about the final appearance of the code's interface, yes, there are several aspects of TDD that may seem a little unusual, and it takes time to become accustomed to it. But it is worth the effort.

You don't have to start writing all your code using TDD right now. Instead, I recommend gradually starting to apply TDD. Just try to use TDD for a certain feature for which you know the expected outcome. Starting like this is really good practice, as you'll learn how to work in a more structured manner.

If you don't manage to do TDD all the time, don't worry too much. First, it takes some time to get used to it. Second, once you are used to TDD, you automatically start writing code that is easy to test, and doing TDD is not absolutely needed anymore.

How TDD Works

There is a simple pattern for writing code in TDD.

1. Write a failing test.
2. Write code until the test passes.
3. Refactor if necessary.

These three steps must be repeated over and over again until you have completed your ticket.

You should write one test for the feature you want to implement and every bug you want to fix. I repeat: one and only one test. If you have functional and unit tests (which I hope you do), you might have one pending test case for each of them. There should be a test case that currently fails.

If a test passes for an unknown reason, this is a serious issue that you have to investigate. Perhaps a feature has already been implemented, or your test may not

---
[13] https://en.wikipedia.org/wiki/You_aren%27t_gonna_need_it

be evaluating its intended functionality and needs to be refined. This problem is much more severe if you don't do TDD, as you might not realize a test passes even though it is not testing what it is supposed to. If your tests pass for an unknown reason, the only solution is to make the test fail deliberately by adding a bug into the code.

If your tests fail as expected, you should start implementing the code. Figure out why the test fails. For new features, it's usually obvious. The test is currently evaluating a feature that has not been implemented yet. Now it's your task to write just enough code so that the test passes. No less and no more. You don't have to write great code at this step. Just make sure you find a satisfactory solution to ensure the test passes.

Once the test passes, you might have to refactor a little to get the code back into shape. You have already written all the necessary test cases as a safety precaution. Then, you are allowed to write the next test case until you are done with the feature and the functional test passes as well.

Also, with TDD, you have to do some significant refactoring occasionally. This is inevitable and has to be taken into consideration. These refactorings involve entire components, requiring you to work with multiple classes simultaneously.

The Importance of TDD

As we learned in the section "Interfaces" (p. 25), they should always be defined from the user's perspective. When writing a test first, you are adopting the user's perspective of your code. You are a user of the corresponding piece of code. Therefore, writing your tests before the code forces the programmer to adapt the code to the test. This is a good thing, as it makes the interface of the code more user-friendly. Even if you don't apply TDD all the time, you still get used to writing code that is easy to test and therefore also easy to use.

With TDD, you will automatically write much better code than with classical software development, even if you write tests. In classical code-first development, you can still write code that is difficult to test and, therefore, bad. Meanwhile, with TDD, you force yourself to write code that is easy to test. This is a significant advantage of TDD.

Example of TDD

TDD is best understood by examining a brief example. Let's write a program that converts Arabic numbers (the ones we use) into Roman numerals. As we learned just now, we start by writing the first test case.

```
# inside test_roman_numbers.py
from roman_numbers import *

def test_one():
    assert roman_numbers(1) == "I"
```

Writing Better Code with Tests

If we run the test, it fails as it was to be expected. But we can make it pass easily.

```
# inside roman_numbers.py
def roman_numbers(_):
    return "I"
```

This may look odd at first sight, as the result is obviously wrong for all other values but 1. However, it is perfectly viable code in TDD. You only have to make the test pass, and that's exactly what we did. No more and no less.

As there is nothing to refactor, we can continue with the second test.

```
def test_two():
    assert roman_numbers(2) == "II"

def roman_numbers(n):
    if n == 1:
        return "I"
    else:
        return "II"
```

The code from the initial test is no longer adequate. We have to use at least some if/else clauses. You might feel the urge to refactor this code, but at least for the time being, we will leave it as it is. The need to refactor this code is not yet strong enough.

There is a rule of thumb stating that a one-time repetition of the code is acceptable and does not need to be refactored immediately. Only if the same code is repeated two times or more should it be refactored, as this may lead to a better understanding of the problem. However, this rule contradicts the DRY principle to some extent.

As you can see, we have a few strict rules in software engineering. It is always a trade-off between different principles.

```
def test_three():
    assert roman_numbers(3) == "III"

def roman_numbers(n):
    if n == 1:
        return "I"
    elif n == 2:
        return "II"
    else:
        return "III"
```

Now the `if/else` statements start to take over. We have three possible cases, and with a little bit of thinking, we find an easy way to refactor them away. The new version of the code might look like this:

```
def roman_numbers(n):
    return n*"I"
```

Let's add a fourth test:

```
def test_four():
    assert roman_numbers(4) == "IV"
```

We don't know yet how to deal with `numbers > 4`, so we may return any value we want.

```
def roman_numbers(n):
    if n == 4:
        return "IV"
    return n*"I"
```

Here, it doesn't matter if we use `n == 4` or `n >= 4` as we don't have any specifications on what should happen for values greater than 4.

For 5, we can just continue with the same pattern.

```
def test_five():
    assert roman_numbers(5) == "V"

def roman_numbers(n):
    if n == 5:
        return "V"
    elif n == 4:
        return "IV"
    return n*"I"
```

Two tests later, we are again at the point where we have to refactor. This time, we have to think a little harder about how the logic of the function really works. One possible outcome of this refactoring is the following code:

```
def roman_numbers(n):
    num = ""
    while n >= 5:
        num += "V"
        n -= 5
    while n >= 4:
        num += "IV"
        n -= 4
    while n >= 1:
        num += "I"
        n -= 1
    return num
```

In a second refactoring step, we wrap the whole while loops into a single for loop.

```
def roman_numbers(n):
    roman = ""
    arabic_to_roman = {5:"V", 4:"IV", 1:"I"}
    for arabic in arabic_to_roman:
        while n >= arabic:
            n -= arabic
            roman += arabic_to_roman[arabic]
    return roman
```

Now we are pretty much done. Supporting larger numbers can be achieved by adding them to the beginning of the `arabic_to_roman` dictionary.

Note that I used a dictionary instead of a list of lists. This is because, as I mentioned on p. 39, all list elements should be treated equally. Thus, having a list of lists, `[[5, "V"], [4, "IV"], [1, "I"]]` would violate this principle.

On the other hand, this approach using a dictionary is a little bit fragile. It is only guaranteed to work for Python versions $>=$ 3.7 because dicts are guaranteed to maintain their order only since then. The following solution would probably be the best option, as it is more robust, even though it is slightly longer. Though here we go into the realm of premature optimization.

```
from dataclasses import dataclass

@dataclass
class NumberPair:
    arabic: int
    roman: str

def roman_numbers(n):
    roman = ""
    arabic_roman = [NumberPair(5, "V"),
                    NumberPair(4, "IV"),
                    NumberPair(1, "I")]
    for number_pair in arabic_roman:
        while n >= number_pair.arabic:
            n -= number_pair.arabic
            roman += number_pair.roman
    return roman
```

The remaining tests and implementations are straightforward. In order to save paper, I'll leave them as an exercise for the reader.

Fakes, Mocks, and Dependency Injection

Dependency Injection is a 25-dollar term for a 5-cent concept.

—Reddit

In many instances, you may need to write a test, but the code you intend to test includes elements that you prefer not to test, such as a database or an Internet connection. You want to create a fake database that returns the expected value and never fails. The solution is to create your own database – not a complete one, of course, but one that does only what you really need for this test case: a fake in-memory database. It implements every function you call and returns the values you desire. Depending on the complexity of your test cases, you may need to incorporate a significant amount of logic into the fake database to achieve the desired behavior. Perhaps you need separate mock databases for various tests, or you might need a dedicated database that throws an exception in some special cases. Programming fake objects altogether is a lot of work, and it makes the code rigid because not all the functionalities of the fake object are implemented.

There are many ways to set up a fake object. We will only look at two of them: faking and mocking.

Mocking

The first approach is to utilize mocking.[14,15] You can take, for example, an existing database and modify some of its functionalities by using a mocking framework. In the following example, we simulate the result of reading a CSV file. In Python, this can be easily achieved using the Mock library. Most other programming languages have similar mocking libraries, too.

```
from important_stuff import read_csv

from unittest.mock import Mock

def read_csv(file_name):
    return [1,2,3]

def test_mock_important_stuff():
    # Override the read_csv function defined in
    # important_stuff.py and return some values.
    read_csv = Mock(return_value=([4, 5, 6]))
    assert read_csv("unexisting_file.csv") == ([4, 5, 6])
```

In this example, we override the `read_csv` function defined in `important_stuff.py` and return the values [4, 5, 6] instead of [1, 2, 3].

This test passes even if the file passed to `read_csv` as an argument does not exist. An alternative to using the mocking framework is to use dependency injection. This is explained below.

---

[14] Clean Craftsmanship, Robert C. Martin.

[15] Software Engineering at Google, Winters et al.

Fakes, Mocks, and Dependency Injection

Mocks have some predefined behavior. In this case, they simply return the values defined in the code. Mocks are different from fakes, as they mimic real behavior to some extent. Setting up mocks is much easier compared to fakes.

However, there is a better solution than using mocking libraries: dependency injection (DI, p. 134). I like DI much better than using mocking libraries. In my opinion, using mocking libraries is a hack to get away with suboptimal code and should not be used unless you have to work with existing code where DI is not an option. Though even there, it is generally not that much effort to implement DI afterward (p. 216).

Here is what the code looks like with DI instead of mocking:

```python
def read_csv(filename):
    # ...
    return [1, 2, 3]

def mock_reader(_):
    return [4, 5, 6]

def read_data_from(reader, filename):
    return reader(filename)

def test_mock_important_stuff():
    data = read_data_from(mock_reader, "")
    assert data == [4, 5, 6]
```

With this code, you can define your own reader function without the use of a mocking library. I think the code has become much clearer.

Faking

A fake[16] is a somewhat more sophisticated version of a mock. It's a simplified functional replica of the object you intend to substitute. For example, the fake CSV reader in the following example does not read a file from the disk; instead, it simply returns a string stored in the code. When running tests, this approach is typically sufficient without the inconvenience of managing the file system, where your original data could be easily deleted or tampered with by others.

The following example is the classical example of a fake. The `FakeCSVReader` does not write the data to a file but stores it in a local variable and returns it if you "read" it out.

```python
class CSVReader:
    def __init__(self, filename):
        self.filename = filename

    def write(self, data):
```

---

[16] Clean Craftsmanship, Robert C. Martin.

```
        with open(self.filename, 'w') as f:
            f.write(data)

    def read(self):
        with open(self.filename, 'r') as f:
            return f.read()

class FakeCSVReader:
    def __init__(self, _):
        self._data = None

    def write(self, data):
        self._data = data

    def read(self):
        return self._data
```

This `FakeCSVReader` clearly does not have a complete implementation of the `CSVReader`. It has just enough capacity to store some data and retrieve it later, but this might be enough to make your tests pass. Fakes should be used whenever a mock is not sufficient for your test case, as the fake has much more functionality.

Dependency Injection

Faking and mocking are closely related to dependency injection (DI), also known as the Strategy Design Pattern.[17]

When using DI, you can create a new object from scratch, for example, an object that returns an API key. Now let's first look at the code without DI.

```
import os

class ApiClient:
    def get_api_key(self):
        return os.getenv("API_KEY")

def main():
    print(ApiClient().get_api_key())

if __name__ == "__main__":
    main()
```

The API key is generated within the `ApiClient` class. This is bad for several reasons. Testing it is challenging, and it is not easy to replace the API key with a fake one. Secondly, it is difficult to reuse. If you want to use the same API key in another class, you will need to copy the code.

---

[17] Design Patterns. Gamma et al.

If you want to change the `api_key` for testing purposes, one thing you can do is make the following selection:

```
import os
import sys

class ApiClient:
    def get_api_key(self, is_testing):
        if is_testing:
            return "1234"
        return os.getenv("API_KEY")

def main(is_testing):
    print(ApiClient().get_api_key(is_testing))

if __name__ == "__main__":
    is_testing = "testing" in sys.argv
    main(is_testing)
```

This, however, is considered bad practice. As we learned in the section "About Booleans" (p. 44), such selections should not be postponed. Don't pass around Booleans or strings. Even if you replace the Boolean with an `enum`, you should still avoid postponing this decision.

A better solution is using DI. Already in the line `is_testing = "testing" in sys.argv`, we know whether we want to use a fake API key or the real one. Thus, we can already at this point select the corresponding `ApiClient` and then pass it on, rather than some flag. Like this, the decision is resolved at the highest level of abstraction, inside the main function.

```
import os
import sys

class ApiClient:
    def get_api_key(self):
        return "API_KEY"

class FakeApiClient:
    def get_api_key(self):
        return "1234"

def main(client):
    print(client.get_api_key())

if __name__ == "__main__":
    if "testing" in sys.argv:
        main(FakeApiClient())
    else:
        main(ApiClient())
```

In DI, you pass a higher object, like a class instance or a function, as a function parameter, as done here in the call of the `main` function. Here, we used the `api_client` as a function argument, which can be either a `FakeApiClient` or a normal `ApiClient`.

DI is a little odd at the beginning. I recommend you read this section again, search for some additional examples online, and play around with them. The important part is that you select the relevant behavior as early as possible in the program, rather than passing around Boolean variables.

Using DI is generally a highly recommended practice and should always be employed when dealing with I/O, time, random numbers, API keys, selecting an algorithm, etc. This is because you can easily replace the injected code with something else. You don't have to go down in the code to where the object is actually used. Just implement it at a high level and inject it.

The only drawback of DI is that the object has to be passed through the entire stack until it reaches the point where the API key is actually used. This leads to functions containing many arguments. But what would the alternatives be?

1. Do not pass any additional argument through the stack. This would prevent you from altering/testing the code.
2. Pass a string, integer, or Boolean through the entire stack and make a selection based on its value, similar to how it is done with the `"testing"` value in the second example. This wouldn't be any better than passing the `ApiClient` object. Rather the opposite. It is better to pass a high-level object than passing a string, as this allows for making a selection based on it.

When you need to make a selection, such as when you want to change a value for testing purposes, using DI is the optimal choice. Delaying the decision would require you to pass around a Boolean or string instead, which is considered bad practice. Selections should always be resolved promptly, and DI allows you to do exactly that.

One of the few downsides of DI is that it may make the code slightly harder to understand. In order to understand what's going on, you have to look through many functions to figure out which code got injected. For this reason, it is recommended to use DI only for things that are expected to change. It should be mostly used for the reasons mentioned above: I/O, time, random numbers, API keys, and other things you want to change when testing or running the code, respectively.

DI is an extremely useful tool when it comes to writing polymorphic code. It allows you to select completely different behavior of the system at runtime. However, it should only be used for that purpose. Don't use DI when there is no reason to. You can still implement DI later on, as explained on p. 216.

It is important to use DI for things you cannot test otherwise, for example, input/output (I/O), time, random numbers, etc. However, you can overdo it. There might not be a reason to dependency inject the `engine` into a car.

```
class Engine:
    def start(self):
        pass

class Car:
    def __init__(self, engine):
        self.engine = engine

    def start(self):
        self.engine.start()
```

This is, of course, perfectly viable code, but it's not necessarily always better than constructing the engine inside the constructor. If there is no reason to use DI, then don't use it. Only once you want to make `Engine` polymorphic should you use DI, for example, if you want to create a `FakeEngine` for testing purposes or distinguish between a `GasolineEngine` and an `ElectricEngine`.

DI with Functions

So far, we have looked at DI with classes. In most programming languages, you can also pass function objects as function arguments and therefore use DI with functions instead of classes. The API key example on p. 135 can be rewritten using functions as follows:

```
import sys

def api_key():
    return "API_KEY"

def fake_api_key():
    return "1234"

def main(api_key_getter):
    print(api_key_getter())

if __name__ == "__main__":
    if "testing" in sys.argv:
        main(fake_api_key)
    else:
        main(api_key)
```

This is perfectly viable code. It is a good alternative to injecting objects with only one method. The only reason why I mention this so late in this chapter is that you don't really need to know about DI with functions. It's just another way of doing DI.

Summary

Don't worry if you haven't understood everything. I just briefly explained dependency injection, faking, mocking, etc., some of which are fairly advanced topics. I hope you have grasped some of the fundamental ideas I attempted to explain here. They can be useful, and the ideas behind them are very important. Especially, TDD and DI were crucial topics in this chapter. If you want to have an in-depth look at some of the things we discussed here, I recommend exploring these two topics. There is plenty of literature available that delves into much more detail than I have provided here.

Design Principles 5

There are several design principles that one should adhere to, with the most renowned being the SOLID principles formulated by Robert C. Martin. The significance of the Single Responsibility Principle (SRP, see p. 13) cannot be overstated. However, for interpreted languages, the relevance of the other principles has diminished considerably. Nevertheless, they remain valuable to understand, particularly if you are working with a compiled language.

Besides the SOLID principles, we discuss several other guidelines that can assist you in writing better code.

SOLID Principles

It is not enough for code to work.

—Robert C. Martin

The SOLID principles[1] were written down by Robert C. Martin. SOLID is named after five general rules for how to write *compiled* OO code. These are

1. Single Responsibility Principle (SRP, p. 13)
2. Open-Closed Principle (OCP, p. 140)
3. Liskov Substitution Principle (LSP, p. 142)
4. Interface Segregation Principle (ISP, p. 143)
5. Dependency Inversion Principle (DIP, p. 145)

These five quite general rules describe mostly how classes, and also code in general, should be structured and interact with each other. Obeying them helps with the design of the code.

---

[1] Agile Software Development, Robert C. Martin.

Interestingly enough, many people agree on the fact that these principles are, or at least were, important, but there are different opinions on what they exactly mean. I, for example, am not taking the definitions as strictly. The original definition of the SRP was, "A class should have only one reason to change." However, it is not apparent why this rule should only apply to classes. In my opinion, this should be a universally applicable rule. This makes this rule much more important than the other rules of SOLID, and therefore the SRP deserves its own section at the beginning of this book (p. 13).

The other principles are nice to know, but they are not as important as the SRP.

Single Responsibility Principle

The SRP is the only principle here that is universally applicable and does not depend on OO code. This makes it significantly more important than the other principles. As mentioned above, the SRP therefore deserves its own section (p. 13). At the time of writing, I counted 80 occurrences of the abbreviation "SRP" in this book!

Open-Closed Principle

> *Software entities [classes, modules, functions, etc.] should be open for extension but closed for modification.*
>
> —Bertrand Meyer

The Open-Closed Principle (OCP) was first mentioned by Bertrand Meyer in 1988. It states that an object should be open for extension and closed for modification. The original version suggests using implementation inheritance to achieve this goal.[2] This is an unfortunate choice. Robert C. Martin suggested using interfaces instead. Interfaces allow you to add multiple implementations at a relatively low cost, while modifying the interface itself can be quite expensive. Each class implementing that interface would also need to be modified.

Our code should be stable with respect to extensions in the future but allow changes. If the requirements change, we must also modify our code. This is inevitable. However, we shouldn't have to change our code if someone else wants to extend theirs. Therefore, the solution is to utilize abstractions at possible abstraction points. This allows the user of our code to extend it without requiring any modifications to our code.

Let's consider a brief example. We have a class containing some postal codes of Swiss cities. If we want to add another city, we would need to include an extra function in this class. The class `Cities` is not open for modification. We have to modify it every time we add another city. This class does not adhere to the OCP.

---

[2] Object-Oriented Software Construction. Bertrand Meyer.

SOLID Principles

```python
class Cities:
    def zurich_postal_code(self):
        return 8000
    def bern_postal_code(self):
        return 3000

def print_all_postal_codes():
    cities = Cities()
    print(cities.zurich_postal_code())
    print(cities.bern_postal_code())
```

If the user of this code wishes to add another city, they will need to do so within our own code inside the `Cities` class. We have to *modify* the class `Cities`. This is the opposite of what the OCP wants to achieve. The OCP wants to separate the user code from the interface.

Instead, we can create an interface called `City` and implement it for every city we are interested in. We are free to add an additional city if we choose to. We don't have to change any existing class or interface. Instead, we can create a new object to *extend* the implementation of the city interface. The code below adheres to the OCP.

```python
from abc import ABC, abstractmethod

class City(ABC):
    @abstractmethod
    def postal_code(self):
        pass

class Zurich(City):
    def postal_code(self):
        return 8000

class Bern(City):
    def postal_code(self):
        return 3000

cities = [Zurich(), Bern()]
for city in cities:
    print(city.postal_code())
```

Now, this code fulfills the OCP. If the user wants to add another city, they can create as many additional cities as they want, and we don't have to worry about it. The base class `City` defines the interface, which is sufficient for us to work with any class the user adds. Of course, there are many other possible implementations of the OCP, especially in a dynamically typed language like Python. The code above is just an example.

If you like design patterns, the code here is a classic illustration of the OCP. It is the strategy design pattern[3] (p. 185). However, you might also consider using the decorator pattern, which also satisfies the OCP.

Liskov Substitution Principle

> *If it looks like a duck, quacks like a duck, and needs batteries, you probably have the wrong abstraction.*
>
> —Wisdom of the Internet

Implementation of interfaces should not blindly adhere to the "is a" principle. This is only a rule of thumb and is not sufficient. Instead, the implementations really have to share the same interface.

For example, credit cards and PayPal should not implement the same payment system interface, even though they are both payment methods. The credit card requires a card number, while PayPal requires an email address.[4] This leads to a situation where you are unsure about what the payment interface should accept as an input argument.

```
class Payment:
    def make_payment(amount, card_number_or_email_address)
```

This logical contradiction regarding whether the second argument should be (email address or card number) violates the Liskov Substitution Principle. Credit card payments and PayPal payments should not use the same interface, at least not at this level. Instead, you have to define an interface that defines a general payment method. The selection of the credit card number or the email address should be done later, within the specific classes. It is there that these credentials have to be requested from the user.

```
from abc import ABC, abstractmethod

class PaymentSystem(ABC):
    @abstractmethod
    def make_payment(self):
        pass

class PayPal(PaymentSystem):
    def make_payment(amount):
        email = ask_for_email_address()
        make_paypal_payment(amount, email)

class CreditCard(PaymentSystem):
    def make_payment(amount):
        credit_card = ask_for_credit_card_number()
        make_credit_card_payment(amount, credit_card)
```

---

[3] Design Patterns. Gamma et al.

[4] https://youtu.be/pTB30aXS77U?t=455

SOLID Principles

Figure 5-1 File A is imported by many other files

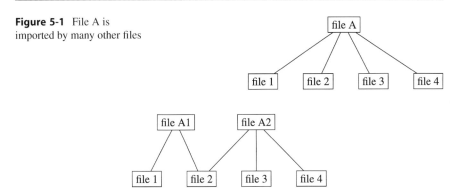

Figure 5-2 File A is split up into two files, A1 and A2. Most other files import only either A1 or A2. They relied only on a fraction of the interface of A

Interface Segregation Principle

Clients should not be forced to depend upon interfaces that they do not use.
—Robert C. Martin

The Interface Segregation Principle (ISP) is similar to the SRP for interfaces. Interfaces should be split up into many small parts. This is important in order to maintain low coupling. You don't want to import and compile a huge library solely for one small feature. If there are separate logical blocks within a library, ensure that they are also made available separately.

In the example below, file A does not comply with the ISP. It does two independent things. Most code only uses one of these functions. They are independent. Thus, they should be in different files.

```
// C++
// file A.h
int function_1(){
    return 1;
}

int function_2(){
    return 2;
}

// and many more functions
```

Now in Python, this is not such a big deal because you can import each function individually. Even if you import the whole file A, it's not a big deal. It's not becoming slow. In C++, on the other hand, adding unrelated functions in the same file is really a no-go. In C++, you always include an entire header file at once, and you will have to compile everything that is included with it. There might be a hefty price to pay if file A is too large.

The solution is to split file A into two subfiles, A1 and A2. The goal is to find a way to achieve this so that the majority of the other files utilize only one of the newly created files, A1 or A2. A1 and A2 should exhibit high cohesion within themselves, but there should be low coupling between them. Ideally, the amount of code that you'll have to import is reduced by roughly half.

This process of breaking up files can be repeated until it is no longer possible to reduce the amount of imported code, or the number of imports is growing unreasonably fast. At this point, you have finished segregating file A. The resulting files have high cohesion and low coupling.

```cpp
// C++
// file A1
int function_1(){
    return 1;
}

// file A2
int function_2(){
    return 2;
}
```

A well-known example of interface segregation is the standard library in C++. All the functionality is defined inside the std:: namespace (std:: is a namespace, not a class!), but the whole library is split up into many different files. Importing the entire standard library solely for the sake of using a small portion of it would increase compilation times tremendously.

Another common example is defining an enum inside a class, while other parts of the code might also need access to this enum. This section of the code needs to import the entire class that contains the enum, even though it only requires this simple enum and nothing else. This code imports more modules than necessary.

```python
# inside ImportantStuff.py
from enum import Enum

class BigClass:
    class Color(Enum):
        RED = 1
        GREEN = 2
        BLUE = 3
    # and much more code here

# inside SomeOtherFile.py
from ImportantStuff import BigClass

color = BigClass().Color.BLUE
```

Here, we first need a class instance of `BigClass` because the enum is encapsulated within the class definition. This issue could be avoided by moving the enum outside the class. This would reduce the coupling of the code because the user code would only depend on the enum and not on the entire class surrounding it.

SOLID Principles

The code would be much better as follows:

```python
# inside ImportantStuff.py
from enum import Enum

class Color(Enum):
    RED = 1
    GREEN = 2
    BLUE = 3

class BigClass:
    # much more code here

# inside SomeOtherFile.py
from ImportantStuff import Color

color = Color.BLUE
```

By doing this, you have segregated the interface, and you don't have to import the `BigClass` anymore in order to access the `Color` enum.

Dependency Inversion Principle

> 1. *High-level modules should not depend on low-level modules. Both should depend on abstractions.*
> 2. *Abstractions should not depend on details. Details should depend on abstractions.*
> —Robert C. Martin

The Dependency Inversion Principle (DIP) consists of two parts that we need to look at separately.

The Second Rule of the DIP

Let's start with the second part, as it is easier to understand. It states that the engine of a car shouldn't know anything about the car because otherwise the engine cannot be reused; it would be bound to the car. The code becomes extremely entangled. The car contains the engine (e.g., as a member variable), and the flow of data always goes from the car to the engine. The engine should only respond to requests from the car. The engine never does anything by itself. Breaking this rule immediately leads to circular dependencies (p. 172).

According to Robert C. Martin, this used to be a very common problem. Therefore, he came up with the name. He wanted to highlight the inverted direction of the dependency. Even though, to me, it seems absolutely normal that the engine should never know anything about the car.

The First Rule of the DIP

The first rule of the DIP is a bit more difficult to understand. It states that high-level modules should not depend on low-level modules. They should depend on abstractions (interfaces in Java, abstract base classes (ABC) in Python, etc.). The reasoning behind this argument is that interfaces are more stable than implementations. However, I don't understand why one would have to define an ABC for this purpose. The following class is perfectly viable code and doesn't need an ABC:

```
class Math:
    def add(a, b, c):
        return a + b + c
```

Every class inevitably has an interface. In this case, the `Math` class has one function, `add`, with the function signature `add(a, b, c)`. I can easily change the implementation without changing the interface. As we are working in Python, we also don't have to worry about compilation times.

But also in C++, I couldn't find any issues with this code. You define the interface in a header file, which contains only the function signatures of the class methods. This header file will be included in other files, so you are free to change the implementation files as much as you want. The interface is stable, and there is no recompilation of the entire codebase necessary.

As far as I know, most other modern programming languages also don't need to recompile the entire code if you change some implementation.

Of course, there are times when it's reasonable to write an ABC, interface, or however it's called in your programming language. But I wouldn't say that you should always do it. There are plenty of cases where this is a case of YAGNI (p. 166). Just write the concrete class, and you are done.

Other Software Engineering Principles

I came, I saw, I conquered.

—Julius Caesar

In this chapter, I explain some very general design principles that I learned from a YouTube video titled "10 Design Principles For Software Engineers"[5] published by the channel Tech with Tim. I really liked these principles and therefore decided to write a section about them.

Divide and Conquer

If you have a huge problem to solve, you won't be able to do it all at once, down to the last detail. It's too difficult. But what you might be able to do is break out pieces of this problem and solve them. This is generally how software is designed: break the problem into small pieces and then reassemble them. This is valid for both the design of software and some algorithms.

---

[5] https://youtu.be/XQzEo1qag4A

Common examples are the Fast Fourier Transform (FFT) and merge sort. Usually, a divide and conquer algorithm is applied if the classical algorithm scales with $O(N^2)$ but can be subdivided into smaller problems. Divide and conquer algorithms typically scale with $O(N \log N)$, which is generally deemed acceptable. Furthermore, divide and conquer algorithms can be parallelized to some degree, which can significantly enhance overall performance.

Increase Cohesion

Cohesion is closely related to the section "Correlation" (p. 165) that we previously discussed in Chapter 6. Similar things that possibly depend on each other should belong together. Mathematical functions are stored together in the math library, and I/O functions are in the I/O library. This makes it easier to search for some functions. Mixing these two libraries would only cause confusion because it would make it difficult to find what you are looking for; see also p. 164.

Reduce Coupling

Reducing coupling is an important topic in classes (p. 65), but also in code in general. Ensure that your code is as independent as possible. You don't want your math library to depend on the filesystem library. Even if it might make sense from a developer's point of view (although it would be difficult to explain in this context), you should minimize the number of dependencies as much as possible. Only import other libraries when it is absolutely necessary.

The same holds true not only for libraries but also for all other code that you write. Try to keep them all as independent as possible. Ensure that you properly structure the levels of abstraction in your code. Low-level code should not depend on high-level code, and so forth. Otherwise, your code may become a Big Ball of Mud.[6]

Increase Abstraction

Abstraction is about omitting unnecessary details and instead focusing on the essential elements. You have to design interfaces that are sleek and highly versatile. For example, let's consider a car once again. You should aim to make the parts as generic as possible. You want to fit any engine into any car. This can only be achieved by unifying the interface of the engine, the brakes, etc. All the details of the engine are abstracted away and hidden inside the engine so that the chassis of the car does not interact with its internals. If you don't abstract all the details, you

---

[6] https://en.wikipedia.org/wiki/Anti-pattern#Software_engineering_anti-patterns

may end up with multiple functions to manage various engines due to the need to address specific characteristics. If this is the case, you'll have to write an adapter for each engine to abstract away their peculiarities. Otherwise, you will face the $N \cdot M$ problem, where N is the number of engines and M is the number of cars. This leads to $N \cdot M$ versions of code, which makes it extremely difficult to maintain.

On the other hand, if you have a common interface, you only need $N + M$ adapters, which is significantly better than having $N \cdot M$ implementations required without a common interface. This common interface is the abstraction of the problem at hand. This is the power of abstraction.

Increase Reusability

Reusability comes hand in hand with increased abstraction. Leaving out all the details of an object reduces it to a fundamental building block that can be more easily reused. General objects are more likely to fit as a building block than something very specific. Just take, for example, all of the commonly used libraries. They all perform one fundamental task: interacting with the file system, conducting mathematical operations, or generating random numbers. Of course, it would sometimes make sense to combine these into a new library, but that would probably not result in reusable code anymore because it is too specific. Only write such specific code if you really need it.

Design for Flexibility

Your code will change. This is inevitable. Start living with this fact. Requirements and libraries may change, and code will change as well. You'd better ensure that your code can adapt. Therefore, it's important that your code follows the rules that are explained in this book. You need tests to be able to modify your code without living in fear of breaking it. To prevent your code from becoming solid as a rock, you must follow best practices. You want your code to be fluffy and easy to modify.

As an example, you might use a Fourier Transform or a sorting algorithm in your code. Well-written code is flexible enough to replace these algorithms without much fuss. You won't have to change code in multiple locations. It's more like a surgical operation where you change only one thing: one function call. Adapt one data structure, and your change is complete.

Designing for flexibility is strongly linked to the SRP (p. 13). Making changes is hard if the corresponding code is scattered all over the codebase. However, if you implement it nicely in one place, you won't struggle to replace it.

Anticipate Obsolescence

Code you use will become obsolete. Version changes, bugs, and security issues are not fixed; license fees are becoming too high, you name it. There are plenty of reasons why you need to adapt and modify third-party libraries or at least adjust to new syntax. So, you should anticipate that you may need to replace some libraries by adding an adapter between the library and your code. This will simplify reacting to changes. You can simply create an adapter for the new library, eliminating the need to modify all the existing code.

You have to anticipate obsolescence by keeping your code flexible and reusable. The database code should not be scattered throughout your entire codebase. This would be the exact opposite of what we desire. It would take enormous effort to replace it. Instead, you should be able to replace it easily. There are cases where you might think you'd never have to replace a piece of code. How wrong you are. No matter how important a library may seem to you, at some point, you will have to replace it. For example, many companies have written their code with an Oracle database in mind, and now they would like to change it because of the high fees. But they can't because the Oracle database code is spread all over the codebase, and changing it would be a nightmare.

If you designed your code for flexibility, you automatically also anticipate obsolescence.

Design for Testability

I believe this is the most evident point in this chapter. I have explained numerous times that you need to write tests. If writing tests for your code is easy, then writing code using the interfaces of your code is also easy. Or even better, use Test-Driven Development (TDD, p. 126). TDD forces you to write code that is easy to test. Thus, it forces you to write good code.

Hand in hand with testing comes dependency injection (DI). There are many things for which writing tests can be brittle. Files can be deleted, the network connection might fail, and timestamp comparisons will return a different result at some point, etc. These are all issues that should be addressed with DI. Inject a mock file or a fake timestamp into the function, and your tests will become much more stable.

Pay Now or Pay More Later

Pay now or pay more later is a very well-known issue, not only in software engineering. If you hurry writing code, you pile up technical debt that will slow you down in the long run. If you don't fix it now, you will pay the price along the way. Now, this sounds terrible, and it may be. But it's not always as terrible as it sounds because later your company will have grown, and you will have more resources to fix the technical debt.

Just imagine Amazon. The first version of their website was very basic. It was just a list of books that you could search using the author name or the book title. Of course, from a current point of view, this is unimaginable. But it was enough to get the company started. And now, 30 years later, Amazon has rewritten the entire website several times. I guess Jeff Bezos doesn't care anymore about the few thousand dollars he paid for the first version of his website. It was money well invested. Fast time to market was more important.

That being said, you have to know where you can go fast and where technical debt will bite you right away. For example, it is always worth setting up your CI/CD environment properly, unless you work on a really small project. Unit tests also pay off quite quickly. In my opinion, code is generally fine if it is covered with unit tests because it forces you to write better code (p. 123). On the other hand, it is not worth searching for appropriate variable names for hours. Okay is usually good enough.

Summary

There are many design principles that you can adhere to. They help you write better code, though these rules are generally quite vague and can be interpreted in many ways. The SOLID principles by Robert C. Martin are the most well-known ones. However, some of these principles are outdated. Still, it may be useful to know them, just as you learned the different sorting algorithms at university. They help you understand some underlying principles of software engineering.

Programming 6

Some people may believe that Java is the best programming language in the world and that one must write object-oriented (OO) code at all costs. I disagree with this point of view. While there is nothing inherently wrong with Java or OO programming, it is misguided to claim that it is the best language or that OO is the superior programming paradigm. The reality is much more nuanced. Flexibility is key; at times, writing OO code is effective, but there are instances where your code may improve by utilizing procedural or even Functional Programming approaches.

Programming Paradigms

> *Object-Oriented programming at the edges of your system always has side effects. Because otherwise, it wouldn't do anything.*
>
> —David Farley

There are several different programming paradigms. For several decades, object-oriented (OO) programming was the generally preferred paradigm. However, it turned out that OO programming has its own set of problems as well. As I have already mentioned several times, our goal is to write code that is easy to understand. It is not our goal to write OO code at all costs. Procedural and Functional Programming are equally valid programming paradigms, depending on the problem at hand. Nowadays, there are also multi-paradigm programming languages like Python and even the good old C++, where you can combine these three different programming paradigms to some degree.

Here is a very short list of what the different programming paradigms offer:

- OO programming: Classes; mutable, non-constant variables; loops
- Procedural programming: Data classes; mutable, non-constant variables; loops
- Functional programming: Data classes; constant variables; recursion

Functional programming is a subset of Procedural Programming, which in turn is a subset of OO programming (I neglected some details here). But this doesn't mean that Functional or Procedural Programming is necessarily inferior to OO programming. Limiting the number of possibilities can make the code easier to understand, just as avoiding global variables makes your code easier to understand. For example, the fact that Functional Programming does not have mutable variables excludes many possibilities that you need to consider when reading procedural or OO code.

Object-Oriented Programming

> *I made up the term 'object-oriented', and I can tell you I didn't have C++ in mind.*
> —Alan Kay

Object-oriented (OO) programming started in the 1960s. It peaked with the still very widely used languages C++ and Java. Somehow, the entire software developer community became absolutely ecstatic about it. OO programming is great. It is the natural representation of things. It makes everything so easy. It will save the world!!!

It still amazes me how some half-baked promises can create such dynamics in a group of highly intelligent people. Come up with some buzzwords, and the crowd will do the rest.

As always, the truth lies somewhere in the middle. Yes, OO programming can make things easier, but it did not save the world. Many of the concepts that were developed alongside OO programming are simply not useful. Without the hype surrounding OO programming, these concepts would never have gained widespread usage. People stopped thinking critically and just started using all kinds of OO features that turned out to lead to terrible code.

In my opinion, most features that came along with OO programming facilitated writing code – bad code. As always, everything that facilitates writing code is done by giving you access to things you shouldn't have access to. For this reason, I regard it as unlikely that there will be any new programming paradigm in the next few years. I think it's rather the opposite. It is more and more apparent that having access to a lot of things leads to bad code, and therefore one has to restrict oneself. This is one of the reasons why I think the usage of OO programming will somewhat decline over the next few years, and there may be a revival of multi-paradigm programming. Writing code without classes also has its merits.

And if you do use OO programming, always remember: don't use any OO feature other than plain classes and abstract base classes or interfaces unless you are sure of what you are doing. Don't forget to make everything private that should be. And always keep the SRP in mind: classes should be small!

Procedural Programming

While OO programming is mostly based on classes, class instances, and methods, Procedural Programming[1] depends mostly on functions and logical operations. Though you can still define your own data types, such as structs in C, in Procedural Programming, functions are more important than data types. Contrary to Functional Programming, you are allowed to have modifiable variables and output arguments. OO programming may be easier to write code, but on the other hand, it may make the code hard to understand if the classes are too large.

In C++, using only structs instead of classes apparently has some drawbacks. Though you could write all the variables and functions in a struct, this has the drawback that everything is public. Therefore, this is not a good coding practice. Instead, you have to adapt to a different coding style. You have to find a way around using classes with private members. As we have seen in Chapter 3 (p. 65), classes can be replaced by data classes and functions.

As you may have noticed, I am not a big fan of OO programming. I've just seen too much bad OO code, and there is no need to do OO programming. The only thing I don't know how to replace in procedural code is classes doing memory management in the constructor and destructor. It seems like this was managed in pure C as well, but I can't go further into details.

It takes some adaptation to get used to Procedural Programming, but it certainly has its advantages and is worth the effort.

As a summary, I can say: yes, it is obviously possible to write good code in C. Otherwise, the Linux Kernel would have been written in an OO programming language to begin with. It's just that some things got more convenient with more modern programming languages.

Functional Programming

The main difference between Functional Programming and Procedural Programming is the absence of non-constant variables. In Functional Programming, data structures cannot be changed once initialized. This restriction imposes significant limitations on the programmer, making programming more challenging. On the other hand, it also has its advantages. You don't have to pay attention to things like output arguments. Functions do not have side effects. Functions *can't* have side effects. The only thing that changes is the return value. Furthermore, the return value of the functions depends only on their arguments. These are called pure functions.

---

[1] https://en.wikipedia.org/wiki/Procedural_programming

Having only pure functions has several advantages. Pure functions are much easier to deal with than functions that depend on some hidden state. They are also much easier to test. You will never have the issue of not knowing how to test a pure function. Call the function with various arguments and verify that the return value is accurate. It won't get any easier than that. It is generally recommended to use only pure functions wherever feasible, including in OO programming.

Due to the nature of pure functions, functional code is generally easier to understand than, say, OO code. This is because Functional Programming relies solely on states that are always explicit and easy to comprehend.

One drawback of Functional Programming is that it does not support the use of for loops since they require a non-constant counter. Instead, you have to use recursion, which can be a little tedious at times. Furthermore, it requires you to use a programming language that supports tail call optimization.[2] This technique allows the compiler to optimize recursion into a loop. Without tail call optimization, recursion can be very slow and may even lead to a stack overflow. I prefer to write for loops instead of using recursion. Furthermore, input/output (I/O) is a big hassle in Functional Programming. For these reasons, I'm not a big fan of pure Functional Programming.

In most programming languages, you can emulate Functional Programming to some extent by writing pure functions. I highly recommend doing so because you will be left with only pure functions, making testing very easy. Using only Functional Programming, however, is, in my opinion, not worth it. It is overly restrictive and makes programming needlessly challenging. At least somewhere in your code, you need to have some effect, like writing data to a file. Otherwise, your program will not do much. This is where Functional Programming reaches its limits.

Temporal Coupling

Temporal coupling occurs when tasks can be performed in an incorrect sequence. Sometimes the code enforces the correct order, and sometimes it does not. Now you might be asking yourself, "What does temporal coupling have to do with programming paradigms?" The answer is: a lot.

Most notably, temporal order can be enforced by Functional Programming, but it is not enforced by OO programming. This has to do with the explicitness of these different programming paradigms. Functional Programming enforces the order in which functions are called by always creating new objects. Class methods, on the

---

[2] https://stackoverflow.com/questions/310974/what-is-tail-call-optimization

other hand, can usually be called in any order. There is nothing enforcing the correct order. The class variables are there all the time. Let me make a brief example:

```
class Shopping():
    def get_money(self, amount):
        self.money = amount

    def create_shopping_list(self, shopping_list):
        self.shopping_list = shopping_list

    def go_shopping(self):
        # use the shopping_list and money
```

At first sight, there seems to be nothing wrong with this inconspicuous class. However, there is one issue: it is not foolproof. The correct usage of this class is as follows:

```
shopping = Shopping()
shopping.get_money(50)
shopping.create_shopping_list(["apple", "banana"])
shopping.go_shopping()
```

This sequence of function calls follows the natural order of the shopping process. First, you need money and a shopping list before you go shopping. However, this order is not enforced by the code. One could also swap two of the function calls as follows:

```
shopping = Shopping()
shopping.get_money(50)
shopping.go_shopping()
shopping.create_shopping_list(["apple", "banana"])
```

Now you go shopping before creating a shopping list. The shopping list is either empty or non-existent. Either way, this behavior is apparently undesired. It would probably be best if an exception were raised as it is undefined behavior. In this example, this would actually be the case as the `shopping_list` is not yet instantiated. But it could be much worse than this. The code could fail silently, causing undefined behavior.

This is one of the drawbacks of OO code. Methods change the state of the object; therefore, it is very difficult to enforce that the methods are called in the correct order.

One advantage of procedural or, even better, functional code is that such issues are less likely to occur. Code doesn't always have to be OO. Sometimes, other paradigms produce better code. Let's examine the procedural version of this code.

```
money = get_money(50)
shopping_list = create_shopping_list(["apple", "banana"])
go_shopping(money, shopping_list)
```

In this case, it is physically impossible to go shopping without having a shopping list, as shown below:

```
money = get_money(50)
go_shopping(money, shopping_list)
shopping_list = create_shopping_list(["apple", "banana"])
```

After having swapped the last two lines, this code cannot be executed anymore because the variable `shopping_list` is not initialized at the `go_shopping` function call. When executing the code above, you will get an error: `NameError: name 'shopping_list' is not defined`. This prevents you from calling the functions in the wrong order.

Long story short: Because methods in OO programming can change hidden states, they are susceptible to temporal coupling.

Ensure that your functions never have side effects. Functions and methods should only affect the class instance or, if necessary, mutable arguments. If possible, enforce temporal order by utilizing Functional Programming.

Another source of temporal coupling is global or static variables. This is just another reason why you should avoid them.

```
counter = 0
def log_in(email_address):
    counter +=1
    check(email_address)
```

Here, the value of the `counter` depends on how often `log_in` has been called before. Now, it might make sense to have such a counter in your code; however, this may lead to all kinds of problems, for example, when testing it (p. 93).

Conclusions

All different programming paradigms have their advantages and drawbacks. Statements like "You have to use OO programming because it mimics the real world" are certainly outdated. It is best to be acquainted with various paradigms to enhance flexibility and adapt your style to current needs. The times when you were only supposed to write procedural or OO code are over. If you are flexible and understand the advantages and drawbacks of different programming paradigms, you can write better code.

I would generally recommend staying at the lowest programming level (Functional Programming) for as long as possible. Only switch to higher levels (Procedural or even OO programming) if the task would otherwise become too complicated to implement.

Programming Languages

> *I think I'm a much better programmer now than I used to be, even though I know less about the details in each programming language I work in.*
> —Michael Feathers

A very common question among beginners is: "Which programming language should I learn? Some may have read somewhere that programming language A is better than language B for some very obscure reason. The very simple answer is it doesn't matter too much. Most OO languages are similar enough, and the differences in programming philosophies are fairly small – small enough to understand the programming examples in this book, I hope.

For example, many of the low-level C++ features can be encapsulated within a higher-level object, giving the appearance of an intermediate-level language, though it's still not quite at the same level of sophistication as Python.

I really want to emphasize that you shouldn't delve too deeply into learning a specific programming language. Reading a small book about the language you want to use is certainly a good start. A small book, not a big one. The rest you can search on the Internet as you stumble upon specific problems along the way. Google and Stack Overflow are more helpful than relying on your vague three-year-old memory, and AI code generation is also becoming a valuable resource. It is much more important that you learn programming concepts in general. The concepts are easier to understand and more powerful than some syntax. Syntax can easily be looked up or suggested by your preferred AI code generator, whereas concepts must be understood. And this is what this book is mostly about: teaching you the concepts.

Nevertheless, I would like to briefly share my perspective on which programming language to learn. Although it is my personal opinion, and it's highly biased, I know mainly C++ and Python, and a little bit about Java and JavaScript from the programming books I have read. If you work in a field where a specific programming language is used, you should definitely learn that language, even if it's just Matlab. You can still learn other languages later on.

As a scientist, I recommend Python as a first programming language. JavaScript is a viable alternative for web developers. Both are scripting languages that do not require a compiler and are relatively easy to get started with. Dynamic typing (duck typing) eliminates the need for inheritance to define an interface. Any two objects that have the same interface can be interchanged in the code. There is no need to learn anything about pointers or memory allocation as in the past. These things are outdated, as explained in the section "Levels of Abstraction" (p. 17).

At the same time, it has to be said that dynamic typing also has its drawbacks. Having type information is not only helpful for the compiler but also for the programmer. Understanding a function's purpose is simpler when you are aware of the types of its arguments. For instance, there are methods to include type hints in Python, but I often find myself too lazy to add them. If you want to learn JavaScript, consider learning TypeScript instead. I think strong typing is a good thing.

Same for the compiler. It may be useful that the Python code doesn't have to be compiled after changing a single line of code, as you save time. But at the same time, a compiler can also give useful insights. A compiler can be a huge aid when refactoring code. Furthermore, running unit tests will take much longer in Python, negating the advantage of not having to compile the code.

Altogether, I would recommend learning a language that is statically typed and has both a compiler and an interpreter – something modern like Rust or Go.

Existing Programming Languages

Programming languages and APIs share a common destiny. Creating a new programming language that is clearly superior to an existing one would be easy. But there are millions of software projects that already use the current languages and depend on the current functionality. Their code is worth billions. You should not update large amounts of code just because of a minor issue in the programming language. Instead, there are thousands of developers making suggestions on how current programming languages could be improved without breaking compatibility. A team of experts will debate all kinds of possible issues before a new feature or internal change is accepted into the standard of a programming language.

For example, in C++, there is the Boost library. Pretty much everyone programming in C++ knows it. It is one of the most commonly used third-party libraries and is known for its high-quality standards. The Boost library contains hundreds of very important sub-libraries that are not part of the C++ standard library. Usually, new features are first implemented and tested as a Boost library. Only after a new feature has been used and tested by the community for a few years might it be accepted into the C++ standard library. This is how smart pointers and the filesystem library were incorporated into the standard. It is important to note that these are all extensions of the programming language, not changes. They don't break any existing code.

Code Examples in This Book

There are quite a few code examples in this book. Most concepts that I explain here can be illustrated with real-world examples. The syntax I used is kept as simple as possible because I want to focus on teaching you concepts, not syntax. I tried to make this book as language-agnostic as possible. The code examples are mostly written in Python and occasionally in C++ to explain some low-level features. It's not a deliberate choice to use Python and C++; those are just the programming languages that I know. I'll try to explain the examples so that you can roughly understand them, even if you don't know the corresponding programming language that well. I promise that the syntax will be very simple to understand. It requires only a fundamental knowledge of the relevant programming language.

Python

Even though Python is a fairly easy programming language to learn, there are some language-specific concepts that are worth learning. For more advanced topics, there is the Google Style Guide.[3]

Type Hints

Python is dynamically typed. At first sight, this seems like a great thing. A function can be called with many different argument types, so you don't have to specify them, as long as the argument supports the required functions called. However, it also comes with its drawbacks. Types are an important part of the information regarding arguments and return values. With types, you know what kind of operations you are allowed to perform or what the expected outcome of an operation will be. For example, the + operator behaves differently with floats than with strings. So, at times, it would be useful to know the type of a variable.[4]

While it is not possible to enforce types in Python, and according to Guido van Rossum, it will never be as it is not Pythonic, it is possible to write type hints. A simple : str following a function argument indicates that it should be a string. Though type hints have the problem that they do not enforce the types, you can still pass a different type, and Python will accept it.

Here is an example using type hints:

```
def digits_of(number: str) -> list[int]:
    return [int(d) for d in number]
```

But, as I mentioned, this does not enforce that the argument of digits_of is a string. You could also pass a list of floats instead and get a perfectly valid result. It's just that this was apparently not intended by the author of the code.

```
digits_of([1.0, 2.0, 3.0])
digits_of("123")
# both return [1, 2, 3]
```

I generally recommend using type hints, as they make the code more readable, even if I'm sometimes too lazy to do it myself and even if it moves the syntax much closer to C++. C++ is not such a bad programming language after all; it's just a little bit old-fashioned.

Typing would be the first reason why I recommend against using Python. The lack of a compiler is the second one. And the fact that Python is sometimes too dynamic, as shown below, is the third one.

---

[3] https://google.github.io/styleguide/pyguide.html

[4] https://youtu.be/dgBCEB2jVU0

Slots

Python is a very dynamic language. It allows you to do things that wouldn't be possible in other languages. For instance, you may add fields to a predefined class like this:

```
class Apple:
    def __init__(self, price: float, weight: float):
        self.price = price
        self.weight = weight

apple = Apple(price=1.0, weight=0.5)
apple.hi = "hi"
```

Adding the member variable `hi` to an existing class instance wouldn't be possible in almost any other language, and this is for good reasons. It might seem tempting to add a new variable at any point in time, but it's generally not good coding practice to do so. Furthermore, you could accidentally misspell `apple.pice = 2.50`, and Python doesn't complain. Instead, it creates a new member variable `pice` and assigns it a value of `2.50`.

This issue can be prevented by using slots.

```
class Apple:
    __slots__ = "price", "weight"

    def __init__(self, price: float, weight: float):
        self.price = price
        self.weight = weight
```

Slots[5] fix the available member variables. In this case, only the variables `price` and `weight` are allowed. (Accidentally) adding other member variables to the `Apple` class is no longer possible.

The following code returns an error:

```
class Apple:
    __slots__ = "price", "weight"

    def __init__(self, price: float, weight: float):
        self.price = price
        self.weight = weight

a = Apple(1.0, 2.0)
a.pice = 2.0
# AttributeError: 'Apple' object has no attribute 'pice'
```

Abstract Base Classes and Protocols

Defining base classes as an interface is not required in Python. However, I still recommend using abstract base classes (ABC) if there is more than one class implementing an interface. Although it is not required in Python, defining the

---

[5] https://youtu.be/Fot3_9eDmOs

structure of the interface you are going to use and implement makes the code slightly more readable. It also prevents you from making mistakes that might be difficult to track down.

An alternative to ABCs is Protocols, which were introduced in Python 3.8. Protocols have some advantages when working with type hints, although they are mostly equivalent. This is a highly advanced topic; I cannot delve into details here. Instead, I recommend the interested reader some YouTube video.[6]

C++

C++ has some peculiarities, such as a preprocessor, header files, pointers, and arrays, that make the language unique nowadays. Thus, I'd like to explain some of the differences between C++ and other programming languages.

C++ was developed by Bjarne Stroustrup and first published in the 1980s. He enhanced the existing C programming language by incorporating OO programming, along with other modifications. So, yes, it is an old language, but it is still in use and will continue to be with us for several more decades. Thanks to the constant development of the language, many of the ancient problems it once brought along have been overcome. At the same time, C++ is a very good example to learn a lot about programming languages and how they have evolved. As I used C++ in some of the examples here, I'm going to explain some of the particularities of this programming language.

For more information about C++, I can recommend the Google C++ Style Guide.[7]

Vectors

In C++, people used to work with pointers and arrays. But these times are long gone. Nowadays, we have vectors, which are a higher-level version of arrays, as explained in Chapter 1, section "Levels of Abstraction" (p. 17). There is no longer a need to use arrays in C++. You don't even have to learn about them; it would be a waste of time.

Some libraries require the use of plain old arrays instead of vectors. This, however, is not a reason to use arrays throughout your code. Instead, you can use vectors as usual and convert them to arrays using the `data()` and `size()` functions as needed.[8]

```
#include <iostream>
#include <vector>

void some_old_C_style_library(const int* data,
                              std::size_t size)
```

---

[6] https://youtu.be/dryNwWvSd4M

[7] https://google.github.io/styleguide/cppguide.html

[8] https://en.cppreference.com/w/cpp/container/vector/data

```
{
    for (std::size_t i = 0; i < size; ++i)
    {
        std::cout << data[i] << ' ';
    }
}
std::vector<int> v {1,2,3,4};
some_old_C_style_library(v.data(), v.size());
```

This approach allows you to work with vectors for as long as possible and only convert them at the very end when you really have to work with an array. Of course, this is not the only way to convert a vector to an array. There are many other ways to do this, but I recommend using this one.

Smart Pointers

Smart pointers, `std::unique_ptr`, `std::shared_ptr`, and `std::weak_ptr`, are replacements for plain old pointers. Smart pointers are a higher-level implementation. They have built-in features like reference counting, and they automatically clean up when they go out of scope. There are still some things to know, such as weak pointers, but these are mostly details that you don't have to worry about in the beginning.

There are libraries that require plain old pointers as function arguments. There is no reason to use plain old pointers throughout all your code. Instead, you can convert the smart pointer into a raw pointer using the `get()` function.

```
auto foo = std::make_unique<Foo>();
some_old_C_style_library(foo.get());
```

This prevents you from having to deal with old-school pointers until the very end, where you call the other API. Don't use raw pointers throughout your code just because some library uses them. Only convert them once you have to.

Passing Function Arguments

In order for an object to be an output argument, it can be passed by pointer or by reference. Passing by raw pointers is outdated. Objects should always be passed by reference. Passing an object by reference means that you essentially pass the object itself, allowing it to be modified. If the object is passed by const reference, it cannot be modified. Passing by const reference is done very frequently. Passing an object by value creates a copy of the object and requires a significant amount of memory.

This is one point for criticism of the C++ standard, as passing by const reference should have been the default. The compiler won't complain if you forget to use `const`, even though you should have used it. It would be much safer to use the programming language if `const` were the default property and you had to specify an argument as `non_const`. This would cause a compiler error if you changed the corresponding variable, and therefore it would be much safer.

Classes

C++ was one of the first mainstream programming languages to support classes, inheritance, and more. Probably, C++ became so widespread because most things worked out pretty well, except for some details about multiple inheritance.[9] But as I advised you not to use inheritance, you don't have to worry about such details (p. 85).

There is one thing, however, that was done better in other languages, such as Java. In Java, defining an interface is actually called this way, while in C++, one must define an "abstract base class." Interface inheritance is the only type of inheritance that I recommend using. Remember when I say you shouldn't use inheritance: the entire concept of abstract base classes should be named differently and is not impacted by this rule. It is fine to use interface inheritance.

Structs

Structs are essentially the same as data classes in Python (p. 68). These are classes where all members are public. In general, structs are used to store various data types, although, theoretically, structs may also include functions. The latter is only forbidden by general agreement.

Structs are very useful data structures, as explained in Chapter 3 (p. 65). It's a pity that struct-like objects are barely used in Java and some other languages. In Java, a struct can be defined as a normal class containing only variables without any getter or setter functions. Since Java 14, one can use a `record`, which is similar to a struct.

Const

In C++, you can make a variable constant by using the `const` keyword. While at first it may be confusing ("what if I still want to change this variable later on?"), it is actually a very useful feature. There are many variables that should never be changed at all. One common example is `const double pi = 3.14`. In fact, the const property is so useful that, in my opinion, it should be the default for any object, and you should only be able to change it if you explicitly declare it as non-const. This would make the code much safer.

Learning Low-Level Languages

I would not recommend learning "low-level" languages such as C++ (or Java) as a first programming language, even if I included some C++ code in this book to explain some details. Java and C++ are too complicated to be learned as introductory languages, and it takes much more time to understand the languages themselves rather than learning the principles of programming. The C++ examples throughout this book are only meant to explain low-level details that you generally don't need

---

[9] https://www.geeksforgeeks.org/multiple-inheritance-in-c/

to worry about in Python. Instead, you should learn how to apply the higher-level principles taught in this book to improve your coding skills.

Of course, later in your career, it makes sense to learn many more languages. Java and C++ are still among the most widely used programming languages, not because these languages are superior to more modern languages, but simply due to the abundance of old projects.

C++ and Java are both statically typed. They have to be compiled and use inheritance to define interfaces. In C++, you have to deal with pointers. The pointers are certainly a drawback of C++; however, the fact that C++ is a compiled, statically typed language also has its advantages. Types and the compilation may give you valuable hints in case something is wrong with your code.

Learning new languages will expose you to alternative ways of approaching problems. Switching from Python to C++ will require you to learn many fundamental aspects of software development. It also opens up more job opportunities. But it's not worth bothering with when you are a programming novice.

Physical Laws of Code

Only entropy comes easy.

—Anton Chekhov

Entropy

Entropy is the physical law of disorder. The second law of thermodynamics states that entropy will always increase. Fighting entropy is a challenging task. It is like cleaning up your room every week. If you don't clean your room, it will become dirty, and you won't be able to find your stuff anymore.

In software engineering, we have a very similar phenomenon, and it has very severe consequences. As we write code, more and more disorder is created. On the one hand, this is very natural, as a growing codebase automatically attracts more disorder. There is simply more stuff around that you have to take care of. On the other hand, this disorder is also man-made. The entropy only grows significantly if you allow it to. You have to fight entropy in your code the same way you fight entropy in your bedroom. You have to clean up regularly. You have to sort all your belongings. You have to throw away things that you don't really need or that are duplicated. This will take time and effort. But such is life. You don't get a well-paid job in IT without doing the dirty work as well. What you have to do is explained in Chapter 8 (p. 203).

Correlation

Similar things belong together. It may sound trivial, but it is extremely helpful when designing code. And it's true for pretty much any aspect of programming. Not only code objects but also abstract concepts.

There is a market for food, and further down the road, there is a store selling electronics. Each type of store is located in its designated area. If you find a market store selling apples, chances are high that the next store sells apples as well. It is normal for similar things to align together. This makes them easier to find.

The same holds true for code. Functions are bundled together based on their functionality, just like classes. This makes them easier to find when searching for specific functionality. At the same time, they should also have the same level of abstraction. The main function, for example, consists of only a few high-level function calls. Avoid any string manipulations or other low-level operations. These low-level functions are buried deep within a lower level of abstraction.

Bugs also tend to cluster inside your code. Did you find a bug in a very complex part of the code? Chances are you will find more bugs in the same area of the code. Probably, it's some kind of complex algorithm or the implementation of a little-understood requirement.

Once you start thinking about this rule, you will automatically structure your code in a much better way. It becomes much tidier. It will feel more natural and won't require too much effort to improve. By checking the complex parts of the code earlier on, you will be able to find your bugs faster.

Quality

There were studies on what must happen for an area of a city to start decaying.[10,11] They came to the remarkable conclusion that one broken window is a sufficient signal for other people to start breaking windows as well. In no time, an entire area gets ruined and abandoned.

Accordingly, when writing code, it is crucial to maintain high quality. Don't write poor code, or it will feel neglected too. Some individuals may become careless when they feel that maintaining code quality is not worthwhile, leading them to write poor code. And trust me, I've been there as well. You really start lowering your standards when the code quality is already poor.

On the other end of the quality spectrum, you have the issue that some developers persist in improving their code indefinitely. This is, of course, also an issue. There is always something that you feel could be improved. But at some point, you have to come to the conclusion that your code is good enough. Or, as Steve Jobs said, "Real artists ship."

---

[10] The police and neighborhood safety. Willson and Kelling.

[11] The pragmatic programmer. Thomas and Hunt.

These two things, broken windows and good enough code, are another example of opposing principles. It is your task to find the right balance between them, as it is in many things I teach throughout this book. Obviously, this is a very difficult task and takes a lot of experience. I cannot give precise explanations on how to find the right balance.

Overengineering

Software engineering is a constant trade-off between speed and quality. There is always something that you can improve, but on the other hand, your customers would like to have the product as soon as possible. You have to find the right balance between these two extremes. Fix what has to be fixed, and leave the code as is where you won't improve it significantly.[12]

In my opinion, it's always worth having good test coverage with unit and functional tests. You write your tests before the code, don't you? Working without tests is dreadful. You'll live in constant fear because you don't know if your changes will break anything. Furthermore, unit tests force you to write good code. They force you to structure your classes and functions in a way that they can be tested. This is usually the quality of code that you need, and it gives you a certain standard that you can adhere to.

On the other hand, you can spend days searching for the perfect variable names. You'll never find them. The software works without them and could be shipped instead. If you have proper test coverage, you can still improve your code later on.

It is important that you are fast at writing code because being fast gives you more feedback. Therefore, it is important that you eliminate things like extensively searching for variable names or hours-long code reviews because they slow you down, and the costs are higher than if you are able to just move on and possibly fix the code later on if needed.

Whether something is overengineering or not is also a question of what stage in the project you are in. In the beginning of a large project, you certainly have to invest more time into planning your code. Making mistakes at the beginning can be really costly later on. Meanwhile, toward the end of a project, you don't have to be that strict anymore. You should still write tests and make sure you don't introduce bugs, but you don't have to be as strict as in the beginning.

Another thing you should avoid is future proofing. YAGNI: You Aren't Gonna Need It. It happens more often than not that you write code that you think you will need in the future, but you never do. And then you have to maintain this code for the rest of your life. This is a huge waste of time. Make sure that you write your code to the best of your knowledge now and cover it with tests. Then you can still improve it later on if needed. Only the architect is allowed to make some decisions that may affect your code in the future.

My personal experience is that you should focus on quality with the fundamental structure of the code. Once you have found it, it resembles the actual problem at

---

[12] https://youtu.be/FLe5dvqV6xs

hand, and most problems seem to fall into place. Furthermore, you should write plenty of unit tests. Other things, like naming local variables, are not that important. In peripheral code, you can also write somewhat longer functions. You can still improve these things later on if you have to.

Complexity

> I choose a lazy person to do a hard job. Because a lazy person will find an easy way to do it.
> —Bill Gates

Complexity of Code

As we write software, we have to deal with two different complexities: the complexity of the problem we want to solve and the complexity of our code. As the code encompasses all the features of the real problem, the complexity of the code will always be at least as high as the complexity of the actual problem. This becomes apparent when one product manager generates an excessive amount of work for several programmers. The complexity of implementing a feature is much higher than its actual complexity.

The goal of writing software is to minimize complexity as much as possible, close to the complexity of the real problem. If possible, it should be equivalent to the actual problem. The code should replicate the real problem one to one. Unfortunately, this will never happen. There is always some overhead when programming, not only boilerplate code but also conceptual overhead. How should you map a real problem one to one into code? How should an apple ever become code? The answer is it depends on your requirements. This is where object-oriented programming originated. It claimed to be the natural representation of things because you could create a class called `Apple`, and this would solve all our problems. But it did not. We still don't know how this apple should interact with all other objects in our code. We don't even know how this `Apple` class should really look!

I cannot deny that OO programming makes some things easier, and having an `Apple` class is a good start. But it doesn't explain all the logic behind it. You have to figure it out yourself. You have to try to explain what the apple really does. Maybe even write it down. Engage in conversations with others, including experts. It takes time to build up knowledge of what is important and how everything is connected. This is a fundamental requirement for writing high-quality code with minimal complexity. And always remember: an `apple` only needs the properties for your current purpose. Inside a cooking recipe, you don't care about the price of an apple. So neither should you in your code!

As a next step, you have to figure out how to convert all this knowledge into code. Explore various ways to connect all the objects involved. Change the order of statements and the way data is passed between the objects. When done correctly, you will end up with code that closely resembles the explanation provided by domain experts. The objects have the same properties, the functions perform the same tasks, and you use the same names. Your code seems to directly map to the real problem. Eric Evans referred to this as a domain model.[13] Handle it with care. The domain model is very valuable, and you can easily compromise it by incorporating code that does not align with the model.

Having a domain model is a very valuable asset. It forces you to understand the problem thoroughly and write the core of your code first. At the same time, it prevents you from getting lost in low-level details.

Estimating Complexity

Estimating the complexity of a task is extremely difficult, not only due to technical considerations but also because of pressure from management. Frequently, the process of estimating a feature follows this dreadful pattern:[14]

Project Manager: "Can you provide me with an estimate of the time required to develop feature XYZ?"

Programmer: "One month."

Project Manager: "That's far too long! We've only got one week."

Programmer: "I need at least three."

Project Manager: "I can give you two at most."

Programmer: "Deal!"

Estimating the complexity of a task is typically very challenging. Some developers might have an idea of what needs to be done, while others do not. But nobody really knows exactly, and everyone is a little bit scared of that task. No one knows for certain how to break the complete problem down into smaller components. However, some uncertainty always remains. I have to admit that there are companies that frequently get it right. Yet still, I know of numerous IT projects that went significantly over budget.

Generally, there are two different methods to estimate the amount of work required for a certain task. The first approach involves breaking down the entire topic into smaller components and then aggregating the efforts of each individual piece. This task requires a significant amount of expertise, and there is a common tendency to underestimate the actual workload involved. When breaking down a task into smaller pieces, many subtasks are often overlooked, or the overall complexity is usually underestimated significantly.

The second method to estimate the amount of work is based on comparing it with similar tasks. This is generally the more accurate approach, although there is still some uncertainty remaining. It works best if you engage in repetitive tasks, such as building a house or creating a home page. However, for more unique problems, such as developing custom software, this approach usually doesn't work because there is

---

[13] Domain-Driven Design, Eric Evans.

[14] 97 Things Every Programmer Should Know. Henney et al.

no previous work available for comparison. Therefore, estimating the amount of work required for a certain task is still quite tricky.

Many projects underestimate the workload required by a factor of two to four.[15] It really takes a lot of experience to get the estimates right. And there are companies that frequently get it right. Still, I know of numerous IT projects that went significantly over budget.

Precision and Accuracy

> *Saying that pi = 17.630231 is more precise but less accurate than saying that pi = 3.*
> —David Farley[16]

There are many companies prioritizing precise answers over accurate ones. This is nonsense. The precision should always be as good as the accuracy. If someone asks you how long it will take, you should provide an estimate in terms of an order of magnitude: hours, days, weeks, or months. Only if you have several different options to compare, you can determine which one will take the least time.

Single-Line Complexity

A common subject of discussion is the level of logic present in a single line of code. There are very different opinions. On one side, we have Linus Torvalds. In the Linux kernel, the maximum line length used to be 80 characters when using the C programming language, and the length of indentations is 8 spaces. It is absolutely impossible to write more than one or maybe two operations on a single line of code. Try it yourself. It is really worth writing such code once in a while. You will learn quite a bit about what code can look like.

On the other end of the spectrum are some Python programmers or, even worse, web developers. It seems like turning the addition of as much logic as possible into a single line has become their goal. Honestly, I believe this is a rather unhealthy habit. You don't gain anything by saving lines of code. At the same time, every single line becomes increasingly convoluted. You won't understand it anymore. For this reason, the maximum line length set by the Google Style Guide is 80 characters for both Python[17] and C++.[18] Additionally, there are restrictions on list initialization.

---

[15] https://youtu.be/v21jg8wb1eU?t=414

[16] https://youtu.be/v21jg8wb1eU?t=469

[17] https://google.github.io/styleguide/pyguide.html Section 3.2.

[18] https://google.github.io/styleguide/cppguide.html#Line_Length

For example, it may not loop over two different variables, as shown in the following example:

```
[[[0] * (i + j) for i in range(2)] for j in range(3)]
```

One alternative is to refactor out one of the loops:

```
l = []
for j in range(3):
    l.append([[0] * (i+j) for i in range(2)])
```

Or we can do it the old way using two for loops:

```
matrix = []
for j in range(3):
    row = []
    for i in range(2):
        row.append([0] * (i + j))
    matrix.append(row)
```

When in doubt, resist the temptation to split up the code and avoid using single-line initialization. Here, I would prefer the second solution using list initialization with one variable.

Personally, I don't work with a strict limit, though I try to keep the lines below 100 characters.

Black Magic Code

Your code will contain some complexity. It's inevitable. The only question is how you deal with it. One point is that you have to be honest. Some programmers try to hide complex code using all kinds of black magic. This approach may work at times, but the code will be cursed. You can keep working on the code, but occasionally you see this black magic, and you'll become petrified. Your only thought will be "I hope I'll never have to touch this."

One example of hiding complexity is template metaprogramming in C++ where you let the compiler calculate things intstead of running the code afterward. This has some applications in highly optimized code, but it is terrible to debug because the compiler was not optimized for such kind of operations. Only use such techniques if you really have to.

It is much better to be honest. The problem has a certain complexity, and we break it down into smaller pieces that we can solve. Do not hide the complexity; make it apparent.

Dependencies

If you automate a mess, you get an automated mess.

—Rod Michael

In this section, we are discussing files that depend on each other – an inevitable evil.

The Early Days

In the early days, people wrote code in a single file. This has several drawbacks. It's very easy to lose track of the code, and it can be challenging when you need to replace a part of it. For example, if you find a faster library or, even worse, if the library is only available as a binary, then you cannot use it at all.

These are some of the considerations that led programmers to split their code into multiple files. How do you instruct the computer to compile the complete code from these files? Apparently, there are some build tools available nowadays, but this is an ongoing discussion.

All programming languages have some sort of import or include statements at the beginning of the files. Even with the build tools of C++, you still need them. They might bother you, but at times, they are quite handy. They are a good indicator of some very bad patterns in your code.

The Dependency Graph

If you draw a plot with all the files represented as circles and their interconnections as arrows, you should obtain a directed acyclic graph. The trunk of this graph is the file containing the main function, representing the highest level of abstraction. As you move down the graph, the level of abstraction decreases, and the object becomes more concrete.

Now, the first thing to look out for in this abstraction graph is an arrow pointing in both directions as shown in Figure 6-1. This means that two files are importing each other. Depending on the language, this may result in anything from normal

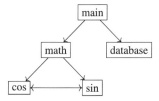

Figure 6-1 The dependency graph of a small project using a database and the math library. We assume, for whatever reason, that the definitions of sin and cos depend on each other ("cyclic dependency," the arrow points in both directions)

behavior to undefined behavior or errors. But even if it works, it is a sign of very poor design. If you have mutual dependencies, there is no clear distinction between the levels of abstraction. It's just a mess that will be very hard to understand.

The simplest solution is to merge these files causing the circular dependency. However, this is only a superficial fix. You really have to determine the relationships between the functions and classes in the files. Maybe you need to reorder them, or perhaps you have to rewrite the corresponding code from scratch.

Breaking Up Dependencies

Circular imports are easy to spot; therefore, experienced programmers typically do not encounter such issues. With good coding habits, circular dependencies won't occur, as mentioned in the section "Levels of Abstraction" in Chapter 1 (p. 17). The much more common problem is having too many dependencies, which makes the code very sticky. It is challenging to provide specific numbers to quantify the problem because it depends on numerous factors. Breaking up a file is usually beneficial, but it also leads to an increase in the number of dependencies. This is inevitable. Breaking a file into two is a good thing if the number of dependencies increases only a little, and it should be reconsidered if the number of dependencies almost doubles. The latter means that most code requires all the code from this file, so it makes sense to have it all bundled together.

How you break up a file is an even harder question. Sometimes you can easily group the code into clusters, while other times it is challenging to discern what belongs together. If you have divided a class into two classes, you can definitely separate some of the code into a new file.

The most important step toward reducing dependencies is to focus on your code. Ensure that similar code fragments are placed in the same location. For example, having direct database access spread throughout the code is typically a significant issue. The logic of your code should be concentrated in a few key areas. Make all the database requests at once, whenever possible, and store the results in an instance of a data class. Afterward, you can pass around this class instance, and there is no need to think about the database anymore. And just like that, you have eliminated many dependencies while simultaneously enhancing your code. One possibility to achieve this goal is to use a wrapper that wraps all database access.

The most challenging aspect is reducing dependencies by enhancing the overall structure of the code. Good code has simple logic, which, in turn, has few dependencies. This, however, is quite tricky to achieve, and even if I could, explaining it here would be barely possible.

Circular Dependencies

Circular dependencies typically occur when two classes exchange data between each other. Class A requires data from Class B, which in turn requires some data from Class A. You should be able to determine whether Class A or Class B corresponds to the higher level of abstraction. Let's assume that Class A is the higher-level class calling Class B at some point. Now, Class B should never have to call Class A. Class B is at a lower level and knows nothing about the high-level Class A. This leads to only one solution: Class A has to call Class B exactly once and hand over all the data that Class B needs to return the final result.

Long story short: The high-level object calls the low-level object and passes all the necessary data at once. The low-level object returns the final result at the end of the calculation. This resolves the problem of circular dependencies and organizes the levels of abstraction.

Example
An engine is on a strictly lower level of abstraction than a car. We could also say that the car is the parent object of the engine. Therefore, an engine should not know anything about the car it belongs to. This is a common antipattern and leads to circular dependencies.

```
class Car:
    def __init__(self, engine):
        self.engine = engine

class Engine:
    def __init__(self, car):
        self.car = car

    def start(self):
        # This is really bad code.
        # The tail wiggles with the dog!
        self.car.drive()
```

An engine should never execute a function that needs access to the car. The communication all goes in one direction: from the car to the engine. The engine only responds to commands from the car.

Another question is how would you access the engine if it knows about the car? In reality, the engine is an integral part of the car, so it is never possible to directly access the engine. And as we have learned, your code should be as close to reality as possible. Don't allow other programmers to access the engine without knowing about the car surrounding it.

As a summary, one can say that circular dependencies should be avoided altogether. This task is usually not too difficult if you use proper levels of abstraction, and it significantly enhances the readability of the code. Even a single recursive call can often be refactored to improve code readability.

Decoupling

Before software should be reusable, it should be usable.

—Ralph Johnson

Coupling is a crucial aspect of software engineering. Without coupling, it would not be possible to write code. Coupling is the glue that holds everything together. But too much glue is bad because everything becomes sticky. In bad code, everything depends on each other. Every module or file imports dozens of other files. This is a significant issue because if you want to change one file, you might have to change a dozen others. Ensure that the coupling is minimized. This keeps the code soft and flexible. It is the ultimate goal to have completely decoupled code. This makes it easy to work with and reusable.

This is one of the reasons why global variables and inheritance are not recommended. Global variables are detrimental as they tightly couple the entire codebase. It's worse than importing something everywhere. All your code dependencies start intertwining with each other. This is absolutely deadly. Never use global variables.

Inheritance is almost as bad. Everything that depends on a derived class also automatically depends on its base class. You are not only coupling the derived class to the base class but also vice versa. You can barely change one without changing the other. This is not how flexible code is supposed to be. Avoid using inheritance.

Microservices, on the other hand, are loosely coupled. They are chunks of code that can be called and executed independently. Microservices are somewhat similar to Functional Programming, where you have independent functions that run autonomously. Microservices and Functional Programming both involve calling a function or a piece of code that returns a value.[19]

Only ask for things you directly need. This is another advantage of Functional Programming or microservices. If you need to validate an email, you can utilize the email validator, which can be either a microservice or a pure function. The email validator returns a result and resets. You only receive what you asked for, nothing more. There are no semi-useful objects wobbling around that you don't know how to deal with. You need exactly what is around. This is the strength of Functional Programming.

Bugs, Errors, Exceptions

One in a million is always next Tuesday.

—Gordon Letwin

Even if you write absolutely pristine code, some things will still go wrong. Some of these things are no problem at all, while others can be extremely dangerous –

---

[19] https://youtu.be/4GnjjocWGOE

literally. Problems are less critical if you find them early on in the development cycle, and they are immediately recognizable. If your compiler finds an error, the costs are barely worth mentioning. Triage the source of it and fix it. However, if your software is already in production, the costs can be significant.

I would like to briefly go through the different cases.

Syntax Errors

Syntax errors happen to anyone, even the most experienced programmers. It's normal and not a problem at all. You are not even able to run the code in its current state. Enhance your skills and deepen your understanding of the programming language you are using. Syntax errors are the best example of how problems do not cause any harm if they are caught early on. In compiled languages, the compiler will find the syntax errors, while in Python, the parser checks the correctness of the syntax at least to some degree. Either way, you'll receive an error message immediately.

At the beginning of our programming careers, we were probably all bothered by syntax errors. We were happy once the program was running. Our programming skills were insufficient to realize that the compiler or interpreter was assisting us in writing a functional program. It is a good thing the compiler pinpointed the errors because they might have prevented us from creating serious bugs that could have been difficult to find later on. Nonetheless, this didn't prevent us from creating bugs. As we learn here, you can still create bugs even if the syntax is correct.

Bugs

Many people underestimate the issue of bugs. They are easy to ignore because they might not show up too often, and at times they are not too severe. They are just some glitches. But this is exactly why bugs are so catastrophic. You don't necessarily know when something went wrong. You might have a sense that something is amiss, but you are not certain. Or you don't know at all. This is the worst-case scenario that can occur in your code. You may think everything is all right, but in fact, it is not. Your hard disk was deleted, a bank lost dozens of million dollars, or an airplane crashed. Everything is possible, and it has all already happened. Bugs are the worst possible issue that can occur in your code. Sure, most bugs are not that terrible. But don't take them lightly.

One property of bugs is that the programmers in charge can usually tell you in advance where bugs most likely occur. This is because they know that they haven't understood a certain part of the code completely and the code is therefore convoluted.

Cost of Bugs

The cost of bugs can be enormous. It may take hours, if not days, to track down a bug. In bad code, it's frequently unclear how it should be fixed. Furthermore, the cost of bugs increases exponentially over the course of the development cycle (p. 109). This is due to the growth and increased complexity of the code.[20] This is why syntax errors are so cheap: you are forced to fix them immediately.

I hope you got the memo. You always have to make sure you don't create bugs. Write good code and ensure it is well covered by tests. This is the only way to keep the number of bugs low (although it will never reach 0) and to stay as far away as possible from the exponential growth of the costs they cause.

Is It a Bug or a Feature?

In theory, it's very simple. Either some behavior is documented, or it's a bug. But in practice, it is not. First of all, not all behavior is documented. And secondly, not all undesired behavior is a bug, or at least it is not always advisable to fix it. The users of your software may have become accustomed to the faulty behavior and have implemented a workaround. So, fixing the bug could actually introduce new bugs in your clients' code.

Bugs can be classified by their severity. A bug resulting in a crash of an airplane is one of the worst-case scenarios and must be fixed, regardless of how unlikely it is to occur. Meanwhile, if you are developing an Android game, a bug that causes the game to crash every thousand hours or so may be considered acceptable. The potential inconvenience caused by the user may not justify the effort required to fix the bug. It is very common for only critical bugs to be fixed. All other bugs may be documented along with a workaround, but they will not be fixed due to economic reasons. Only in safety-critical systems, such as the airplane industry, must all bugs be resolved.

Bug Reports

Depending on the software, writing good bug reports may range from straightforward to nearly impossible.

Good bug reports explain the problem clearly and unambiguously. They follow a simple pattern: "If you do A, then B happens, but it would be expected that C happens." Unfortunately, describing A may be very difficult, depending on the software. If your software has an API that can be used to trigger the bug, you are usually in a good position because it is very simple to reproduce the bug. Just hand over all the relevant source code and files.

On the other hand, if it is, for example, a game without an API that crashes under very specific circumstances, it may be extremely difficult to reproduce the bug. Maybe some log files may help, but even that is not always sufficient to track down the bug.

---

[20] Software Engineering at Google. Winters et al.

Writing good bug reports is challenging. A bug report should be written with scientific accuracy so that anyone can reproduce the bug. Any factors that could potentially cause the bug must be reported, such as the software version number and even the version numbers of third-party libraries. The more information you provide, the easier it is to track down the bug.

Tracking Down Bugs

Debugging is the process of finding and resolving bugs. If you spend too much time debugging, it's a clear indication that your code quality is poor. Your code has no clear structure, and it lacks tests. Even with good code quality, some bugs are inevitable. But at least it is usually fairly obvious where they are trying to hide because they also have to follow the logic of your code.

The very first thing you always do when dealing with a bug is write an automated test. This is the only way that you can be certain the bug really exists. Furthermore, you have to make sure that the bug is reproducible. In most cases, this is not an issue, but when working on a distributed system, you may encounter race conditions and similar issues. These bugs are extremely difficult to track down, especially since they are not always reproducible. We will not discuss such bugs here, as they are out of scope for this book.

For debugging, you have a debugger to help you out. It allows you to set breakpoints and inspect variables. So far, so good. But if you find yourself using the debugger frequently, it may indicate poor code quality. If you had structured your code better and had higher test coverage from the beginning, you probably wouldn't need to rely on a debugger. Using a debugger is a clear indication that you lack an understanding of the task at hand. Meanwhile, this may happen occasionally. You should ensure that using the debugger is the exception rather than the rule and reconsider the way you write your code.

There are many different ways to track down bugs. Most importantly, you need to have an idea of which part of the code may have caused the bug under investigation. In well-written code, it is apparent where it comes from because of the SRP. The behavior of the bug can only originate from one location.

If you have a code example using the API of your software, you can attempt to simplify it while checking whether the bug still exists. This usually gives you a good idea of what the bug depends on. In most cases, the bug depends only on one specific setting in your API file. For example, the user may have used an option that is rarely utilized, and you anticipate it being buggy for some reason. Once you have minimized the number of API calls, there are two ways to track down the bug:

1. You can set a breakpoint where the value of a variable is assigned. If you have already reduced the code from the bug report to the smallest possible case, you should not need to iterate over the breakpoint too frequently to identify the faulty behavior.
2. You can bisect the bug. You set a breakpoint somewhere in the middle of the code to check if the bug already exists. If it does, you bisect the first half of the

code; otherwise, you bisect the second half of the code. This is a very powerful technique, as you can track down the bug in $\log(n)$ steps.

Now, as I already mentioned, the most important thing is to have as much information about the bug as possible. You need to have a clear idea of which part of the code may have caused the bug. If your code is badly structured and you have no idea whether some value returned by the debugger is correct or not, you will have a very hard time debugging it. You'll have no choice but to guess, and guessing is an extremely tedious process. Always make sure you understand the problem at hand as well as your code!

However, some bugs are very challenging to track down. These are the bugs that are not reproducible, such as race conditions in a distributed system. Utilizing log files may help; however, in complex cases, it takes an enormous amount of time to track down the bug.

Fixing a Bug

As mentioned earlier, you should never immediately fix a bug that you have just discovered. Users may rely on this faulty behavior, and fixing the bug may interfere with their workarounds. Consistency may be more important than correctness. Fixing the bug may break user code!

Once you have a bug ticket, the first thing to do is to write an automated test using the minimal API code that causes the faulty behavior. This helps a lot in tracking down the bug and prevents future changes to the code from reintroducing the bug. Bugs that have appeared once are very likely to reappear in the future.

Next, you have to track down the source of the bug, as mentioned above. Once you have found the bug, you can start fixing it. However, there are still some things to be considered. It is not advisable to simply insert a random hack into the code to solve the issue. You need to identify the faulty logic in your code! This is the only place where a bug can truly be fixed permanently. When looking at the code, you should have no idea that this is a bug fix applied later on. It should integrate into the code seamlessly, as if it had always been there.

Exceptions

Exceptions may occur once in a while. They occur when the computer is supposed to perform a certain task but is unable to do so. For example, errors can occur if a network connection cannot be established, the hard disk is full, there are divisions by zero, there are logical errors in your code, etc. These cases need to be addressed. The user must be notified to fix the problem.

User input should always be validated immediately. Are all values correct? When writing and supporting your own code, this is not a big deal, but users need human-readable feedback. A "division by 0" error message is not helpful because there may be no input value of 0; it could be the result of a lengthy calculation. The user should know which combination of variables caused this exception. Check the sensitive values and provide a meaningful response. "Invalid input: the number of 'shopping_items' cannot be 0" makes it much easier to track down the source of the problem. Check the values that are sensitive and promptly return an appropriate error message. If there is an invalid state, you should throw an exception as early as possible. Check if there is enough disk space before you start writing a file. Check if a division by zero can occur before you start your calculation, and return a meaningful error message.

Wrapping Exceptions

You don't want exceptions to escape your code. This code will cause the software to crash when executed. It is not a significant issue for a small stand-alone project, as it should probably be terminated anyway. But in serious software development, you cannot allow this to happen. Your software must be able to recover from an exception. The user has to be informed about what went wrong and given the possibility to fix the issue.

It is recommended to define your own error types. Put a try-except block around the entire code to handle all custom exceptions. Custom exceptions indicate that the user made an error, and you anticipated this incorrect behavior. You should provide the user with a meaningful error message explaining why the exception occurred and what they should do to resolve it.

Add another `except` block at the end of the program to catch any other types of exceptions. These are errors you didn't anticipate – bugs. Write a different error message and kindly instruct the user to contact your support team. The cause of this error message is a logical issue in your code.

Raise exceptions immediately if the program enters an invalid state and provide a clear error message to the user explaining what went wrong. It is not worth trying to deal with a semi-invalid state. You will not be able to rectify the situation. Exceptions should result in a message explaining the cause of the issue.

As stated in C++ Core Guideline E.31, "Properly order your catch clauses."[21] This means that you should always catch specific exceptions first and then more general ones. This is because specific exceptions allow you to provide the user with more detailed information about the problem, enabling them to resolve it without requiring your assistance. General exceptions, for example, a `division by zero` exception, indicate that the problem was unexpected, and the customer is not expected to resolve it by themselves.

---

[21] C++ Core Guidelines Explained. Rainer Grimm.

The try-catch block around the main function should ensure that no exceptions propagate out of the program. Following the above rule, it should look something like this:

```thon
if __name__ == "__main__":
    try:
        main()
    except CustomException as e:
        print("Unable to process user input:")
        print(str(e)) # for example: "InvalidInput: length of
                      # 'shopping_items' cannot be 0"
    except Exception as e:
        print("""Unknown issue. Please contact our customer
                 support.""")
        print(str(e)) # for example: "ZeroDivisionError:
                      # division by zero"
```

Other Things to Consider

Try-except blocks have some similarities to if-else or switch-case blocks. They are susceptible to bad code, especially violating the SRP. Therefore, apply the same rule to try-except blocks as to if-else blocks. There should be very few lines of code within each case, typically a function call or a short error message. Furthermore, try-except blocks should be the only content within a function. The sole responsibility of this function is to manage the try-catch block.

One common pattern is catching and re-raising exceptions. This allows you to add additional information, depending on the type of exception. This is not worth the effort. This additional information is not particularly helpful to the user. Instead, you should define a custom exception type and print a corresponding message when catching it, with all the information you have at the time when the exception was thrown.

Make sure your unit tests also cover exceptions. Exceptions are an integral part of the code specification and therefore have to be tested. In some cases, it is not possible to write a unit test. For example, you should never read a file in a unit test. Instead, you should dependency inject a file object that throws an exception. We delve into more details in the section "Dependency Injection" on p. 134.

Exceptions and Goto

By the way, you might have heard of the `goto` statement that was widely used until the 1970s. Then Edsger Dijkstra wrote the famous paper "Go to Statement Considered Harmful" which basically ended the usage of the goto statement. As always, there was a lot of truth behind his argument, but there are cases where goto statements are a legitimate choice. The Linux kernel is written in C, which does not support exceptions. Therefore, the Linux kernel uses goto statements instead. The goto is called when an error occurs and redirects the code to the equivalent of a catch block. Thus, goto statements are not always that bad. Otherwise, Linus

Torvalds would have chosen a different language. But you can certainly write terrible spaghetti code if you abuse goto statements.

Summary

There are also other programming paradigms besides OO programming. I generally prefer Procedural Programming over OO programming. This is due to the fact that good classes are small. However, if you make them smaller and smaller, at some point they disappear, and you are left with Procedural Programming.

Don't spend too much time thinking about which programming language you should learn. Once you know the basic principles of software engineering, you'll be able to learn other programming languages as well.

If your code is perfect, the complexity of the code is exactly equal to the complexity of the problem. And in most cases, this is much simpler than the code turns out to be. Vice versa, if the code seems utterly complicated, chances are high that you don't yet understand the problem and you haven't found the optimal solution. Rethink the problem and try to find a better solution.

High-Level Design   7

There are various perspectives from which you can examine the high-level design of your code. In addition to the essential software architecture, topics such as design patterns and Domain-Driven Design (DDD) can assist you in structuring your code effectively.

Software Architecture

> *Architecture: The decisions you wish you could get right early.*
> —Ralph Johnson

In this chapter, I am only providing a high-level introduction to what software architecture is, in my opinion. Many times, I'll leave the details to more specialized books.[1,2]

There are many people who misunderstand the work of "real" architects. Architects do not simply create a plan and pass it on to the construction company. Instead, they closely monitor the construction because there are always questions and problems arising that need to be addressed. And there is no one better suited to answer these questions than the architect.

In software engineering, it is similar. As far as I understand the expression "software architecture," architects are not only responsible for designing the cornerstones of the software; they also have to monitor the entire process of software development, as there will always be fundamental questions along the way.

Here is an example of how I understand the term "software architecture" based on my work experience: "I worked on a quantum compiler. We used an Abstract

---

[1] Clean Architecture. Robert C. Martin.

[2] Fundamentals of Software Architecture. Richards and Ford.

Syntax Tree (AST) to represent the gate operations. The quantum gates were then translated into electrical pulses that were played by our devices. The compiler was comprised of numerous visitors who traversed the AST and sequentially conducted all calculations and optimizations." Anyone familiar with an AST and the visitor design pattern will have a good understanding of the code I was describing. In four sentences, I described the basic data structure (the AST) as well as the fundamental structure of the algorithm (the visitor pattern) used in the code.

The End of Architecture

One question is where does architecture end? How detailed does it get? In my opinion, the answer lies in how far the architect plans it. There is no fixed boundary. What is clear, however, is that the architect cannot work out all the details by themselves. If they did, there would no longer be a need for software engineers. So, unless a project is very small, they only have time to focus on the high-level design. All the technical details have to be worked out by the engineers. The architecture is never perfect, and there will always be implementation questions from the software engineers. One way architects can stay connected with the development team is by writing code themselves. They can write code examples or tests that use the code and do something interesting with it.[3]

Designing Interfaces

One of the primary responsibilities of a software architect is to define the building blocks (data structures and libraries) and interfaces of the entire software system. Some of the interfaces may be only "partial interfaces," indicating that they are interfaces within a library. It fulfills all the requirements of a real interface, and the library could easily be divided into two parts at this point. It is an internal interface that is not exposed to the outside.

A partial interface has the advantage of requiring only a limited amount of maintenance for versioning, etc. However, there is a risk that the interface may become obsolete over time as programmers begin to work around it.

It is the architect's job to determine at the outset where and what kind of interfaces are required. They have to foresee the future. The YAGNI principle (p. 166) does not always apply to an architect because what if it turns out that we really needed that interface after all? Implementing an interface in existing code will be very costly.

---

[3] Domain-Driven Design, Eric Evans.

Separate Libraries

Increase cohesion within a library and reduce coupling between them. It's exactly the same principle as for classes and files, just on a higher level.

In every large codebase, you will have to work with multiple libraries. Some of the software components are developed internally, while others are third-party libraries. There are many factors to consider when making such decisions. The very first question is do you need another library? Can you implement the required functionality within an existing library? There are mechanisms that favor either smaller or larger libraries.

These advantages for either side lead to trade-offs in library sizes. Generally, it is advantageous to establish a dedicated library if there is a suitable opportunity.

Coupling

Interestingly, all the explanations about coupling and cohesion made for classes are also applicable to libraries. It is important to note that libraries should not become too large and rigid. You don't win a prize for writing the largest library in the company – one library that covers every object that exists. It just won't work!

An apple can have a color, a flavor, and a price. There can be three different areas: graphical rendering, food, and shopping. Each area uses exactly one property, and it makes no sense to mix them up. Keep the libraries separate and write glue code between them if needed. That's the only way to go. Just trust me. Don't write monolithic software that tries to replicate the entire world.

Design Patterns

> *A design that doesn't take change into account risks major redesign in the future.*
> —Erich Gamma

Design patterns[4] refer to a specific arrangement of classes, methods, and inheritance that give rise to unique properties in the resulting object. There are about two dozen commonly recognized design patterns and numerous books explaining them. I have neither the space nor the knowledge to write about all of them. I just added this chapter so that you can get an idea of what they are about.

Factory

I'll show the so-called factory pattern as an example to give you an idea of what design patterns are all about. It's a very simple pattern. Chances are that you have

---

[4] Design Patterns, Gamma et al.

already implemented a factory before, even if you were not aware of this pattern. Similar to the fact that DI is a design pattern, we just didn't call it this way.

```python
from enum import Enum

class Vehicle(Enum):
    CAR = 1
    SPACESHIP = 2

class Car:
    def move(self, speed):
        if speed > 200:
            raise Exception("Cannot move that fast")
        print(f"Car is moving at {speed} km/h")

class SpaceShip:
    def move(self, speed):
        print(f"SpaceShip is moving at {speed} km/h")

def factory(type):
    if type == Vehicle.CAR:
        return Car()
    if type == Vehicle.SPACESHIP:
        return SpaceShip()

vehicles = []
vehicles.append(factory(Vehicle.CAR))
vehicles.append(factory(Vehicle.SPACESHIP))

for vehicle in vehicles:
    vehicle.move(100)
```

When looking at this code, you might ask yourself, "what is the point?" This is because the factory in Python doesn't seem to be anything special. In Python, implementing a factory is particularly easy due to duck typing. In strongly typed languages like C++, you would have to use a base class and pointers to implement the code above.

The crucial point of the factory is that you can create objects of different types depending on a string or whatever else you provide. Factories are generally very useful for the creation of objects. They take some arguments and return an object. In some cases, factories are classes, but there is nothing wrong with defining them as functions.

One last remark: Instead of using the if statements in the factory, you could also use a dictionary. In my opinion, this makes the code better and shorter.

```python
factory = {
    "car": Car(speed=100),
    "spaceship": SpaceShip(speed=100)
}

vehicle = factory["car"]
```

The End of Design Patterns

Design patterns were specifically designed for OO programming. The original book also contains a lot of UML diagrams. This, however, leads to the inevitable question: What do we do in Functional or Procedural Programming?

The answer is simple: in many cases, we don't need design patterns. At least the few patterns that I can remember, you can easily write the code without them. At times I even have the feeling that design patterns solve problem with OO code that didn't even exist before OO code.

One example is the decorator pattern. The decorator pattern adds some functionality to an object. Typically, the decorator does something before or after the execution of the object. One common example is the `timeit` decorator in Python. Note that the decorator pattern is so common in Python that it is built into the language. You don't have to implement it yourself. You only have to install the `timeit` module using `pip install timeit-decorator`.

Here is an example of how you can use the built-in `timeit` decorator:

```
import logging
import time
from timeit_decorator import timeit

logging.basicConfig(level=logging.INFO)

@timeit(runs=10, log_level=logging.INFO)
def sample_function():
    time.sleep(0.1)

sample_function()
```

I won't go into the details of how you could implement the decorator pattern yourself. It is out of the scope for this book.

In Procedural or Functional Programming on the other hand, implementing the decorator pattern is straightforward. You only have to define a function that takes a function object, and you're done.

```
import time

def timeit(func):
    start = time.time()
    func()
    end = time.time()
    print(f"Execution time: {end-start}")

def sample_function():
    time.sleep(0.1)

sample_function = timeit(sample_function)
```

With a little more code, you can also pass `args` and `kwargs` to the function, and you have a general `timeit` decorator for functions.

Domain-Driven Design

The heart of software is its ability to solve domain-related problems for its user.
—Eric Evans

This chapter is highly influenced by Eric Evans' book *Domain-Driven Design*.[5] The book covers mostly conceptual topics such as the domain model and bounded context. This, along with the concept of "Ubiquitous Language" (Evans), forms the heart of the book and will be explained in this section, though there are some more resources on this topic by now.[6,7]

Ubiquitous Language

In software engineering, there are very few topics that are described purely mathematically, most notably finance, physics, and engineering. Most other topics are described using natural language. This is a significant challenge because it is difficult to incorporate such a topic into code. How do you implement an apple? The answer is it depends on who you are talking to.

It takes a lot of effort to understand a topic well enough to be able to implement it. Engaging in extensive discussions with domain experts about the topic is essential. Only through these discussions can you learn how their domain model is built up and what the underlying mechanisms are. This common language between developers and domain experts was named "Ubiquitous Language" by Eric Evans. It is of utmost importance that the development teams learn this language used by the domain experts. The development team should communicate using this language and implement it into the code. A domain expert must be able to understand the high-level discussions among developers. They have to be able to tell when something is off because there is something that doesn't make sense to them, for instance, if the developers mix up the usage of atoms and molecules in a chemistry simulation. Usually, domain experts can detect issues much earlier than developers. If there are expressions used in the code that do not exist in the domain, the model is most likely incorrect.

Developing this Ubiquitous Language is of utmost importance for the whole project. Only a well-developed shared language between developers and domain experts enables high-level discussions about the domain required for the success of the entire project. Developing such a language requires a significant amount of effort. Developers and domain experts need to stay in constant communication and continuously refine their language usage to enhance the model built upon this language. Play around with this language. Attempt to alter the vocabulary. Try to

---

[5] Domain-Driven Design. Eric Evans.

[6] https://github.com/ddd-referenz/ddd-referenz/blob/master/manuscript/

[7] Learning Domain-Driven Design. Vlad Khononov.

create new phrases. This is an important aspect of the Ubiquitous Language. You have to develop this language like children learning to speak a natural language. Find easier and more effective ways to express your thoughts, regardless of how silly they may seem initially. Utilize the insight gained in this way to enhance the domain model. Ensure that the business experts understand what you are discussing.

Thinking about the code in the English language also helps, even if you don't do much DDD. The following explanation from the book *The Art of Readable Code*[8] can help you improve your coding skills significantly:

1. Describe what code needs to do, in plain English, as you would to a colleague.
2. Pay attention to the keywords and phrases used in this description.
3. Name your variables and functions to match this description.

Especially if you're struggling to translate your thoughts into code, these steps may help you organize your ideas, making it much easier to write the code. If you cannot articulate the problem or your design in words, there is likely something flawed. This technique also allows you to avoid comments as you name your variables the way you would describe them in the English language.

The Domain Model

A model is a selectively simplified and consciously structured form of knowledge.
—Eric Evans

A model is a simplification of something real. A computer game, for instance, is always a model of some kind of reality. Interestingly enough, a computer game does not necessarily become better if the model or the graphics are more realistic, but rather if the model is more focused on making a point – if it emphasizes the core domain of what the game is all about while leaving out unnecessary details.

When writing code, we implement a model of reality – a model that closely resembles the problem we are trying to solve, not one that is closest to reality. The model must cover the domain of interest, the field in which you are working. It needs to simplify the domain to the bare minimum required to fulfill your programming task.

Along with the domain model comes the question of how to plan and document it. These are also problems which are not easy to solve.

UML Diagrams
The domain model is a high-level concept that needs to be described. This can be done in several different ways. Very common descriptions are UML diagrams. These are commonly used to illustrate the relationship between different classes and

---
[8] *The Art of Readable Code*, Boswell and Foucher.

instances. However, UML diagrams are not always the ideal choice for describing code. UML has several limitations. Personally, I don't like UML diagrams too much; that's why you don't see any of them in this book. I prefer to write code instead of drawing UML diagrams. I simply find code easier to understand. Ultimately, you'll have to decide for yourself whether UML diagrams are useful for you. And if they are not, you have to be flexible enough to use other methods to describe your code.

The first limitation of UML diagrams is that they support only a somewhat limited amount of interactions between classes or class instances. There are often more effective ways to describe code than using a class diagram. Maybe a piece of text or a diagram illustrating the temporal dependency of a process would be suitable. It does not really matter how you represent the domain model, as long as it helps you understand your code.

Secondly, one always has to consider that UML diagrams should remain small. Some development teams have printed out their entire codebase as a UML diagram, but this practice is largely ineffective. There are too many objects and interactions between them in such a graph, as if it could be useful. It's just like a map with too many details. Buried in all the information, you won't find what you are looking for. A map should be simple and easy to understand. It should only show what you are interested in, such as the subway stations. The same applies to UML diagrams: keep them concise and focus on what you are interested in, for example, the high-level structure of your code or a small subset of it.

There have been attempts to create a programming language similar to UML, but they have all failed for various reasons. Graphical programming simply isn't any better than textual programming; on the contrary, graphical programming generally lacks important tooling like version control or testing frameworks. Furthermore, a significant amount of information may be lost during the creation of the diagram. UML is not a complete programming language, and it will never be. UML diagrams cannot explain the entire functionality of your code. Thus, keep UML diagrams small if you ever happen to use them.

Documentation

Instead of using UML diagrams, you can use any type of document you prefer to document your code. At times, it is better to create a temporal order of a process than a class diagram. Or you can create a diagram with class instances instead of class definitions. After all, it's called object-oriented programming, not class-oriented programming.

As with all documents, the documentation of the domain core should be kept up to date or archived. There is a risk that the documentation and the code may diverge over time. Documentation has similar drawbacks to those described in the section "Comments" (p. 237). It takes a lot of effort to keep documentation up to date.

Though documentation has its merits, code is often too detailed to effectively explain its functionality. There are plenty of things that code alone cannot explain; it has to be complemented, possibly by comments and some additional documentation.

Ensure that design documents extensively utilize the Ubiquitous Language. If the documentation does not use the same terms as defined in the Ubiquitous Language,

Figure 7-1 The nonlinear progress over time. At some point in time, you'll have a breakthrough and understand the problem

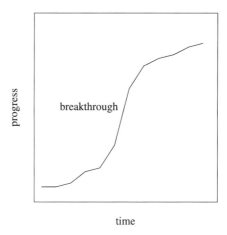

it is not useful. It doesn't help to explain what you are trying to implement; it only creates confusion.

Implementing a Model

There are cases where you cannot implement a model you have developed. It would be simply too complex. It just doesn't work as planned. This is a clear sign that your model is not optimal. If a domain expert can explain it, you should be able to implement it. In theory, the complexity of the domain model should not exceed the complexity of the problem it tries to solve. This is the optimal scenario where a developer can explain the code to the domain expert, and the domain expert can understand it. They would simply talk about the same thing, the same logic. In this case, the development of the code would feel very easy as everything just falls into place.

In reality, finding the optimal model is a challenging process. Most likely, you'll end up in an iterative loop, switching between coding, modeling, and refactoring until you have a breakthrough when you suddenly realize what the optimal model should look like.

Decouple the domain-model code from your other code, as explained in the section "The Abstraction Layers" in Chapter 1. This is important for maintaining clean and concise domain code. Violating this rule would also violate the SRP, as the domain model is located on a different abstraction level than, for example, the database code. The domain model contains the actual conceptual complexity of the final software. Therefore, it should not be cluttered with non-model-related things such as infrastructure or GUI code. Keep the domain model slim.

Domain Levels

Not every part of the software can be treated with equal priority. You'll have to prioritize what is important. There will be various domains in your project, for example, the core domain. The core domain is the most crucial domain of your project and must be treated as such. The core domain is what your company makes money with; it is the unique aspect that sets your company apart from other companies. Try to keep the core domain concise; only the most essential elements should be included in it. Your most experienced developers should be working on this topic.

Around the core domain, you will have several other domains. Each domain typically implements one class of features to support the core domain. For example, an infrastructure domain may involve managing the database or the math library. Keeping the domains separate is important as it prevents you from creating a Big Ball of Mud.

Each domain corresponds to a piece of code, such as a library. The different domains are fairly independent of each other. They are only linked through their interfaces. Otherwise, there doesn't have to be much resemblance between the different domains. For example, the Ubiquitous Language does not have to be the same across different models. On the contrary, the Ubiquitous Language is expected to vary among different models, and at the interface, there is an adapter that functions as a translator between the different languages.

As one example, a flight may refer to the time between takeoff and landing. But there may also be direct flights or flights with stopovers. This is an example where one expression may have different meanings, depending on the type of model you are working with. Therefore, it is always important to keep in mind the type of domain model you are currently working in and the specific type of flight you are discussing. Otherwise, you may end up confusing yourself.

Domain-Specific Language

A Domain-Specific Language (DSL) is a language specifically tailored to the needs of a certain problem. This DSL has to resemble very closely the Ubiquitous Language, as it should be the code version of how marketing people would talk about the problem. However, it is not exactly defined how this language should be implemented. Obviously, it has to be a programming language of some sort. It can be one relying on heavy usage of preprocessor macros or a language like Gherkin that resembles spoken language. Yet, it can also be a normal API using function calls or a simple JSON file.

Honestly, I don't like the preprocessor nor the Gherkin approach. If that were the best way to program, our programming languages would all work this way, which is not the case, probably for a reason. I prefer to design a dedicated API using a "normal" programming language. When using this API, a marketing person can still get an idea of what the code is about. That's also way less work than developing a preprocessor or Gherkin language, which both have its limitations as well.

Domain Boundaries

As your codebase grows, it becomes more and more difficult to keep working with a single domain model. There are processes that tend to tear the domain model apart. An object may have very different properties, depending on what part of the code you are working on. For example, a `user` has different properties in the payment domain than in the GUI domain. Of course, it would be preferable to have a single domain model for the whole codebase, but this is not a requirement for good code. The `user` would become much too big. Instead, you may have several different models, depending on which part of the code you are working on. There will be interfaces between the different models. And the big question is how do you deal with the different models?

Bounded Context

A bounded context is everything within a boundary. Typically, a domain model corresponds to a bounded context, where the boundary represents its interface. The interface regulates what goes in and out of the bounded context. Bounded contexts are important as they separate specific problems from the enterprise-wide codebase. One example of a bounded context is the math library. The names used in this library may also be applied in other contexts, but `sin`, `cos`, etc., have a very specific and well-defined meaning within this bounded context. These expressions should not be reused within the math library. On the other hand, the terms `sin` and `cos` may be utilized in other bounded contexts and carry a completely different significance.

Typically, domain models consist of one bounded context each. All the problems mentioned so far for the domain models are true for the bounded contexts as well. Mostly, if they get too large, they tend to be torn apart and that objects carry too much information.

Unified Model

The attempt to keep the model unified is the most obvious one, though it is challenging to sustain the necessary level of communication to uphold this condition. A good way to enforce this communication is through Continuous Integration (CI). CI compels the team to merge frequently and at an early stage, making any disparities between the model and the actual code evident at an early stage. The automated tests enforce the behavior of the model and warn the developers if they are inadvertently changing it.

On the other hand, working on a unified model is not always possible because, for larger projects, the forces that tear the single model apart become too large. In enterprise-scale software, it is simply not possible to work in a single model. The various requirements for the code may become too extensive, and classes are becoming too large. In a single model, the `user` object, for instance, becomes too complex as it continues to grow over time. At some point, it is easier to work with several different `user` objects, each of which is smaller and has different attributes, making them easier to manage.

Context Map
A context map is important when a model is divided into two or more parts. All parts are now separate bounded contexts. They are individual domain models with clearly defined boundaries. You'll need a translation map to convert one model to the other. The translation map is similar to an adapter pattern; it converts one interface to the other.

Shared Kernel
Two bounded contexts may share a common sub-context. This is typically the core domain utilized by various domain models. Having a shared domain core means that all involved models must ensure that the domain core is always in sync. This can be done by the CI. Additionally, it requires considerable communication between teams. Otherwise, the core domain may become fragmented. The shared kernel can also be regarded as a unified model that is used by both teams, embedding it into their own models.

Anticorruption Layer
The anticorruption layer is similar to the adapter design pattern. You add a small layer around your context. If the other code changes, you only have to adapt your anticorruption layer and not the entire codebase. This can save you a lot of work.

The anticorruption layer can be located on the outgoing part of an interface, though typically the users of an interface write it themselves, just to make sure that their code won't break if the developers change something.

Separate Ways
Sometimes, the burden of maintaining models collectively becomes too big, and it becomes apparent that collaborating further is no longer worth the effort. There is very little overlap between the two models, so cutting them apart is not a significant issue. If you need a feature from another model, simply re-implement it. Having a little bit of redundancy between two models may be preferable to coupling them together. If the redundancy becomes too significant, it may be worth implementing a shared kernel.

Developer-Client Relationship
The model is split into two parts, and one development team is relying on the other team's model. If the upstream team (the developers) is willing to cooperate (for financial or political reasons) with the downstream team (the client), the two teams can establish a developer-client relationship where the downstream team can request features for implementation by the upstream team. The success of this relationship hinges on politics and the cooperation of the upstream team within the company.

Conformist
The conformist is a model where the downstream team just follows the upstream team. The downstream team doesn't have anything to say. Needless to say, this is

Building Blocks of DDD

In *Domain-Driven Design*, Eric Evans introduced, among others, the terms entities, services, value objects, and aggregates.[9] These are various models used to differentiate between objects with diverse properties. Generally, the building blocks of Domain-Driven Design are implemented in OO design. In most cases, this is the easiest choice to model the functionality of the building blocks. However, other programming paradigms may also be chosen.

I'd like to point out that you don't have to implement everything using entities, value objects, etc., as explained here. It should be regarded as just a different way to think about how to structure your code.

Entities

Entities are unique objects. Their lifetime typically spans most of the code's lifespan, and they possess unique properties such as an ID. Humans are a very simple example. Every human is unique, and there are efforts to assign some form of identification to each individual, though this is harder than it sounds. Obviously, names are not suitable as unique identifiers. The social security number is used in some places, but not everyone has one, and there is nothing comparable in many countries outside the United States. For many websites, the email address is used, and sometimes the phone number is also required.

Another example of entities is seats in a stadium. Each customer buys a ticket for a specific seat. Thus, the seats and the customers are both entities. They are both unique objects. For each customer, exactly one seat is reserved. Every seat has a unique ID. Two seats are only considered equal if their IDs are the same. Even if all other properties are the same, if the IDs are not identical, the seats are not considered equal.

Now, it is different if the tickets are not assigned to a specific seat (general admission). If the customers can sit in any available seat, then the seats and customers are no longer considered entities. They are just one object among many. They become exchangeable. They become value objects.

Opposite to value objects, entities are not constant. They may have an internal state that changes over time. Only their ID has to remain constant. Whether this ID is really required depends on the situation. Generally, it is sufficient that you have access to a variable. The name of this variable already serves as an ID inside your code. However, if you want to store this object in a database, you certainly need some ID to retrieve this object later on.

---

[9] https://stackoverflow.com/questions/77425208/when-do-you-use-entities-value-objects-and-aggregates-ddd

Value Object

Value objects[10] are essentially the opposite of entities. Value objects are defined solely by their properties. They do not have a unique ID. One example is apples in the supermarket. We can regard them as indistinguishable. The only interesting aspects of an apple are its flavor and price. Other than that, they can be replaced at any time.

Value objects are immutable. You can only set the properties of a value object during its creation. Thus, if you don't like your apple, replacing it with another one is the only option you have. It's not possible to change its properties.

Having value objects is extremely useful, even if you don't care much about DDD. Value objects are generally small custom types, such as a price. The price is set in its constructor and cannot be changed thereafter. Furthermore, the constructor can ensure that the price is valid; for example, it cannot be negative. Therefore, the constructor takes care of the checks, and you won't have to bother with it any longer. Another example is the usage of an email address object. This object can ensure that the email address is valid. Therefore, using value objects is much better than using a string for the email address.

Value objects also help against the primitive obsession. Here is a small example of an email address as a value object:

```
def _check_email_address(address):
    assert address.count("@") == 1
    assert address.count(".") >= 1

class EmailAddress:
    def __init__(self, address):
        _check_email_address(address)
        self.ADDRESS = address
```

It fulfills the requirement of a value object. You can only set the value once in the constructor, and the validity of the address is checked there as well. It is not possible to change the address afterward. Class instances of `EmailAddress` are immutable. Value objects are therefore perfectly suited for use in Functional Programming.

As you may have noticed, value objects don't fit into any of the class types we have discussed so far. A value object is a data class with additional checks in the constructor.

Now, the question remains: When should an object be considered an entity or a value object? As I mentioned before, value objects are immutable. So, if you have an object, like the apple mentioned above, that will never change its properties, it is likely to be a value object. On the other hand, if something is important enough to change its properties, it should be considered an entity. In general, you should have many more value objects than entities in your code.

---

[10] https://youtu.be/P5CRea21R2E

Services

Services are used for operations on value objects or entities. A service has three properties:

- The operation does not naturally align with an entity or a value object.
- The interface of the service is defined in terms of the domain model.
- The service does not have any internal state that can change over time.

A service is an operation on the domain model. Its name is part of the Ubiquitous Language. Services are typically represented by pure functions.

While entities and value objects are generally too fine-grained to be reused, services are of medium granularity and are thus appropriate for reuse.

Aggregates

Aggregates are a special type of entity. They typically consist of other entities and value objects. The goal of an aggregate is to form an object whose operations never violate the system's invariants. A very common example of an aggregate is smart pointers or the vector class in C++. They are both implemented following the "Resource Acquisition Is Initialization" (RAII) pattern.[11] Both store some data and encapsulate memory management at the same time. When using the interface of a vector, the mechanisms underneath it always make sure there is enough memory allocated and that it will be deleted once the vector goes out of scope. And as a user, you don't even have to think about these invariants. They are hidden within the implementation.

Another somewhat more general example of an aggregate is my favorite example: a car. The car has a global ID. It consists of an engine, a chassis, and four tires. Let's say that the tires wear out, and occasionally you have to replace them. This makes them entities. Meanwhile, the engine and the chassis never change their state. These are value objects. The entire car can only be accessed from the outside. The engine, chassis, and tires can only be accessed from within the car object.

Once the tires are worn out, they are disposed of at the recycling plant. The recycling plant is likely represented by a different domain model compared to the car. At the recycling plant, no one cares anymore about how worn out a single tire is. The recycling plant simply consists of one huge pile of old tires. The tires become valuable objects. For the sake of simplicity, we are not going to model the recycling plant in our code here.

Here is an example of how the car entity could be modeled in code. `engine` and `chassis` are value objects; `tires` are entities.

---

[11] Effective Modern C++. Scott Meyers.

```
MAX_DISTANCE = 1000

class Tire():
    def __init__(self):
        # invariant: self._distance_remaining >= 0
        self._distance_remaining = MAX_DISTANCE

    def drive(self, distance):
        self._distance_remaining -= distance

    def get_distance_remaining(self):
        return self._distance_remaining

def replace_tire_if_needed(tire, distance):
    if tire.get_distance_remaining() < distance:
        tire = Tire()

def drive(tires, distance):
    for tire in tires:
        replace_tire_if_needed(tire, distance)
        tire.drive(distance)

class Engine():
    # ...
    pass

class Chassis():
    # ...
    pass

class Car:
    def __init__(self):
        self._tires = [Tire() for _ in range(4)]
        self._engine = Engine()
        self._chassis = Chassis()

    def drive(self, distance):
        drive(self._tires, distance)

batmobile = Car()
batmobile.drive(100)
```

You might have realized that Car is a delegating class. Delegating classes typically meet the requirements of an aggregate. A delegating class hides all the functionality within the class so that it is only accessible through the class instance itself. The car instance is accessible as it is a variable. A unique ID would only be needed for saving the car object in a database and retrieving it. If you want to save the car information to a database, you would need an identifier, such as the license number. The entire car would be saved intact under this ID. In this example, we would have to add a self._ID to the Car class.

It is not possible to modify the instance of the Car and its internals in any other way. It is not possible to violate the car's invariants. All the variables are encapsulated within the Car, and the methods are guaranteed to maintain the invariants.

The class Car may have the following invariants. It needs

- A unique identifier (as it's an aggregate)
- Four tires (entities) with the invariant _distance_remaining >= 0
- One engine (entity) with an ID
- One chassis (value object)

Upon construction, these invariants are guaranteed by the constructor of the class, assuming that the ID is indeed unique. All the other functions (services) that act on the car must ensure that these invariants are not violated. The method car.drive() calls the function to replace tires if they are worn down, but there are still four tires with a positive _distance_remaining after the replacement and driving some distance.

Aggregates should always be treated as whole objects; for example, they should be saved to or loaded from a database. Aggregates are always entirely within the domain level of your code. It can't be any other way because all parts of an aggregate are on the same level of abstraction. Having one element of the infrastructure level inside an aggregate would violate the SRP.

As the root entity is the only thing accessible from the outside, it is comparatively simple to enforce the invariants of the aggregate. For example, every car has four wheels that are not yet worn down. All accessor functions must pass through the root entity, the car. Thus, this is the place where you can enforce the invariants. In the car, you can define functions such as drive that take care of ensuring the wheels are in good condition and replace them if necessary.

Aggregate instances are often created by a factory or another creational design pattern. These patterns allow us to outsource the creation of a fairly complex object. This is in accordance with the SRP. If the instantiation of an object is fairly complex, it is a noteworthy task and should be handled in a dedicated object. Furthermore, the factory can also take care of the invariants of the class instance at its creation.

Just to clarify the concept of an aggregate, let's consider an example where it is violated.

```
class Engine:
    _is_started = False

    def start(self):
        self._is_started = True

    def is_started(self):
        return self._is_started

class Car:
    def __init__(self, engine):
        self._engine = engine
```

```
    def start(self):
        self._engine.start()

    def get_engine_status(self):
        return self._engine.is_started()
engine = Engine()
car = Car(engine)
car.start()
print(engine.is_started()) # this is bad code
```

Now that the engine is started, we can use it. This, however, is bad code. The engine is now part of the `car` aggregate and should only be accessed through the `car` interface. Here, it is accessed directly. You can also think of a real car where you install the engine, start the car, and then remove the engine for inspection. This feels wrong. And as it's wrong in the real world, it is most likely wrong in the code domain as well.

The solution is the function `get_engine_status()` that I defined in the `Car` class. Now, the aggregate is properly encapsulated, and you can access the relevant properties of the engine through the car's interface. Note that this way, we don't need the intermediate `engine` object. Instead, we can directly instantiate it inside the `Car` constructor.

```
car = Car(Engine())
```

Of course, it is sometimes more convenient to have an `engine` as a temporary object. For example, if the readability is affected because the engine is created by a function with a very long name, you should create the mentioned object along with the `car` instance within a specialized factory to encapsulate this temporary object. There, you construct the `engine` and then pass it on to the `car` constructor. The engine should never be visible from the outside; it should be accessible only through the `car` interface.

Third-Party Software

Prefer Visa over Power Shell

—YouTube

There are thousands of companies selling software parts. For many problems, there are open source solutions available. This is great, but as always, there is a price to pay.

No airplane engineer would start developing their own jet engine, and no programmer would write their own database software. Even if they don't like the products available, they can still purchase something from the market. Everything else is simply crazy; it's too expensive. Other companies are developing databases, and you are not going to compete with them. You want to do other things instead. You have found your niche elsewhere, and you plan to remain there unless there is a compelling reason to completely change your business. You outsource everything that you don't really have to do yourself.

In software engineering, there are not many products available to address all possible problems. But still, there are quite a few suppliers who can assist you in solving some of your issues, especially when it comes to infrastructure and tools.

It is possible that you have a bad feeling about this approach. You want to do everything by yourself. You don't want to pay other companies for their libraries. I can assure you that your feelings are natural. But you have to get over it. It's just not worth doing everything by yourself. You haven't developed your own operating system, the database, nor the cloud service you're using. Instead, you earn a good amount of money every year by working on your core domain. You do what you can do best. And if you can save time by outsourcing other parts of the code, that is great. This also allows you to save on maintenance costs, which are typically even more expensive than the actual development of the software.

Using third-party libraries or software is great – most of the time. But sometimes it also has its issues. Some companies did not adhere to coding standards, and now they are in trouble – most famously, all the customers using Oracle databases who didn't decouple the database from the rest of the code. The code extensively utilizes Oracle database queries, making it challenging to switch to a different database vendor. These companies now pay substantial licensing fees and cannot evade them.

Another problem is libraries with comparatively few contributors. At some point, there might be no one left to maintain the code. In most areas, you can still use such a library for a while, but you should look out for a different solution. A lot of problems can arise when using software that is no longer supported. If you truly require this software, you may want to consider becoming a contributor yourself.

Everything explained here is also true for IT services and infrastructure (Amazon Web Services (AWS), GitHub, Google Maps, etc.). These services are great, but you should always have the ability to change your supplier. For example, there are medium-sized companies that require a significant amount of computing power. They started the company using AWS, just like everyone else does. It's just too convenient. As the company grew, the AWS bill reached millions, prompting the company to migrate to its own server infrastructure.[12]

In short, third-party software and services are generally excellent. They may save you a lot of work and money, but they come along with their own set of problems. You have to make sure you don't get stuck with them. You have to stay flexible. Decouple the third-party library from your code. Write a lightweight adapter between your code and the library. And if you don't, make sure that you really want to stick to this specific third-party code for a long time. As always, if you can write tests using dependency injection and similar techniques, you are probably fine. In order to mock the database, you need an interface that can be used to support other databases as well. So, you are flexible.

---

[12] https://world.hey.com/dhh/why-we-re-leaving-the-cloud-654b47e0

The very big question is always when you really need such an adapter. Most of the time, I am too lazy to write one. But you certainly need one when dealing with databases. Call all the database-specific queries only within this thin layer. The entire remaining code is a database-syntax-free zone. This makes it very simple to exchange the database. You only have to replace the wrapper. You might have to modify some of the implementation since the functionality varies slightly between databases. But this is a small price to pay compared to the millions you have paid to Oracle so far.

You should reconsider using a third-party library if it has only a few developers. If there is a reasonable alternative, you might be better off avoiding it. On the other hand, if this code is crucial for your software, it would be beneficial to participate in the project and contribute as a developer. In fact, pretty much all major software companies support the software projects they rely on. Some projects received so much additional manpower that they ran out of work to do. And even the unthinkable happened: Microsoft became a contributor to the Linux kernel!

Summary

The topics discussed in this chapter are somewhat more complex than the ones discussed in other chapters. The most important section here is the one on Domain-Driven Design (DDD). I think Eric Evans had some great ideas, though it took me a while to understand them. Most importantly, the Ubiquitous Language describes how the naming of objects in the code should be done. Define your own vocabulary and stick to it. If possible, use the vocabulary that is also used by the domain experts.

Entities, aggregates, and the other components of Domain-Driven Design are a great way to structure your code. You can write great code without knowing about them. However, they represent a different way to think about how to structure your code – a very useful one. It forces you to structure the code in a similar way to how I did throughout this book.

Refactoring

8

Refactoring is the process of enhancing the structure of existing code without altering its functionality. In older codebases, this practice was often neglected due to the absence of tests that covered the code. Consequently, modifying the code was risky, as it could easily introduce bugs. As a result, the common approach was to avoid refactoring and instead add new features wherever it seemed feasible.

Refactoring Fundamentals

If you wait until you can make a complete justification for a change, you've waited too long.
—Eric Evans

There are books about refactoring[1] by Martin Fowler teaching some basic techniques. Still, the most important aspect of refactoring is that you know what good code looks like (and that you have plenty of tests to back you up). If you have a vision of how the code should look, you are always going to find a way to make it better.

There Will Be Change

If code exists for a long enough period (which is usually sooner rather than later), it will need to adapt to changes. When you add new features, the build system might change, the database could be altered, libraries get security updates, and you will need to adjust your code to fit the new environment. This is inevitable. Only if you write extremely low-level code with minimal dependencies might you be safe

---

[1] Refactoring: Improving the Design of Existing Code. Martin Fowler.

from changes, or if you develop mobile apps that are expected to last only one or two years. In all other cases, you have no choice but to adapt to the changing environment. Your code has to remain flexible. You have to keep it in shape. Ensure that you can adapt to change.

Don't Let Your Code Rot

The most fundamental rule about refactoring is that you shouldn't let your code rot to begin with. Always make sure your code, or at least its foundation, is well tested and well structured. This will save you a lot of pain in the future. Once you reach the point of having classes that are a thousand lines long, you will struggle to regain control of your code. By writing properly tested code from the beginning, you'll save a lot of time in the long run. Not only will it be easier to refactor your code, but your code quality will also improve, requiring less refactoring.

Even without external changes, it is important to refactor your code once in a while. We have to face the sad fact that our perfect code deteriorates over time. Every line of code you add is a potential source of deteriorating code quality. You may introduce duplication, enlarge the class size, or disrupt the logical order in your code. Over time, the code becomes messy and needs to be cleaned up. Sometimes it is also compared to entropy (p. 164), the physical law of disorder.[2] Fighting entropy is hard.

About Refactoring

Refactoring means to change the code without altering its functionality. This is what people didn't do in old code. They were afraid that they would break the existing functionality and introduce bugs. It's as if they didn't clean up the kitchen because they were afraid they might break something. They didn't see the reason why they should have cleaned up the kitchen to begin with. They only had a nagging doubt that something was wrong, but they couldn't pinpoint the exact issue. Long story short, the next person had to cook in a dirty kitchen. At some point, there were so many dirty dishes in the kitchen that they didn't even notice the bugs that could hide underneath each and every dirty plate. People using the kitchen were afraid of introducing bugs when refactoring, but in the end, they still ended up with bugs. They didn't clean up the kitchen or refactor the code. They started encountering numerous bugs further down the road because the whole thing became a mess.

I really hope you understand that not refactoring is not an option. A cook has to clean up the kitchen continuously, just as you have to refactor your code all the time. Refactoring is an integral part of your job, not just an optional feature. You are responsible for refactoring your code. Therefore, we have to help you overcome your fear of refactoring and introducing bugs. You need a safety net – something that automatically notifies you when you introduce a bug. You need automated tests!

---

[2] The Pragmatic Programmer. Hunt and Thomas.

Unit tests, functional tests, performance tests, etc. Just make sure your automated tests cover pretty much all the functionality of the code you want to refactor. There are tools available to highlight the lines of your code that are covered by tests. Alternatively, you can modify one line of code and check if any of the tests fail, although this approach is not very productive.

If you are confident about the test coverage, you can do pretty much anything you want. Whenever you dislike some piece of code, simply discard it and rewrite it from scratch. Or even better, utilize a third-party library if one is available. As long as the tests pass, you are most likely fine.

Keep Refactorings Small

Most refactoring is usually minor in scale: renaming a variable, breaking up a class into two new ones, removing duplicate code, and extracting functions. Meanwhile, rewrites of entire features are relatively uncommon.

The biggest mistake one can make with refactoring is waiting too long. If you have a gut feeling that your fundamental data structure could be an obstacle, you should act right away. Discuss with your colleagues whether this is truly the correct choice and explore alternative options. Peripheral code can still be refactored later on. But if the core of your code is rotten, you will have a big issue fixing it, and it will only get worse if you don't act quickly. As always, the core of your code needs the highest priority.

Probably, you do some smaller refactorings quite often, but not really in a structured manner. You refactor code as soon as you encounter something you don't like. This is honorable, but there is a very simple workflow that I can recommend to everyone: write code – test – refactor. For every feature you implement, you should follow this pattern. Or even better, you can also write tests – code – refactor, as explained in the section "Test-Driven Development" (TDD, p. 126). This pattern is great because you can focus on one thing at a time. You can start by writing mediocre code. Maybe you are unsure about how to name a variable, or you might be inclined to create a class that is too large. There may be duplicated code. Certainly, it would be better to write flawless code from the outset, but you cannot multitask. Most people can't. You cannot develop code and make it perfect at the same time. You're not perfect. Learn to deal with your imperfections and refactor your code in a dedicated development step.

Then you write the tests. Some tests may fail because your imperfect code might contain bugs. When you fix the bugs, the code becomes even messier. Even if you had written sublime code to begin with, due to the inevitable changes, you would still have to refactor at some point. This is something that was overlooked by the waterfall development process. You never write perfect code to start with. You always miss some details that you have to fix later on. It always takes some refactoring to end up with good code.

Finally, you refactor. You review all the code you have written since the last time you refactored. Possibly, there is also existing code that has been around for a long time and could be merged with your new code because it is very similar. The code will probably look more complicated than you would expect. Then you try to rethink the logic of the problem you just solved. Can you modify the algorithm so that you can eliminate all the `if` statements for the corner cases? Do you need to sort your data structures differently to improve the code?

There are hundreds of things you could do to improve the quality of the code. When examining the code, identify the key elements that require modification. Try to write good code and trust your instincts. But make sure you also get some real work done between the refactoring sessions. The code will never be perfect, but at some point, it will be good enough. Move on once this is the case. Don't get stuck in endless discussions about variable names. Go ahead and write some new code again.

Levels of Refactoring

Maybe you have a simple question: At what level should you refactor? Should you only refactor small elements, or should you delve deep into the core of your software?

Let me provide another brief example. Let's assume you are planning to build a house and enjoy cooking. Ensure that there is ample space in the kitchen for all your equipment. You are very pleased. This is the equivalent of a first draft of your code. Everything looks perfect.

Yet dishes get dirty, so you have to clean up the kitchen every day. Otherwise, you'd be left with a huge mess in no time. This corresponds to the everyday refactoring done by a software engineer. Ensure you eliminate code duplications, name all variables appropriately, and clean up anything you find unsatisfactory along the way.

Over time, as you occasionally purchase additional kitchen gadgets, you may find yourself running out of space. You need to sort out all the old devices you no longer need and utilize your Tetris skills to neatly fit everything back onto the shelves in an organized manner. Make sure you can still find your belongings. This is an intermediate refactoring.

At some point, you buy another device and realize there is not enough space for your equipment anymore. There is only one solution: you need a bigger kitchen. You need to plan how much additional space you will require for the next few years and decide whether to tear down some walls or expand your house. Now, this will be a very demanding and expensive renovation.

I hope you received the memo. Small refactoring should be done all the time, every few lines of code. The costs are low, and it keeps your workspace clean. Intermediate refactoring costs more and affects a significant portion of your codebase. It should be discussed with your work colleagues during the coffee break and may be done together. Large-scale refactoring is really labor-intensive. It is done only every few months and requires careful planning and dedicated meetings because there is a lot at stake.

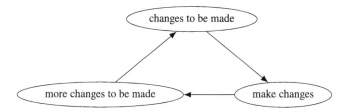

Figure 8-1 The circle of refactoring

Refactoring Is Dynamic

Waterfall refactoring is bound to fail for the same reasons that most waterfall projects do. Refactoring is concrete, just like regular coding. It consists of a learning process; it's a feedback loop. Refactoring usually needs to be done incrementally, and endless planning sessions are a waste of time. You only have to make sure you get the fundamental data structures right. Every couple of lines you write, you learn so many new things that require you to adapt the detailed refactoring plans. Possibly, you may even have to abandon these grand plans altogether because you realize they just won't work. Due to some detail, the fundamental data structure was wrong. You can have as many beautiful plans as you want; if they don't work out, they are worthless.

You have to face the facts. Waterfall refactoring is not working out. Instead, you have to follow the actual dynamics of making changes, learning more about your code, and adapting your future changes. These three steps are the only way refactoring can be done.

Refactoring certainly has the highest impact when you have gained a new understanding of the problem you are trying to solve. This feature allows you to rewrite an entire piece of code at once, enabling you to make significant progress in improving your code quality. Eric Evans refers to this as "Refactoring toward deeper insight."[3]

The Circle of Doom

There is something very mean about refactoring. Refactoring good code is easier than refactoring bad code. The circle shown in Figure 8-1 also operates in the opposite direction and becomes the circle of doom. For example, dealing with code that includes global variables, numerous dependencies, and large classes is always challenging, whether you are writing new code, tests, or performing refactoring. In all cases, you have to understand what the code really does. For writing new code and tests, this is bad enough. But with refactoring, it can become a nightmare. You may find yourself delaying refactoring tasks because it can be challenging to comprehend poorly written code. But over time, this will only exacerbate the situation until you reach the point where refactoring becomes essentially impossible,

---

[3] Domain-Driven Design. Eric Evans.

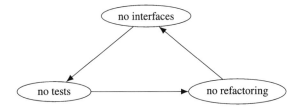

Figure 8-2 The circle of doom

and you are paralyzed. You would need to refactor your code because it is poorly written, but you are unable to do so because it has deteriorated to a point where improvement is no longer possible.

Don't slack off on refactoring. You'll pay the price sooner rather than later. Make sure you always keep your code well organized; this will greatly simplify your life. And always remember to keep writing tests. Missing tests are the most obvious sign that your code is getting out of hand.

However, there is one thing you should always consider while refactoring: even if you don't like the behavior of your code as you are refactoring, you should not change it. The behavior of the software may not be changed. Even if it's a bug, you should first discuss with your team whether you should fix it. Users may rely on that bug, as explained by Hyrum's law (p. 27).

When to Refactor

It is generally a good idea to do refactoring. Most developers do too little refactoring rather than too much. Still, there are some general recommendations on when to refactor or not.

Every few lines of code you write, you should consider refactoring them. It is not always necessary, though it is by far the best moment. You still know what you just programmed, and you might have an idea of what is left to improve. Maybe you just introduced some code duplication or an if statement that you could get rid of? Additionally, you are always working in a tidy workplace, which increases your productivity. Code that is well taken care of is much easier to modify.

As mentioned earlier, you should always refactor the code you have just written. This is the number one rule. Furthermore, you should adhere to the Boy Scout rule:[4] "Leave the campground cleaner than you found it." The same can be said for code. Always refactor a little more than you should. This helps fight code entropy.

Refactor when you find a bug. Don't just add a patch that might resolve the issue superficially. Search for the actual source of the problem. Consider if there is any redundant code that needs to be fixed or refactored for better efficiency. Find a viable solution for the bug, which may involve some refactoring. This is time well spent because, usually, bugs tend to cluster. So, if you found one bug, there might be more.

---

[4] Clean Code. Robert C. Martin.

If you add a new feature, it may not seamlessly integrate into the existing codebase. Most likely, the code has not been cleaned up, or the other authors simply didn't know how the code should look in the future. Hence, the code has a different structure than what is required for this new feature. But now, as you're adding this new feature, you have more knowledge. You might have an idea of how the code should really look for the feature to fit in. Now, don't force the feature into the existing codebase. Refactor instead and ensure the new feature integrates seamlessly. Maybe transform a data structure as explained in the section "Orthogonality" (p. 29). Altogether, this is less work. And especially, the code will ultimately be in a much better condition.

During code review (p. 257), you can also perform refactoring. Team up with the code author and engage in pair programming (p. 253). This type of review is much more motivating than a standard review because it facilitates better knowledge exchange and significantly enhances the review's output.

Last but not least, it is your code. You are responsible. You are the one to decide when it's time for refactoring. Don't ask your boss for permission to refactor; just do it when you have to.

What to Refactor

Generally, you should refactor the code that you work with. In some cases, you may refactor code that you have just walked by, but this should not be the rule. If there is no reason for you to touch that code at the moment, you shouldn't refactor it. It is important in software engineering to know when to postpone certain tasks, and this is one of those cases. If no one is currently working with a particular piece of code, there is no immediate need to refactor it.

Once in a while, you have to do a significant refactoring – one that you don't just do between writing a few lines of code, but that will take considerable effort to get done. You should probably discuss this topic with your work colleagues, as opposed to the smaller refactorings that you do on your own.

Refactoring Process

Writing code follows a similar process to the one I use when writing this book. I first started by jotting down the basic ideas: a rough draft of the content I wanted to include in this book. Some ideas I had for a long time, while others I acquired while reading other books. Then I tried to connect all the different parts. I read the text repeatedly, reworking it several times. I clarified points, removed redundancies, rearranged chapters, and added explanations where necessary. Every time I started to understand my text better, I could further improve it until I reached the point where the text said what I wanted it to – until I had gathered all my knowledge from my head and organized it into a human-readable text. Or, as Ward Cunningham put it, "By refactoring, I move the understanding from my head into the code."

Refactoring Techniques

> *Whenever I have to think to understand what the code is doing, I ask myself if I can refactor the code to make that understanding more immediately apparent.*
> —Martin Fowler

The techniques explained here mostly require an existing set of automated tests because changes to the code may introduce bugs otherwise. Some refactoring can also be done without tests, but in most cases, this game is very dangerous to play. Even if some techniques seem safe to apply without tests, there is always some latent danger of breaking the code in some way. Especially if you have global variables or overridden functions, it becomes tricky. Refactoring code in compiled languages is easier than in interpreted languages because the compiler performs valuable checks on names, functions, types, and so on.

There is a wide range of concrete refactoring techniques to be applied in specific cases. I will only briefly explain some of them. Most of the concepts originate from the book *Refactoring* by Martin Fowler.[5] In the following, I will group these techniques into two categories: refactoring for good code explained in this section here, while refactoring bad legacy code with global variables, inheritance, no tests, etc., follows in the next section.

The techniques explained in this section are unlikely to create bugs. Good refactoring usually consists of a sequence of small changes, and the code should almost be in a working state all the time. However, you never know. In very convoluted code, I wouldn't dare to break a class into pieces without having it covered with unit tests.

When following the rules taught in this book, you should be writing good code. It is well tested, contains clear interfaces, has no global variables, and has no side effects. Still, you have to refactor once in a while. But it's comparatively easy because you can focus on the refactoring part. The tests are already in place to ensure that you don't break anything. In this section, you will learn some techniques that you can apply when refactoring.

Where to Start

Usually, it takes me very little time to see whether some code needs to be refactored and, if so, what the problems are (p. 6). The most frequent problem is classes and functions that are way too long. As we have learned, functions should be short, generally below 20 lines, though less is better (p. 57). Classes may be only slightly longer than that. Too long functions and classes are also very easy to spot, but, unfortunately, they can be very challenging to fix. Along with too long functions

---

[5] Refactoring: Improving the Design of Existing Code. Martin Fowler.

Refactoring Techniques

comes the problem of too many levels of indentation. This is another sign that the logic of the code should be simplified.

Missing unit tests is also a very common problem, though this one is even harder to fix. You simply lack information on what a piece of code does. Especially for long functions and classes, it is nearly impossible to find out what the code does. Furthermore, it is certainly the task of the original programmer to write tests, not yours.

Another common problem that is easy to spot is comments. If the expression used to explain something in a comment is different from the name of the variable, something is off. Usually, the variable should be renamed, though renaming is not the highest priority. The highest priority is fixing the logic of the code. This is where you can really improve your code.

Breaking Classes

Breaking classes into smaller pieces is one of the most commonly used refactoring processes. As it is tempting to write too big classes to begin with, and due to the fact that classes tend to grow over time, they have to be split once in a while. Classes should be small. In my opinion, the best classes are the ones that don't exist. Use data classes and a few functions instead to organize your code. Functional Programming does have its merits, after all.

Too Many Methods

One issue with classes is the excessive usage of methods. As I've already explained before, I prefer having freestanding functions over methods. They are decoupled, and you can deal with them more freely. For instance, you can move these functions into a new class if you like, with only minor effort. Furthermore, it is easier to write unit tests for freestanding (and preferably pure) functions compared to methods. The technique behind it is fairly simple. Just search for methods that use only "few" class variables. Remove one of these methods from the class and create a function out of it. Instead of passing the class instance (`self` in Python, `this` in C++), you have to pass all the function arguments explicitly.

```
class House:
    def __init__(self, address):
        self._address = address

    def _print_address(self):
        # do something more with _address
        print(self._address)

    def wrapper(self):
        # do something with _address
        self._print_address()
```

Here, we can refactor the `_print_address` method out of the class. The only variable needed by this method is `_address`. So we have to pass this variable as a function argument.

```
def _print_address(address):
    # do something more with address
    print(address)

class House:
    def __init__(self, address):
        self._address = address

    def wrapper(self):
        # do something with _address
        _print_address(self._address)
```

This is, of course, a very artificial example, and the question is whether it's worth doing this refactoring. If the class is very small, it doesn't really matter. But as the class grows, it becomes more and more important to increase cohesion and refactor out everything that doesn't need to be within the class. Here, `_print_address` is such an example. It requires only one member variable from the class, so it has comparably little cohesion. It is therefore a candidate to be refactored out into a separate function. If you don't refactor such methods out of your classes, your code becomes rigid, and making changes to the class will require a lot of effort.

In our example, we were able to reduce the number of methods that need access to `_address` from two to one. This is a very significant improvement. If you now have to change the shape of the class by changing the `_address` member variable, it has become much easier. You'll only have to change one method in the class.

Of course, this example is so small that you could completely dismantle the class. It has only one variable that is only used in one method. This is not what you should write a class for. The only class-like thing here should be the `address`, which should probably be a data class.

Structuring Variables

If variables are always used together in the same methods, they have high cohesion. This means that they probably belong together. They should be stored in a data class. Let's look at the following example:

```
class Boat:
    def __init__(self, name, age, weight):
        self._name = name
        self._age = age
        self._weight = weight
        self._price = 10.0

    def print_boat(self):
        print(f"""{self._name} is {self._age} years old and
                weighs {self._weight} kg.""")
```

Here, the variables `_name`, `_age`, and `_weight` are all used together. So it makes sense to store them in a dedicated data class. Furthermore, we can implement the new `print` function as the Pythonic `__str__` function.

```
from dataclasses import dataclass

@dataclass
class BoatDetails:
    name: str
    age: int
    weight: float

    def __str__(self):
        return f"""{self.name} is {self.age} years old and
                weighs {self.weight} kg."""

class Boat:
    def __init__(self, boat_details):
        self._boat_details = boat_details
        self._price = 10.0

    def print_boat(self):
        print(self._boat_details)
```

And probably we could rename the `print_boat` method to `print_boat_details` since it only prints the details of the boat. As the `print_boat` method now depends only on the `_boat_details` variable, we could also make it a freestanding function that takes only this variable as an argument.

Possibly, this code above is still coupled too strongly. The `boat_details` and the `price` are not part of the same domain. It might make sense to store the price in a dictionary with the name separate from the other information. So, if you want to have complete information about the boat, you would have to combine the information from the `boat_details` and the `price` dictionary, similar to having the two properties in different tables of a database. That might be the best solution, but this is a different story.

Splitting Classes

One of the hardest tasks is splitting big classes into pieces. Here, we have a very small but suboptimal class that I made deliberately that way. Not every class is that easy to refactor; there is no generally valid pattern.

Here, everything is implemented inside the `Shopping` class. This is bad because, for every comestible, you have to extend the class. This violates the Open-Closed Principle (OCP, p. 139).

```
class Shopping:
    def __init__(self):
        self._apple_tracker = []
        self._eggs_tracker = []

    def get_shopping_items(self):
```

```
        return self._apple_tracker + self._eggs_tracker

    def add_apple(self):
        self._apple_tracker.append('apple')

    def add_egg(self):
        self._eggs_tracker.append('egg')

shopping = Shopping()
shopping.add_apple()
shopping.add_egg()
print(shopping.get_shopping_items())
```

Instead of having a class for each comestible inside the `Shopping` class, you should have only one list for all different comestibles at the same time. The different behavior is implemented inside each individual class, obeying the OCP. This allows you to simply add a new comestible without changing the `Shopping` class.

Also, testing this class in its current state may be hard. Possibly, you'll have to use a mocking library to alter the functionality of some functions that are implemented inside this class. This is a sign that the class is badly designed. Instead, we can use dependency injection to inject the comestibles into the class. Using DI is frequently the easiest solution to break a class (p. 216) into different pieces.

Note that the resulting code is much longer. We don't have separate `apples` and `eggs` lists anymore. We have a list of `items` that can be of any type. Therefore, the order in which the elements are stored may be different. But this is probably not a big deal since all elements inside a list should be treated equally. On the other hand, the `apples` and `eggs` were stored in separate lists, but they were private and never used alone. So there is no problem with storing them in one list together. These are, of course, all things that have to be considered when refactoring a class as they vary from case to case.

```
from abc import ABC, abstractmethod

class Shopping:
    def __init__(self):
        self._shopping_basket = []

    def add_item(self, item):
        self._shopping_basket.append(item)

    def get_shopping_items(self):
        return [str(item) for item in self._shopping_basket]

class ShoppingItem(ABC):
    @abstractmethod
    def __str__(self):
        pass

class Apple(ShoppingItem):
    def __str__(self):
```

```
        return 'apple'
class Egg(ShoppingItem):
    def __str__(self):
        return 'egg'

shopping = Shopping()
shopping.add_item(Apple())
shopping.add_item(Egg())
print(shopping.get_shopping_items())
```

This is, of course, a very simple example, and I made some changes to the functionality, which is usually unacceptable. In reality, the functions may be much more complex than this. But still, I think it was worth splitting up this class into many smaller classes because it can now be extended much more easily.

For testing purposes, you can also create a `FakeShoppingItem` if you want. This entire technique here we have already learned in the section "Dependency Injection" (DI). This code here is similar to a factory (p. 185).

Renaming

Even though renaming barely alters the structure of the code, it should be done frequently, not only for good code but also for legacy code. Finding good names is one of the most challenging tasks in programming because assessing the quality of names is very difficult. There are some general rules on how naming should be done (p. 32); yet, it is still one of the hardest tasks in software development. This leads to the fact that there are many objects with suboptimal names. As you write some code, it may happen that you spot something for which you happen to know a better name. Then, rename this object. This is the only way names improve over time. Don't assume the author of the code knew better. You now have much more information at hand that simplifies finding a good name.

However, you have to pay attention. People get used to names. If a name for an object has become familiar to the entire development team, you shouldn't change it, even if you have a better name. Renaming it would cause too much confusion. It has probably become part of the Ubiquitous Language (p. 188). For this reason, it is better to name central elements of your code at the beginning of the development and not change them later on.

One possibility is to start with mediocre names initially and then search for better names toward the end of programming a few lines. Then, AI code generation can also help you find better names.

Note that renaming is generally a fairly safe refactoring technique, and there are plenty of tools helping you. In many cases, the search function of your IDE may do the job as well. However, things may get tricky if you use global variables or overridden functions. In this case, you should be very careful because it's easy to miss some variables or functions.

Dependency Injector

As we have already seen, dependency injection (DI, p. 134) is a very helpful tool. Among other benefits, it allows us to inject mock objects to test functionality that would otherwise be untestable. It also allows us to break the functionality of a class into two classes. So, the question is: Can we retrofit DI onto an existing class?

The answer is yes. And it is fairly simple. Especially in interpreted languages, it's super simple, though it is also more dangerous than in compiled languages. In compiled languages, the compiler will notify you if you have forgotten to update one of the function calls to match the new signature. So it is fairly fail-safe. In interpreted languages, you have to rely on your tests to find out if you forgot to adapt one of the function calls. This is more dangerous because you may have forgotten a function, and the code will fail in production.

The dependency injector is also called "parameterized constructor" by Michael Feathers.[6]

Let's assume we once again have our `Car` class containing an engine.

```python
class Engine:
    def __init__(self, power):
        self.power = power

class Car:
    def __init__(self):
        self._engine = Engine(power=100)

    def drive(self):
        print(f"Driving with power {self._engine.power}")

car = Car()
car.drive()
```

This is not always bad, but there are some reasons why the `Engine` object should not be instantiated inside the `Car` constructor. Most importantly, the constructor should be as simple as possible. It shouldn't create anything that isn't necessary. If the `engine` is a complicated object, you can either create it in a helper function or pass it to the constructor using DI. Using DI, the `Car` constructor could look like this:

```python
# ...

class Car:
    def __init__(self, engine):
        self._engine = engine

    # ...

car = Car(Engine(power=100))
car.drive()
```

---

[6] Working Effectively with Legacy Code. Michael Feathers.

And that's it. We have implemented DI in about three lines of code: passing the object as an argument and assigning it to a variable in the constructor. Just remember that you not only have to change the constructor of the class (or function) and maybe its implementation but also all the instantiations of the class, unless you decide to use a default value.

Of course, there are many cases where implementing DI is much harder than here. In this example, the `Engine` is already an object that we could simply pass to the constructor, and we were done. In many cases, however, you first have to figure out which functions should be sorted in a class used for DI. This will make it much harder; yet, if done correctly, this process shouldn't introduce any bugs. Furthermore, DI directly allows you to write unit tests for all the methods that are injected without making anything public.

In order to make this technique bulletproof, it is recommended to add a default value to the injected object which is the same value as was used so far.

```python
# ...

class Car:
    def __init__(self, engine=Engine(power=100)):
        self._engine = engine

    # ...

car = Car()
car.drive()
```

If you don't want to use default values, you have to make sure that you really change the function signature everywhere. Here, it is helpful to work in a compiled language as the compiler will notify you if you have forgotten to adapt one of the function calls.

Also note that DI doesn't solve all your problems. It is hard to tell where the boundary lies, but you can overdo it with DI. If you only need one object that doesn't use polymorphism, you don't need to implement DI.

In compiled languages, the dependency injector is once again a little harder to implement. However, at the same time, it is also safer, as the compiler will notify you if you have forgotten to adapt one of the function calls.

In order to make the DI really useful, we have to be able to pass a polymorphic object to the constructor. This means that we need a base class (the Java folks would say: an interface). In C++, the code above would roughly look as follows:

```cpp
class Engine {
public:
    virtual void increase_speed() = 0;
};

class ElectricEngine : public Engine {
private:
    float power;
public:
```

```
    ElectricEngine(float power) : power(power) {}
    void increase_speed() override {
        // do something
    }
};
class FakeEngine : public Engine {
public:
    FakeEngine(float) {}
    void increase_speed() override {
        // do something else
    }
};

class Car {
private:
    std::unique_ptr<Engine> engine;
public:
    Car(std::unique_ptr<Engine> engine) : engine(engine) {}
    void drive() {
        engine->increase_speed();
    }
};

// somewhere in your code
car = Car(std::make_unique<ElectricEngine>(100));
car.drive()
```

Now the examples given here were very simple. In reality, you usually have to change a lot more code because an object is not just "lying around" in your code to be refactored out with the dependency injector. You might have to first implement a class containing several methods and then replace them in the code.

In my experience, the dependency injector is a very powerful yet frequently overlooked tool. Especially in compiled languages, the danger of introducing bugs is comparably low, even if the test coverage is not that high.

Scratch Refactoring

In chess, a rule of thumb suggests that you should silently communicate with your pieces during your opponent's turn. You should ask them where they would like to be and thus get a sense of their preferred position.

In programming, there is something quite similar. Scratch refactoring is not about improving code; it is only about getting an idea of how the code could look. Just refactor as you like without worrying about bugs or similar issues. Figure out how the code should look in an ideal scenario. But also try to implement some of the edge cases to challenge your dream implementation and understand its limitations.

I like the concept of scratch refactoring very much because it gives you an idea of how the code could look instead.

Once you're done refactoring, discard everything and do a regular refactoring, attempting to implement the ideas you just acquired. Pay attention to not simply re-implementing the code you envisioned previously. You may have overlooked certain technical details, and the solution from scratch refactoring may not work out as intended. After all, the scratch refactoring was just a dream...

Extract Function

If you have a function or method that is too long or not cohesive enough, you can replace some of the code with a newly created function. This is one of the most important refactoring techniques because excessively long functions are a common issue, and extracting functions is the primary method to manage them. If there are not too many variables involved, the technique is fairly simple. The biggest challenge is finding suitable names for the newly created functions.

Let's consider this very simple code snippet. We have already observed that this violates the SRP since printing a string and calling a function represent two different levels of abstraction.

Here is the code example that we already saw in the section "Levels of Abstraction" on p. 24.

```
def process_email():
    open_email()
    with open('attachment.txt', 'r') as f:
        print(f.read())
    # much more code here
    close_email()
```

As we have already seen, the levels of abstraction do not match. However, due to the added code, the function has become too long. Therefore, we have to take some code and put it into a new function. At the same time, this makes the function `process_email` shorter, which is another advantage of extracting functions.

```
def print_attachment():
    with open('attachment.txt', 'r') as f:
        print(f.read())

def process_email():
    open_email()
    print_attachment()
    # much more code here
    close_email()
```

The code overall has become longer, but this is not an issue. The length of the low-level code usually doesn't matter too much because it is hidden in some file. If you found a good name for this function, you'll barely have to look at the implementation. The function name should be descriptive enough to understand what the function does. Furthermore, you only have to implement the low-level function once, while you may call it multiple times.

You can also utilize AI code generation to extract this function. Just write the command "move the print statements into a dedicated function," and AI code generation will take care of the rest for you. As always, you should pay attention to ensure that the solution is correct. In this case, it happened to me that AI code generation suggested an incorrect solution.

There is not much more to know about extracting functions than what I just showed here. It is a simple yet crucial refactoring technique. This is probably the most commonly used refactoring technique besides renaming. The only thing you have to watch out for is the variables used by the newly created function. If the code is inside a class, you might consider making the function a member function of the class as well. Otherwise, you may end up having to pass too many arguments to the function, though this would be a sign of poor class design because the class has too many member variables (p. 65). You may extract methods from this class later on if needed.

Further Reading

For more refactoring examples, I would like to refer the interested reader to the book *Refactoring*.[7] It contains numerous examples and is an excellent resource for learning how to refactor code. Of course, I recommend doing a lot of refactoring yourself in order to learn it.

AI Code Generation

It seems as if AI code generation sometimes struggles with code refactoring. At times, it doesn't find a reasonable refactoring suggestion. However, with a little experimentation and by providing AI code generation with some hints, it works out quite well. It must be said that AI code generation is not a dedicated refactoring tool, and I don't know how often it introduces undesired behavior. I recommend having good test coverage before using AI code generation for refactoring.

Here is an example:

```
def roman_number(number):
    if number == 1:
        return 'I'
    elif number == 2:
        return 'II'
    elif number == 3:
        return 'III'
    # Code used for later:
    # elif number == 4:
```

---

[7] Refactoring: Improving the Design of Existing Code. Martin Fowler.

```
#       return 'IV'
# elif number == 5:
#       return 'V'
```

I commented out the last two cases that were suggested by AI code generation. Having only the first three cases and asking AI code generation to refactor this code, it makes the following suggestion:

```
# refactor this code to use a dictionary instead of
# if/elif/else
return {1: 'I', 2: 'II', 3: 'III'}.get(n, 'Invalid number')
```

This works out, but it's not quite what I wanted. After commenting out the cases for 4 and 5 and explicitly asking for a while loop, the code looks as follows:

```
# refactor this code using a while loop
roman = ''
while number > 0:
    if number >= 5:
        roman += 'V'
        number -= 5
    elif number >= 4:
        roman += 'IV'
        number -= 4
    elif number >= 1:
        roman += 'I'
        number -= 1
```

This is almost what I wanted, except that one could use a dict with number–Roman numeral pairs. Asking explicitly for using a dict, the code looks pretty much how I wanted it to be.

```
# refactor this code using a dictionary
roman = ''
roman_map = {1: 'I', 4: 'IV', 5: 'V'}
while number > 0:
    for key in sorted(roman_map.keys(), reverse=True):
        if number >= key:
            roman += roman_map[key]
            number -= key
            break
return roman
```

I particularly like the part with `for key in sorted(roman_map.keys(), reverse=True):` where AI code generation makes sure that the entries in the dict are sorted, even if the dict itself is not sorted, as was the case before Python 3.7. In Chapter 4 (p. 93), I used a list with class objects to achieve the same result. But I have to admit that the solution here is quite neat.

This code can be further refactored with the following command:

```
# refactor this code using a for loop
roman = ''
roman_map = {1: 'I', 4: 'IV', 5: 'V'}
```

```
    for key in sorted(roman_map.keys(), reverse=True):
        while number >= key:
            roman += roman_map[key]
            number -= key
    return roman
```

As always, AI code generation works best if you give it some step-by-step instructions. It is not always able to find the best solution by itself, though, at times, it is still a great help for refactoring code.

Changing Legacy Code

To me, legacy code is code without tests.

—Michael Feathers

Up to this point, everything was great. We assumed we were working on a greenfield project. I could tell you whatever I wanted. There were no restrictions because of the existing codebase. I told you to write unit tests, and you started writing unit tests. Now, however, we will start working with existing codebases. We will learn how to handle legacy code: code without tests[8] or, even worse, code without interfaces. However, I have to warn you: refactoring legacy code is hard. "I have nothing to offer but blood, toil, tears, and sweat."[9] You are in the middle of the circle of doom mentioned on p. 207. I can only give you a few hints here. As always, for more detailed explanations, you have to refer to specialized literature.

So far, we have discussed refactoring techniques for code that is covered by tests. Refactoring code without tests would be dangerous. Unfortunately, this is precisely the issue with numerous existing projects. There are so many projects out there without tests. Due to global variables, functions with side effects, complex constructors, and missing interfaces, it is very challenging to write tests for them. In these cases, you may start to feel afraid to make changes to the code as you are supposed to do during refactoring. There's just too much that can break without testing. This is apparently a really bad thing. No one likes to live in fear. In your own code, you can prevent this situation by meticulously testing all the code you write. However, if you work on an existing project, you will have to face the demons.

When you start working on a project with bad code, you might be motivated to suggest a complete rewrite. You may do that, although I do not recommend it. A complete rewrite is rarely an option. It takes years, costs millions, and very often the final code is not significantly better. Generally, it is better to improve the existing code. Once you have identified something you want to enhance, you write tests and start refactoring. This may seem tedious to you, but you always have to consider that the code was written by many programmers over many years. It will not be fixed in a few months.

---

[8] Working Effectively with Legacy Code. Michael Feathers.
[9] Winston Churchill.

Changing Legacy Code

Refactoring untested code is usually a very hard task. There are entire books about it. This section is mostly based on *Working Effectively with Legacy Code* by Michael Feathers.

The most common issues of legacy code on the macro level are

1. No interfaces
2. No tests
3. Obscure code
4. No time (or budget) to fix it

And on the micro level, we have a few more indications that things will get tough:

1. Functions with side effects and global variables
2. Huge classes and functions
3. Objects that are hard to construct
4. Inheritance chains

If you want to divide a large class into smaller parts, consider the following approach. It has no tests, and you are uncertain about the side effects it might have. This is bad because any functional changes you inadvertently introduce are bugs. The only way to prevent these changes is by having plenty of functional tests.

Nomenclature

Michael Feathers introduced various terms in his book Working Effectively with Legacy Code. I will briefly explain them here using the following code:

```
import sys

class Reader:
    def read(self):
        print("reading")

class DebugReader:
    def read(self):
        print("debug reading")

def f(reader):
    reader.read()

if __name__ == "__main__":
    if "debug" in sys.argv:
        reader = DebugReader()
    else:
        reader = Reader()
    f(reader)
```

Enabling Point

The enabling point is the place where you can decide which behavior to use. In the code above, using DI, this is where the code is called from the command line as the functionality depends on `argv`. The enabling point is important because it allows you to change the behavior of your code. Enabling points are inevitably part of some interface that can be used to write a test. This makes them invaluable.

Sensing Point

The sensing point is the place where you can observe the behavior of your code. This is required to test the behavior of your tests. In our example, the sensing point is the output of the print statements. At times, there is no sensing point where you would like to have one. For example, if you want to test some behavior that ends in the middle of a very long function, you might be forced to use some tricks in order to get these values, such as early returns that are called in the tests.

It is a common issue that classes are too long and don't have sensing points because the methods are private. You can fix this either by adding a getter method or by making a private method public. Making methods public is generally not recommended, but if you have to work with legacy code, there might be no other option. On the other hand, this is not as bad as it seems at first sight because most likely the class should anyway be split up into smaller classes, and the method you just made public should be part of a new class.

Seams

The ease with which you can write tests largely depends on the quality of your code. In order to write tests, you need something tangible to work with. Michael Feathers refers to this as a "seam." "A seam is a place where you can alter behavior in your program without editing in that place." Conversely, you can edit it elsewhere, at the enabling point.

There are several different ways to implement seams. The best seams are interfaces using DI, as shown in the example above. They are very easy to deal with and resemble typical code. Just create a new implementation of the interface or inject it, and you are done.

Some of the seams described by Michael Feathers alter the behavior at the compiler level, either through the linker or the preprocessor. Needless to say, implementing such fancy seams is a rather desperate measure. Such techniques strongly resemble black magic and should be avoided. Furthermore, they are only possible in old languages like C++.

The most common scenario of a seam involves passing function arguments. It is not mentioned in Working Effectively with Legacy Code, and the following code is simply a less effective version of using dependency injection, but it still serves as a seam. Here, the seam is the command-line arguments passed to the program.

```
def f(debug):
    if(debug):
        # ...
    else:
        # ...

if __name__ == "__main__":
    debug = "debug" in sys.argv
    f(debug)
```

As we have already learned, this is a place where you should replace the `debug` flag with DI. But that's just a side remark.

Pinch Points

Pinch points are another expression introduced by Michael Feathers. Roughly speaking, pinch points are an interface where a lot of data is bundled together. They are useful as you can write tests for a larger part of your code surrounded by several pinch points. At the pinch points, you can easily observe the behavior of the code, and accordingly, it is quite easy to write tests if you use the pinch points as enabling and sensing points.

Tests making use of pinch points are usually integration tests, as they may cover a lot of code; yet, they are too small to be functional tests. But, as always when refactoring code, you should break down the code between the pinch points into smaller and smaller pieces that you can test with unit tests.

Michael Feathers recommends deleting the pinch point tests once you are done refactoring. I don't like this recommendation. You should keep the tests as they are integration tests, and they are still valuable.

Refactoring Untested Code

How can you refactor legacy code?

Michael Feathers broke the refactoring process for legacy code down into five steps:

1. Identify change points
2. Break dependencies
3. Write the tests
4. Make your changes
5. Refactor

Once you have good test coverage with all kinds of tests, you can do some textbook refactoring, consisting of the last two points. The problem arises if you don't have sufficient test coverage. So let me briefly explain how to get there, if it is at all possible.

No Tests

Let's start with the most crucial point: we need tests. If we have tests, we are fine, as we can start refactoring and don't have to care about anything else.

Now you could argue that writing code without tests wasn't that bad. One could still write the tests later on. This, however, leads often to very bad code without interfaces and very long classes, which in turn makes writing tests extremely difficult.

As such, code has no interfaces, making it very difficult to find useful enabling and sensing points. Accordingly, writing tests becomes a very challenging task. It becomes much harder than writing tests to begin with. So remember, always write your tests right away. And preferably, apply TDD (p. 126).

No Interfaces

Code without interfaces doesn't have tests. Maybe not in theory, but certainly in practice. It's simply too difficult to write tests if you don't have interfaces. And if you started writing tests, you would have defined proper interfaces a long time ago. Therefore, we can say that interfaces are a prerequisite for tests.

Code without interfaces is a nightmare. But maybe you get lucky. Every piece of code inevitably has two interfaces: one for the input and one for the output. If the two interfaces are some sort of API, it isn't difficult to write functional tests. Using these interfaces is far from optimal, as such tests will probably be slow and cover way too much code, but at least they give you a rough idea if the code works.

Generally, it is preferable to have interfaces that cover code on a much smaller level. Fine-grained interfaces allow you to write fine-grained tests. As we have learned in the chapter on testing (p. 97), fine-grained unit tests are the foundation of the testing pyramid. You only want to test the smallest possible unit of code required for the corresponding changes that you are planning to make. This is because small tests are fast, and they pinpoint the source of the problem much more precisely than functional tests.

Problems of Legacy Code

As we have discussed the basic nomenclature, you probably already have a quite good understanding of the problems you are facing when dealing with legacy code.

Extremely Long Functions

Let's be honest. A function, or even worse, a method of about a thousand lines, is an absolute nightmare. It lacks interfaces. It is not tested. No one will ever understand it with all its corner cases. There are so many variables present that it is difficult for anyone to comprehend the state your code is in. It is absolutely impossible to work with. No one is ever going to touch such a function voluntarily. You might be able to make some minor adjustments, but you won't be addressing the core issue. Such a function is impossible to work with. The only way to truly change it is through a complete rewrite. The hardest part is obtaining the specification of what the function has actually done so far. If bugs are absolutely not allowed, which is usually the case, you'd better leave the function as it is. Just work your way around it and accept the fact that at some point you'll have to rewrite it.

Classes Can't Be Instantiated
There are various reasons why classes can't be instantiated. Most notably, this is because they use objects that have a very complex constructor, which in turn relies on many other objects. As we already discussed in Chapter 3 (p. 65), constructors should be simple, exactly for this reason. If a class doesn't have a trivial constructor, you have to create the entire object tree used by the constructor manually. You have to figure out how to instantiate all these objects and what kind of side effects they may have. This can be done, but it may be extremely tedious.

Missing Enabling Points
Usually, just passing a number or a string is not sufficient to fundamentally alter the behavior of the function. It only yields a slightly different result. Variables generally do not alter the control flow of your code. The only two things that should significantly alter the behavior of your code are Booleans and DI objects. And since you are not supposed to use Booleans, you are back to using DI.

The piece of code between the enabling point and the sensing point may be too large, and you may not have a clear idea of what you should test exactly. In the extreme case, the only tests you can write are functional tests. This is the issue of missing interfaces. Writing tests along with, or even before, the code forces you to define enabling points and sensing points that are close together. It forces you to write interfaces, thereby promoting good code quality. If your code doesn't have any interfaces or an API that you can use to write your tests, you are completely screwed. I'm sorry, there's no other way to say it. And no, I'm not exaggerating. Spaghetti code without tests can be an enormous issue, and it appears that there is no clear solution. A friend of mine was developing gas turbines. One individual developed software that could generate a full CAD model of a turbine. Now, the problem was that this person retired, and the code was a 15,000-line-long mess. The company paid millions in a desperate attempt to refactor the code but failed. In the end, they just wrote a wrapper around this piece of code and left it as is.

Missing Sensing Points
If you lack enabling points, chances are high that you also lack sensing points. The problem is very similar, but with sensing points, you might get lucky. Maybe you can make some method public or write a getter method for a variable.

Global Variables
As we have learned in the section on variables on p. 51, global variables and static variables are similar. They are both a nightmare. If the code under test contains a global or static variable, your tests may become very brittle. It starts depending on things that are out of your control. Even with minor changes, such as rearranging your tests, they might start breaking as the value of the variable used changes.

There are techniques to deal with global variables, but they are tedious. For example, you can rewrite the following code:

```
x = 1
def f():
    return x + 1

print(f())
```

to

```
x = 1
def f(x):
    return x + 1

print(f(x))
```

Like this, you converted the global variable into a function argument.

The theory behind converting global variables into function arguments is very simple. But, once again, the problem is the execution. You have to find, somehow, all the global variables and replace them. And, once again, this is much safer to do in compiled languages, as the compiler can help you find all the places where you have to change the code. In interpreted languages, on the other hand, you'll have a serious issue, as you'll introduce bugs if you make a mistake.

How Do I Get the Code Under Test?

As you might already expect, this is another difficult topic. First of all, you have to be aware of the magnitude of the problem you are facing. The code you are working on has probably been developed by a team of software engineers over many years. The amount of code is enormous. In well-written software, the test code is at least as long as the production code. In highly regulated environments such as the aerospace industry, it may be several times longer than that. If you want to write tests for a longer piece of software that has not been tested at all, it will most likely take years. Achieving high test coverage for all your code is generally not feasible. You'll have to be more pragmatic than that.

We can summarize the process of testing legacy code as follows:

1. Figure out where you want to change the code.
2. Search for the closest enabling and sensing points.
3. Write the tests.

As we'll see in a second, the first point is usually by far the most difficult one. If the code is incomprehensible, it is almost impossible to find a place where you can change it according to your needs.

Determining the Area of Change

Achieving reasonable test coverage for the whole codebase is not feasible. It's usually too much work, and there is no reason to write tests for code that you are not going to change. Instead, you have to focus on the parts of the code that you want to change and write your tests accordingly. For example, you should write tests for a class if you are going to add some new functionality to it.

Finding this function or class may be an endeavor in itself. If you are lucky, the variable is named the same way as the real-world object it represents, and you can search for it in your codebase. You might be able to localize the area of the code where the changes should be made and pinpoint the specific usage of this variable. However, this is frequently not the case. The variable may be used in too many places, and you don't know in which area of the code you have to search. You need someone who knows how the code is structured. If these people have all retired, you are in big trouble.

Finding the Enabling and Sensing Points

The enabling and sensing points always come in pairs. Together, they surround the code you want to change. If you are planning to change several things at once, you might need several pairs of enabling and sensing points, depending on what you can test with each pair.

As already written above, the enabling and sensing points should be as close as possible, as this makes the tests much faster to execute and localizes the issue much better. As we have already learned, this is the reason why you should prefer writing unit tests over functional tests whenever possible.

Frequently used enabling points are function calls or class instances. Sensing points are return values of functions and methods. If you have to fall back to functional tests, you may also read files that are created by the code.

Writing the Tests

Once you know what piece of code you want to change and you have found your enabling and sensing points, you can start writing your tests. This is pretty much the same as writing any other tests. The only difference here is that there is too much code between your enabling and sensing points. As you keep refactoring your code, you should try to find enabling and sensing points that are closer together than the previous ones. So, this will be an iterative process until you have refactored your code and achieved good test coverage with unit tests. Once you have written your tests, you have passed the hardest part, and you can start refactoring your code.

Refactoring Techniques Without Tests

As you can imagine by now, writing tests for existing code can be a very tedious task. However, there are also some refactoring techniques that don't require writing tests for existing code. Of course, it is generally better to write tests; however, you don't always have the time to do so. At times, you also struggle to find interfaces that allow you to write tests.

Here are some techniques to add functionality to existing code without writing tests. There are many ways to write such functions, the ones explained here are just some examples. These techniques explained here consist of some form of layered code where you add a wrapper around the existing code. This allows you to add functionality without touching the existing code. Meanwhile, you can write tests for the new code you just wrote.

A very frequent problem is that some refactoring techniques look safe at first sight, but they aren't. Especially once you start working with huge methods, making changes becomes much harder than you might think.

Sprout Method

Let's assume you want to add some functionality to an existing function. How do you do that without deteriorating the code quality any further? The solution is to add a new function or method that you can test and call from the old function. Michael Feathers calls this a "sprout method" (or function).

Assume we have the following code that we cannot test for some reason. In reality, it would, of course, be much more complicated. I have simplified it enough to create a readable example.

```
def post_entries(transactions, entries):
    # ...
    for entry in entries:
        entry.post()
    transactions.get_current().add(entries)
```

Now we only want to add the valid entries to the transactions and execute the post function. It seems as if we'd have to create a temporary list and add an if statement.

```
def post_entries(transactions, entries):
    # ...
    valid_entries = []
    for entry in entries:
        if entry.is_valid():
            entry.post()
            valid_entries.append(entry)
    transactions.get_current().add(valid_entries)
```

This, however, makes the untestable code even more complex. Instead we can create a new function that extracts the new functionality.

```
def get_valid_entries(entries):
    valid_entries = []
    for entry in entries:
        if entry.is_valid():
            valid_entries.append(entry)
    return valid_entries
```

```python
def post_entries(transactions, entries):
    # ...
    valid_entries = get_valid_entries(entries)
    for entry in valid_entries:
        entry.post()
    transactions.get_current().add(valid_entries)
```

This new function can easily be tested, so you can apply TDD.

```python
def test_get_valid_entries():
    entries = [Entry(is_valid=True),
               Entry(is_valid=False),
               Entry(is_valid=True)]
    valid_entries = get_valid_entries(entries)
    assert len(valid_entries) == 2
```

So, we managed to add only one additional line of code to the original function. All the other code was placed inside the `get_valid_entries` function. This new function is now also unit tested.

Wrap Function

As an alternative to the sprout method, there is also the wrap function technique. The principle is very similar. You take the existing code that you don't want to touch, and you add some well-tested code around it.

Let's assume we have the following code:

```python
def test():
    sum = 0
    for _ in range(1000000):
        sum += 1
    print(sum)

test()
```

Now we want to measure the time it takes to execute this function. There are several ways to do this. The first one is to add a timer into the function.

```python
import time

def test():
    start = time.time()
    sum = 0
    for _ in range(1000000):
        sum += 1
    print(sum)
    end = time.time()
    print(f'{end-start}')

test()
```

This, however, has the problem that we have to change the code inside the function that we didn't want to change. Instead, we want to keep the function test() as is and add the timing calculation around it. As we don't want to change anything other than adding this wrapper, the new function should be called test(). Therefore, we have to rename the old function to something else.

```
import time

def original_test():
    sum = 0
    for _ in range(1000000):
        sum += 1
    print(sum)

def test():
    start = time.time()
    original_test()
    end = time.time()
    print(f'{end-start}')

test()
```

This is the functional equivalent of using a decorator. Implementing a proper decorator in Python with the @ syntax is little more complicated.

```
import time

def timeit(func):
    def wrapper():
        start = time.time()
        func()
        end = time.time()
        print(f'{end-start}')
    return wrapper

@timeit
def test():
    sum = 0
    for _ in range(1000000):
        sum += 1
    print(sum)

test()
```

Summary

Refactoring is another complicated topic. Compared to Domain-Driven Design, it is much more technical. There are many techniques you can learn from the literature, but ultimately you probably won't be able to memorize all of them. You only learn refactoring by doing it yourself.

Refactoring is very meaningful, as it is easier to refactor good code than bad code. If code has fundamental issues, it is hard to improve it, and the chances are high that the code will become even worse over time. The most important criterion is whether your code has tests. As long as you have plenty of tests, you can still refactor your code.

If you don't have tests, things become hairy. You cannot refactor the code without constant fear that you might be breaking something, which prevents you from making fundamental changes. You can only stick to some superficial techniques.

Other Common Topics 9

Here are a few more topics that are important for software engineering, but I didn't manage to fit them into any of the previous chapters.

Performance Optimization

Premature optimization is the root of all evil.

—Donald Knuth

No Optimization Needed

Performance is a commonly overestimated topic in programming. This has historic reasons. Computers used to be extremely slow and expensive. Therefore, it was worthwhile to spend a significant amount of time enhancing every aspect of your algorithm. Back in the day, low-level languages like Fortran or even Assembly allowed you to do so. But the performance of computers has been growing exponentially for the last 50 years, while the price of computers has dropped considerably. Modern programming languages, such as Python, are no longer prioritizing performance, but rather usability – simply because it is more important to write readable code than to write fast code.

As we have learned, the primary goals of a software engineer are to create value for the customer by writing code that is easy to understand, correct, and well covered with tests. There are, of course, cases where performance is crucial, most notably when running large-scale simulations or developing a website. For "normal" business software, performance is generally not a concern.

I'd like to point out that the coding style I recommend does not necessarily lead to optimized performance. In my explanations, I didn't care about performance until now. Instead, I was recommending a coding style for readability and reusability. The problem is that all this polymorphism that I recommended requires lookups in the so-called v-table, and this is slow. There are YouTube videos[1] that explain these things in great detail. So, yes, the code I recommend you write is comparatively slow. But it doesn't matter. When do you need millions of function calls for this slow polymorphic code? Probably never. It is unlikely that the code I recommend you write will ever be the bottleneck of your software.

Optimization May Be Needed

Let's say you start developing an application that you believe requires high performance. You may be unsure about when to start optimizing the code. Right from the beginning? Should you plan your algorithms to be faster? How should you proceed?

First of all, it is not recommended to optimize code for performance at all. In fact, it is best to ignore the topic of performance for the time being. Write your code using the typical test-code-refactor work cycles (p. 126). When done well, the result will be code that is modular, stable, easy to understand, and well tested – code that meets all your requirements, except for performance.

You may have felt the need to write highly optimized code to meet the performance requirements, but you didn't know for sure. Now is the time to test your assumption. If you need to execute your code just once and it requires two days to complete, consider running it during the weekend. Spending hours on optimization would be a waste of time. If your code takes an hour to run and you use it every day, it is worth getting a profiler to check the bottlenecks in your code. Most code you encounter typically has very few bottlenecks. Usually, it involves complex calculations on a large data structure that scales worse than $O(N \cdot log(N))$. This is going to be the one and only point where you'll have to optimize. As you have written great code, it is very easy to identify this bottleneck using a profiler. For example, it turns out to be a self-written Fourier transformation operating on a list with 10,000 elements. As you start reading through the code, you realize that the algorithm you have implemented scales with $O(N^2)$. Such poor scaling is typically unacceptable. When seeking advice, you turn to the Internet. You can find Fourier transform libraries that scale with $O(N \cdot log(N))$. As your code is well structured, you can simply remove your custom Fourier transform function call, adjust your data structure slightly, and utilize the library you discovered. Now your code runs within seconds. Done. You won't have to worry about anything else.

---

[1] https://youtu.be/tD5NrevFtbU

Optimization Certainly Needed

Finally, there are a few cases where you have to develop the software from scratch and focus on optimization. These cases are mostly simulation software, games, websites containing a large amount of data, or infrastructure code for huge server farms where not only performance but also energy consumption is a major concern. If the code can be parallelized, it will become much more complicated due to the additional complexity involved in designing data structures and algorithms. As a very rough rule of thumb, it takes approximately twice the amount of time to write parallel (or distributed) code compared to linear code, but it can easily be much more than that. There is a lot to learn if you want to write high-performance code. But you won't be alone. You'll likely be working in a team where every team member knows much more about parallel programming than I do.

Manual Optimization

There are many small things you can do to optimize your code, such as manual loop unrolling or replacing C++ vectors with arrays. Keep your hands away! The performance gains are negligible. When working with a compiled language, the compiler can optimize such things much better than you can. Major algorithms should be the focus of improvement since they typically account for 90% of the runtime. Optimizing the remaining 10% is usually not worth it.

Always keep in mind that code written with a focus on performance rather than readability is always very challenging to maintain. Due to the complexity of the code, it becomes very hard to understand!

Comments

> A common fallacy is to assume authors of incomprehensible code will somehow be able to express themselves lucidly and clearly in comments.
> —Kevlin Henney

As a very short rule of thumb, comments should not explain *what* a piece of code does, but *why*. *What* the software does should be understood by examining the code. With the *why*, this is not possible. Explaining the *why* requires a comment.

Comments are a double-edged sword. While they may be useful at times, they can also be a liability. You always have to make sure you keep them up to date, as you would with any piece of documentation. Additionally, comments tend to be a remedy for fixing bad code, and this is certainly not the intended purpose of comments.

Bad Comments

"Comments? Don't."

"Why?"

```
def add(a,b):
    # This function returns the sum of the two arguments
    return a + b
```

I've seen similar comments before. Apparently, the programmer thought it was a good idea to write this comment.

I do not share this opinion. In my opinion, this is a useless boilerplate comment. Read the function name; it precisely explains the function's purpose. If you are still unsure, refer to the implementation. This is precisely what distinguishes good code from bad code. When you read a function name, you know what it does. Good code is self-documenting. There is barely any need for additional comments. This comment is a violation of the SRP; it's a redundant explanation of the code's functionality.

"Yes, but it's only one line of comment. It can't hurt us," you might say.

"No!"

Sorry, I just lost my temper. I shouldn't be so harsh with you. Many experienced programmers don't know, so why should you? I have to tell you that you are wrong. You can't believe how wrong you are. Maybe I haven't made myself clear enough so far. This comment is an absolutely useless liability. It makes a claim that will not always be true. The code will change, as code always does. But the comment may be forgotten. Unlike function definitions or variable names, you cannot enforce that a comment remains in its correct location. You will eventually end up with a comment that is simply incorrect. It will confuse everyone who works on this code. It will cost time.

Not convinced? Do you believe you won't encounter these issues because you work meticulously?

"Ha ha. NO!"

Now you're certainly wrong this time. By now, you should know better. This is precisely what I'm trying to teach you throughout this entire book. We are all human. We all make mistakes. It's inevitable. Accept your fate and learn how to deal with it. Code is good if you can make as few mistakes as possible. Removing unnecessary comments is essential. They violate the second rule of software engineering: "Write code that can have as few bugs as possible." Such comments are an unnecessary source of bugs and should therefore be avoided.

You want to become a software engineer. So, stop using the English language and start reading code instead. Get used to it. The code contains the absolute truth, not the comments. Here is an example of how to write readable code without comments.

Let's assume we have the following class containing some methods. For the sake of simplicity, I will only show the method and argument names. There is no value in executing this code.

```
class Shopping:
    set_name(name)
    get_age(user)
    add_fruit_to_basket(fruit_type)
    weight_vegetables(vegetable_type)
    withdraw_money(amount)
    make_payment(bill)
    # and many more methods
```

Undoubtedly, this code is bad. It is very hard to read, and it lacks any visible structure.

A first attempt to make it more readable is adding some comments to structure it better.

```
class Shopping:
    # User
    set_name(name)
    get_age(user)

    # get groceries
    add_fruit_to_basket(fruit_type)
    weight_vegetables(vegetable_type)

    # payment details
    withdraw_money(amount)
    make_payment(bill)
```

The code has certainly become much more readable. However, this refactoring can be taken one step further. Adding these comments does not solve the fundamental issue. The class should be divided into three subclasses, with one parent data class containing the class instances. This logically separates the different parts of the class. The comments are just a workaround for suboptimal code.

Instead of adding comments, we can group the code by using subclasses.

```
from dataclasses import dataclass

@dataclass
class Shopping:
    user: User = User()
    groceries: Groceries = Groceries()
    payment: Payment = Payment()

class User:
    set_name(name)
    get_age(user)

class Groceries:
    add_fruit_to_basket(fruit_type)
    weight_vegetables(vegetable_type)

class Payment:
    withdraw_money(amount)
    make_payment(bill)
```

The resulting code is once again longer than the initial version, but it is much better structured, and there is no need for any comments.

Here is another example. The code is clearly bad as it is hardly readable, even though the function is comparatively short and has little complexity.

```python
def get_new_job(user, job_properties):
    jobs_website = search_job("google.com")
    jobs_website.rescale()
    jobs = parse_website("jobs")
    jobs.filter(job_properties.salary)
    jobs.filter(job_properties.location)
    for job in jobs:
        user.review_job(job)
        user.apply(job)
```

One option is to split up the code and comment it.

```python
def get_new_job(user, job_properties):
    # get jobs from google
    jobs_website = search_job("google.com")
    jobs_website.rescale()
    jobs = parse_website("jobs")

    # filter jobs
    jobs.filter(job_properties.salary)
    jobs.filter(job_properties.location)

    # apply to remaining jobs
    for job in jobs:
        user.review_job(job)
        user.apply(job)
```

This looks like a reasonable thing to do; however, this solution is suboptimal. Again, there is a better solution – one without comments. You can use function names to replace the comments.

```python
def get_new_job(user, job_properties):
    jobs = get_jobs_from_google()
    filter_jobs(jobs, job_properties)
    apply_for_jobs(user, jobs)

def get_jobs_from_google():
    jobs_website = search_job("google.com")
    jobs_website.rescale()
    jobs = parse_website("jobs")

def filter_jobs(jobs, job_properties):
    jobs.filter(job_properties.salary)
    jobs.filter(job_properties.location)

def apply_for_jobs(user, jobs)
    for job in jobs:
        user.review_job(job)
        user.apply(job)
```

This time, the code only became slightly longer compared to other refactoring examples. But at the same time, it is much more readable. You can understand its functionality simply by looking at the top-level function `get_new_job`. You don't have to read the details of the function. You can read the function names to understand their purpose. This is what makes code readable, not the comments.

At times, it is very difficult to explain code using code alone. So, there is, of course, the temptation to use a comment to make it clearer.

```
// sort the elements of v by ascending order
// then return a list of all elements that are greater than the
//     threshold
do_something(v, threshold);
```

I tried to explain in the comment what this function does, but I don't know how to call it. This is a clear sign that there is something fundamentally wrong with this function. It consists of a random sequence of function operations that shouldn't belong together. It violates a fundamental rule of good function design: the code explained in this comment doesn't elevate the functionality to a higher level of abstraction. Therefore, we are not able to find a function name that explains what the code does.

There is something else besides comments that can explain code: unit tests. The test cases act as examples of how the code is supposed to be used and serve as an example at the same time. This is often more helpful than a difficult-to-read comment.

Commented-Out Code

Another thing you might have seen somewhere is commented-out code. Someone was developing a feature. Maybe they were replacing some code and weren't sure how to implement the new version. So, they commented out the old code and started implementing. They somehow didn't understand all the details, but at some point, everything seemed to work. They knew that they were more guessing rather than writing structured code. They knew their work was really bad. Therefore, they decided to leave the old code in the repository and just commented it out right beside the new code.

Commenting out code is absolutely dreadful. This is one of the candidates for the worst programming practices. What are you supposed to do with commented-out code? Everyone reads it. Nobody knows how to deal with it. It's just causing confusion and wasting everybody's time. If we only had a tool to browse the history of the code... Something like Git...

You may have commented-out code in your local branch as you might still need it, but never on master. You have my permission to delete any commented-out code that you ever see on the master branch. You may use this book as proof if needed.

TODO Comments

Another habit of questionable value is TODO comments. When you implement a feature, you are responsible for ensuring that the implementation is ready to be merged into the master branch. It's ready to be merged when there is nothing important left to be done that would justify a TODO comment. Make sure you never merge any TODOs into the master branch. These tasks only lead to confusion, and there is never enough time to complete them. You should never implement a feature without a corresponding ticket. Additionally, for code refactoring, there is no need for a TODO comment. You may comment on any code that you think needs refactoring. Therefore, once again, make sure you never merge any TODO comments into the master branch.

During the development of a feature, it is acceptable to use TODO comments. They might help you organize your work. Just make sure to remove all the TODO comments before merging your changes into the master branch.

Comments Replacing Code

Introducing numerous small functions can somewhat hinder readability. It involves keeping track of and navigating through the function calls, though this cost is very low if the functions are named properly. If all the functions perform as described, you can simply read the function names to understand what the code does. This is what makes code readable, not the comments.

Useful Comments

So much about why not to use comments. Now let's discuss situations where using comments is entirely appropriate.

I have explained that you should not use comments for anything that could (or should) be explained by the code itself. Vice versa, this means that comments are allowed to explain things that you cannot express in code. For example, you can add links to the source of a code fragment, library, or an explanation of an algorithm. It may also be useful to use comments in the interface of a library or API when using documentation software. Comments are typically used at the beginning of the file to include the copyright statement.

Requirements

A very legitimate use of comments is to document requirements. Requirements are something that cannot be explained in code alone. They are usually written in a natural language in some ticket. Despite this, they are still highly important for the software. Usually, the requirements are the only thing that can explain *why* a certain piece of code looks the way it does. And the only way to explain this is by using comments. Please add the ticket number to the comment or, even better, copy the requirement text into the comment, as the ticket may be edited later on.

Usually, the requirements are also expressed in a functional test. I hope you do write functional tests, don't you? But functional tests are not sufficient. They are not visible in the code. You have to search for them. It is unclear which functional test corresponds to which line of code. Therefore, comments are the only way I can think of to connect the code to the requirements.

There are several different ways you can add the requirements to the code. The most obvious one is that you simply add a comment.

```
# Requirement: The user should be able to log in.
```

However, this is generally not the best way to add requirements to the code. Instead, you should provide the number of the ticket and the requirement text. This way, you can easily find the requirement in the ticket system.

```
# Requirement 1234: The user should be able to log in.
```

This makes it much clearer where a requirement comes from exactly. Now, of course, the code will become much longer if you add this kind of comments. But this is not a problem. Knowing the requirements exactly outweighs this problem.

One thing you have to consider if you add the ticket number to the code is versioning the tickets. Otherwise, you are left with a bunch of comments that are outdated compared to the state of the ticket they reference.

I hope you grasp the order of complexity in dealing with requirements and linking them to your code.

Docstring

You may use docstring tools, such as Sphinx in Python, for automatically generating documentation. However, there are some things to consider as well. Docstrings should only be used for external documentation. Never use docstrings for internal purposes. Why should you read docstring documentation if you can read the source code and all its comments?

For using docstrings as documentation for external users, comments are also very useful. Furthermore, when commenting on external APIs using docstrings, completely different rules apply than for internal comments. When documenting an API, it is crucial to comment on the *what* rather than the *why*. The user doesn't have access to the code, or at least they're not supposed to read it. So they solely rely on the docstring comments. Therefore, you have to comment *what* your functions and classes do and explain how to use them, possibly by adding examples. The *why*, on the other hand, is not important at all – users certainly don't care about internal ticket numbers.

There are also tools that allow you to write test cases as examples in the docstrings, for example, doctest in Python. I have ambiguous feelings about this. It is nice to have built-in examples in your code. On the other hand, you are mixing two things that should not necessarily be mixed.

As a short summary: Docstrings are very useful for documenting your external APIs, but not for internal code. If you have to use docstrings for internal code, you should probably reconsider the names and contents of the corresponding functions.

Contrary to normal comments, docstrings should comment on the *what* and not the *why*.

How to Write Comments

Just like code, comments should be concise and meaningful. In the following example, we have the opposite. What does "it" in the following sentence mean? Please avoid writing ambiguous sentences.

```
# Buy a melon, but check if it's ripe first
```

better:

```
# If the melon is ripe, buy it.
```

Commenting Magic Numbers

Here, we have an example of poorly written code, this time in C++. I found it in The Art of Readable Code.[2] The authors correctly state that this code is hard to understand, and I suggest some changes to their solution.

```
pay(50, false)
```

This code is bad as it is very hard to understand what `50` and `false` exactly mean. You'd have to look up the function definition to understand it.

AI code generation suggests improving the code by adding a comment at the end of the line. Honestly, this is a pretty bad solution.

```
pay(50, false)  # amount = 10, add_tip = false
```

The suggestion in the book was to add the comments inside the function call. This is possible in C++, but it's not a good solution. It's an attempt to make bad code better by commenting on it.

```
pay(/* amount = */ 50, /* add_tip = */ false);
```

In my opinion, this solution is still far from optimal; it uses comments explaining the what.

There are two better solutions to this problem. In Python, C++20, and most other modern programming languages, keyword arguments are supported.

```
pay(amount=50, add_tip=false)
```

The other solution is creating intermediate variables. The function arguments used here are magic numbers that have to be avoided.

```
amount = 50
add_tip = false
pay(amount, add_tip)
```

At times, it's better to structure them first and hand over the structured variable to the function.

---

[2] The Art of Readable Code, Boswell and Foucher.

```
@dataclass
class Payment:
    amount: int
    add_tip: bool

payment = Payment(amount=50, add_tip=False)
pay(payment)
```

This might be overkill for this simple example. But when dealing with many arguments, this is usually the best solution.

Summary

Use comments only for things that cannot be made apparent by the code itself, yet you think they're still very important. Comment the *why* and not the *what*. If you write docstrings, it's exactly the other way around. Comment the *what*, rather than the *why*.

AI Code Generation

AI code generation is not yet able to write more than boilerplate comments. The following comment was created by the document function of Copilot Labs. AI code generation makes the mistake of commenting on the *what*. Apparently, there is no way for AI code generation to find out *why* you write some code. Therefore, I would recommend AI code generation only to write docstrings.

I find it very remarkable that AI code generation is able to write such a comment; however, it is still fairly useless as an internal comment.

```
def roman_number(number):
    # The roman_map dictionary is a lookup table that maps
    # numbers to roman numerals. It is used by the to_roman
    # function to convert numbers into roman numerals.
    roman_map = {1: 'I', 4: 'IV', 5: 'V', 9: 'IX', 10: 'X'}
    roman = ''
    for key in sorted(roman_map.keys(), reverse=True):
        while number >= key:
            roman += roman_map[key]
            number -= key
    return roman
```

Logging

The basic idea of logging is to provide feedback on the steps that your software executed. It might help you find bugs. Now, this sounds great, but in reality, there are several things to consider.

- The most obvious drawback is that logging requires time to be implemented. It's not a huge amount, but it may add up.
- Logging pollutes your code, similar to comments.
- Logging is typically unnecessary. Most code is deterministic. If you run the same code twice, it will produce the exact same results, with minor differences due to finite precision rounding errors. You don't need the logs. Run the code with the same settings as the user did and inspect your code using a debugger.
- If you struggle to find bugs in your code, you should focus on improving its quality instead. Simplify the structure and write unit tests. You will have fewer bugs, and they are easier to find.

At the same time, there are some cases where you can consider using a logger.

- It may be useful for non-deterministic software. For example, if you have several programs that communicate asynchronously with each other, such as in microservices. Race conditions may occur that you hadn't considered. The result may depend on the precise timing of the messages being sent. A logger can help you trace back to the source of a bug. Though finding such bugs is challenging, even with the best logger. You may be feeling overwhelmed by the volume of log files.
- In a GUI, the logger could store all the actions performed by the user. This may also be helpful if the user encounters a bug.
- Finally, a logger may be helpful for the user to send in auto-generated error reports if something goes wrong. Users can simply click a button to submit an error report containing all relevant data, eliminating the need to manually write the report themselves. This may be very useful as errors are almost inevitable, and the users are a very helpful group to test your software, as long as the bugs are not too subtle or too serious.

Data Files

There are several file formats available for saving data or using them as an interface. A lot of people apparently don't even know the most important ones, so I would like to give you a very short introduction.

The file formats that I have used so far include CSV, JSON, XML, HDF5, and databases, along with some custom file formats. There are, of course, many more, such as YAML, TOML, etc., but for the sake of brevity, I won't explain those. The file formats mentioned here are sufficient to complete your work, and it won't require much effort to learn other file formats if necessary.

CSV

Comma-Separated Values (CSV) is probably the simplest and one of the most common file formats. You can save numbers by separating them with commas or any other character you prefer. It won't get any easier. But this is also one of the weaknesses of CSV. In some natural languages, such as German, the comma character is used as the decimal separator. Thus, you cannot use a comma to separate different values as well. This overload of the comma character could lead to significant issues when reading a CSV file.

There is no standard for CSV files, so you can format them however you like. At the same time, that's the downside of it. People do whatever they want, and for every file, you have to write a new piece of code to read the data. Saving auxiliary data in CSV files is quite challenging. CSV saves only plain, unstructured lists.

Long story short: CSV is the file format commonly used by those who are not familiar with more advanced options, such as JSON, or by someone who works with Excel.

Here is an example code snippet demonstrating how to read a CSV file with two columns separated by commas.

```
def is_comment(line):
    return line.startswith("#")

def read_csv(filename):
    with open(filename) as file:
        x = []
        y = []
        for line in file:
            if is_comment(line):
                continue
            variables = line.split(",")
            x.append(float(variables[0]))
            y.append(float(variables[1]))
    return (x, y)
```

JSON and Co

The JavaScript Object Notation (JSON) file format is probably one of the best file formats for saving structured data. The libraries are very user-friendly. It can save any data structure you want and is extremely widespread and thus supported. There are libraries available to automate the parsing of JSON files for all major programming languages. The output data structure consists of a combination of nested maps and arrays. It won't get any easier to read a file into data.

There are also other file formats which are very similar to JSON, for example, XML, YAML, and TOML. Some of them have advantages like being shorter or better readable for humans. For this reason, YAML and TOML are replacing JSON when it comes to writing, for example, configuration files.

Once you use JSON in a more serious project, you might want to consider using a schema to validate your files for accuracy. You may use different schemas for different versions of your interface. Before you manually write a schema, there are tools available to assist you. You only have to ensure that your JSON file contains all possible fields to obtain a complete schema.

Thanks to schemas, JSON is also a meta-language. It is possible to define a general pattern for how the JSON file should look. This defines a standard that enables easy file exchange between different projects. You can use schemas to define the version of a JSON-based interface.

The following code creates a JSON file:

```python
import json

def write_json(filename, data):
    with open(filename, 'w') as f:
        f.write(json.dumps(data, indent=4))

if __name__ == "__main__":
    data = {'x': [1,2,3], 'y':[4,5,6]}
    write_json("temp.json", data)
```

Meanwhile, this code here reads out the data:

```python
import json

def read_json(filename):
    with open(filename) as f:
        return json.load(f)

if __name__ == "__main__":
    data = read_json("temp.json")
    print(data['x']) # prints [1,2,3]
    print(data['y']) # prints [4,5,6]
```

As you can see, working with JSON files is much easier and less error-prone than working with CSV files. The underlying data structure is a dict, which is a pretty bulletproof way to work with data. There is hardly a way to introduce unnoticed bugs.

Most of the points I just mentioned about JSON also apply to XML, YAML, TOML, and other similar formats. These are simply different dialects of the same type of file.

HDF5

HDF5 is the most commonly used binary file format. It is designed to handle terabytes of data and is optimized for high throughput. While writing CSV files is usually limited by the conversion speed of numbers to strings, writing HDF5 files is usually limited by the write speed of the SSD.

Most research facilities and companies that handle large amounts of data use this file format. It supports structured and auxiliary data. To access the data, you can either utilize the HDF5 library in your preferred programming language or download the free GUI software. Use HDF5 if you need to store multiple gigabytes of numerical data.

Working with HDF5 is, in my opinion, slightly less intuitive than working with JSON files. This is because HDF5 uses datasets that need to be created instead of simply accepting a dictionary. However, with the current version of the HDF5 library, the code becomes quite simple.

The following code saves a list of values in an HDF5 file.

```
import h5py

with h5py.File("temp.hdf5", "w") as f:
    dset = f.create_dataset("x", data=[1, 2, 3])
```

Reading a file returns an HDF5 file object. It may be a little intimidating at first, but it is fairly easy to work with. In many respects, it behaves similarly to a dictionary.

```
import h5py

with h5py.File('temp.hdf5', 'r') as f:
    print(list(f.keys()))
    print(list(f['x']))
```

As HDF5 is a binary format, you cannot look at the data using a text editor. Instead, you have to use the HDFView software.[3]

Databases

Databases (DBs) are used for a large amount of structured data that you want to analyze but don't fit into memory. Databases have a wide range of functionalities that enhance searching and manipulating data within the database. There are several vendors offering different technologies.

I never really cared much about DBs, and I'd like to teach you other things instead. I only know that proprietary DBs can be extremely expensive, and it's important to write your code in a way that allows for easy replacement of the database with another one. Otherwise, you may find yourself locked into paying substantial annual fees.

Also, make sure that a database is not the core of your software. It's just a place to save and access data. It can be replaced with a text file if necessary!

---

[3] https://www.hdfgroup.org/downloads/hdfview/

Here is the code to create a database and add some movie objects in SQLite3:

```
import sqlite3
con = sqlite3.connect("tutorial.db")
cur = con.cursor()
cur.execute("CREATE TABLE movie(title, year, score)")
cur.execute("""
    INSERT INTO movie VALUES
        ('Monty Python and the Holy Grail', 1975, 8.2)
""")
con.commit()
```

Custom File Formats

Similar to the CSV file, you can also define your own file format for things other than just numbers. You can define your own file with structured data. You can even define your own programming language, such as structured text, within your custom file format. You can do pretty much anything you like. You are a free person. Just don't expect to be paid for such a waste of time. If you aspire to become a successful software engineer, you must prioritize delivering value to the customer. You need to utilize JSON, HDF5, or a database. There is no need to define custom file formats.

AI Code Generation

AI code generation is a great help when it comes to using the different file formats. This is a typical problem of *what* you want to do, and AI code generation can help you here. In general, AI code generation "knows" all the file formats mentioned above and can provide you with example code.

Setting Up a Project

> If it's your job to eat a frog, it's best to do it in the morning. And if it's your job to eat two frogs, it's best to eat the biggest one first.
>
> —Mark Twain

Many software developers start by writing code immediately when they have a task to complete, and they postpone all infrastructure work for as long as possible. They continue to compile code using the command line for as long as possible, and they don't use Git. They certainly don't use a Continuous Integration (CI) tool. This is dreadful. Set up these things at the beginning of the project.

Yes, it will take some time to get started. And yes, it's a painful process if you are not accustomed to it. But it is worth it. The very first reason why it is worth it is Do not Repeat Yourself (DRY). If you find yourself repeatedly typing the compilation command into the terminal, you are essentially repeating the same action over and over again. This is going to slow down the development process. This is much worse than spending the same amount of time at the beginning of the process because it interrupts your thoughts.

For small projects, setting up Git and a proper build tool hardly takes any time. After encountering a challenging bug for the first time, you will appreciate having version control in place. This will allow you to easily revert back to your previous changes. The same holds true for the build process. Typing in many long commands not only takes time but is also brittle. It is too easy to make a typo and screw up the build process in some unforeseen way that introduces hard-to-understand behavior. Especially when you have to cooperate with other developers, there is no way around using proper version control software and a build tool.

Similarly, for CI, it will take some time to set it up, but you will save a lot of time later on because you can be sure that the tests you wrote (and I really hope you have tests; otherwise, I recommend you read Chapter 4 (p. 93)) always run. The code committed to the master branch has been compiled, and the tests pass without any errors.

Yes, setting up the infrastructure of a project may take some time. I have already heard that setting up a project may take up to 20% of the total development time! But it is certainly time well spent. There are so many advantages to having a properly set up infrastructure.

- You have to learn how to use Git, CMake, and all the other tools anyway. So, it's good practice to get started with them as soon as possible.
- You will save a lot of time in the future. This will outweigh the time needed to set everything up now.
- Having properly set up tools makes it easier for new team members to get started. Users only need to clone the repository and run the build tool to get started.

Summary

The most important message of this chapter is certainly that you shouldn't optimize your code for performance. It's better to write good code that is well tested and easy to understand. In most cases, you can still optimize later on. There are quite a few cases where you have to optimize for performance from the beginning.

Another important point is that you shouldn't comment on your code. You should make it self-commenting whenever possible. For example, you can define a one-liner function that performs a certain task, and its name makes a comment redundant. Alternatively, you can replace a magic number with a variable.

Collaborating   10

The era of the lone wolf programming alone in their basement is long gone. Professional software development now occurs in teams. This does not simply mean that the work is divided among different programmers. Instead, collaboration is essential. Programmers review each other's code and engage in discussions about how to implement new features. Additionally, professionals from various fields work together. For instance, requirements engineers are responsible for clarifying what needs to be implemented.[1,2]

Nowadays, this process is typically conducted using an agile approach, where the team works in iterations of approximately two weeks, in contrast to the traditional waterfall method, which involved comprehensive planning at the outset.

Working in Teams

Humans are mostly a collection of intermittent bugs.

—Brian Fitzpatrick

A good manager considers how things are done, but a great manager focuses on what needs to be done and entrusts the rest to their employees. They have faith in their team, which is far more motivating than someone who just yells orders.

The era of lone wolf programmers is over. Instead, you will spend most of your career working in teams. The narrative of the solitary prodigy programmer in the basement is a myth. Modern programming is a collaborative effort. Modern software prodigies might write (an elaborate) prototype, but then they hand over their work to the public for further refinement, as has happened to many major open source

---

[1] 97 things every programmer should know. Henney et al.

[2] Software Engineering at Google. Winters et al.

projects. Programmers not only collaborate with their peers but also engage with individuals from marketing, sales, and customers.

Collaborating with other programmers has both advantages and drawbacks. Comparing programming in teams with working alone is akin to comparing a parliament with a dictator. A parliament may take more time to reach a consensus, but the solution is typically superior to a decision made by a dictator.

At the same time, scaling up software projects only works with teams where all programmers are cooperating together. It is not possible for a dictator to work on their own project. They have to adapt and become part of the team.

Team Structure

In most projects, a team typically consists of around three to seven software engineers, one project owner, and one project manager. The software engineers are responsible for the core work, putting in effort to write exceptional code, while the rest of the team also has their own tasks to complete, even if it may not be as visible to the developers.

The project manager (PM) oversees the entire project. They are in charge of communicating with customers to understand what they want and need. These two aspects are not always identical. For instance, before its release, nobody desired a mobile phone without a keyboard, yet everyone eventually needed an iPhone. It is the PM's responsibility to discern such distinctions (p. 242).

The project owner (PO) is responsible for managing the tickets. They act as the interface between the project manager and the developers.

It is important that everybody in the team communicates with each other. Software engineers often discuss their code extensively. However, they frequently have questions about the ticket that the project manager (PM) needs to address. Conversely, the PM needs to be informed about the status of each feature to estimate the progress of the software.

The Bus Factor

The bus factor[3] says how many team members would need to be at least hit by a bus before the project is doomed. The definition of this expression may sound a little absurd. And it is. But it has a point. Fortunately, people don't get hit too often by a bus. But there are other risks to consider, such as team members falling ill or leaving their positions for various reasons. A low bus factor may put the entire project at risk. Make sure the bus factor in your project is as high as possible. Ensure that there is a good amount of knowledge exchange between team members so that everyone has some understanding of all aspects of the project. This way, the entire project won't come to a halt just because one person is sick.

---

[3] https://en.wikipedia.org/wiki/Bus_factor

I encountered many projects where the bus factor was 1. Every programmer had their own domain in the code, and the other developers barely knew what was going on in the other domains. This is a very dangerous situation. If the one developer leaves, the project is doomed. And even if there was some time for a hand-over, the new developer would have a hard time understanding the code. This is why it is important to work on the code collaboratively.

Developers Work

The developers are the ones who do the real work. They are the ones who write all the code. For such hard work, it is important that they stick together. Only a tight pack of dedicated software engineers can accomplish the task. That's at least their perspective. Now, let's get a little bit more serious.

Software engineers have several tasks. The most obvious one is, of course, communicating with each other. This is why any modern software company provides a coffee machine with free coffee. Additionally, engineers need to discuss tickets, determine the fundamental structure of the code, and communicate during pair programming or code review sessions. While talking during code reviews is not mandatory, smaller merge requests (MRs) can be completed with written comments. However, when unsure, it is always preferable to engage in verbal communication. Particularly during times like the Corona pandemic, the personal connection has diminished, and situations can become challenging.

During pair programming, it is essential to communicate. Both participants engage in discussions to determine how the code should be structured. This facilitates crucial knowledge transfer, particularly when both participants are experts in different aspects of the code. Through this collaboration, both programmers gain insights from each other, leading to an enhancement in code quality. Consequently, the need for code review in the MR is eliminated. Although pair programming may require more time than working independently, the benefits often outweigh the additional time investment. It is important to remember that the most valuable resource in a company is not the code itself, but the knowledge. This knowledge is acquired and spread through effective communication and collaboration.

Another fairly big job is going through MRs, also referred to as pull requests. Everyone has to do it, and no one really likes it, but it has to be done. Nobody likes waiting a day for their code to be approved and merged. Therefore, reviewing MRs has to be done quickly. So, get up, open the browser, and select the first MR. Now, doing a code review is a tricky business. You can somehow sense that the code is not good, but it's elusive. It's your job to pinpoint the issues without being too critical. Though, especially for long MRs, the issues can simply be "I don't understand what you did." This is more honest and better than just approving some code you don't understand. Additionally, you may notice some duplicated code that needs to be refactored, among a dozen other things. It might be time to reach out to the author of this MR. Some issues can't be resolved just by writing comments.

Communication

As mentioned above, teamwork is a key element in modern software engineering. Without good communication skills, teamwork is not possible. Therefore, it is important to learn how to effectively communicate with others, understand human flaws, and learn how to address them.

In a team, the most important language is not Java but English (or German in some of the projects I worked on). Use this language to communicate with other team members. If you find communicating with a computer challenging, you should reconsider. With a computer, you can simply up on Stack Overflow what to do, and most of the time it works. However, effective communication with other humans may require significantly more effort.

- Ensure that you have a thorough understanding of the subject matter and are able to communicate effectively with the intended audience.
- Keep communicating. Ask questions. Let the other person talk. Once you stop receiving replies, there may be an issue.
- Make sure the other truly understood what you were discussing.

There are probably hundreds of other rules, but the few mentioned here are the ones I know, even though I'm not that proficient at applying them. As a developer, you don't have to be familiar with all these things. However, if you aspire to manage people, you need to develop a sense of how to communicate effectively with others. Consider exploring books or attending seminars on this topic, as this is not the appropriate place to delve into specifics.

Humans are all inherently flawed. They are insecure and tend to conceal their vulnerabilities. They dislike criticism and fear not being perceived as geniuses. However, being a genius is not a requirement. The majority of work is accomplished by competent, though not exceptional, programmers. However, this fear exacerbates the situation. Effective communication among developers is crucial. A team is significantly more productive when its members engage in constructive criticism and open dialogue.

It is okay to fail. Fail early, fail fast, fail often. Get feedback as early as possible and improve. This is the only way to make progress. Conversely, you always have something to teach. Discuss with your colleagues, and you can learn from each other. Don't be afraid; nobody is perfect.

Don't make statements like "this is bad." Criticism has to be constructive; otherwise, it is pointless. Even worse, it can be seen as a direct attack. You need to be able to clarify why something is considered bad so that the original author has an opportunity to make improvements.

In order to excel, humans need psychological safety. This requires three things: humility, respect, and trust. Effective teamwork is not possible without these elements. Discussions can only be successful if all parties involved are treated equally.

Working with Customers

Customers are only humans. Quite frequently, they don't say what they mean because they may not know it any better.[4] Keep adapting your vocabulary to understand what specific words truly mean from the customer's perspective. Sometimes, this reveals a misinterpretation, for example, if a customer and a client have some completely different understanding of something. Do not assume that the discussion on requirements is complete after just one meeting with the customer. It is essential to stay in touch to receive continuous feedback to ensure that you implement what the customer desires, not just what they say.

Frequently, customers do not prioritize what is important. Or at least, things that are important to customers may not be important to the programmer. For instance, a software is only used if the GUI looks exactly the same as in the previous software. As long as the user does not have to learn anything new. Even if the old GUI was poorly designed, the customer refuses to adapt. You really have to come up with some significant improvements for your version to be accepted.

Code Review

The computer was born to solve problems that did not exist before.

—Bill Gates

Code reviews are important for spreading knowledge and improving the quality of the code.[5] This does not work without some criticism, so it requires a bit of intuition to know how to critique the code without insulting the author. Most importantly, you have to criticize the code rather than the author. But let's first take a look at how the whole code review process began.

A long time ago, in a kingdom far away, software developers began collaborating. They shared their code and worked on the same code simultaneously, which led to problems arising. They required software to manage the various versions of the code.

After some mediocre attempts to fix this issue, our savior emerged. Linus Torvalds, the hero of every fervent Linux developer, rescued us by creating Git. This resolved the issue of version control software definitively.

Unfortunately, Git was not yet the final solution. It was still possible to write poor quality code and merge it into the master branch. The only solution left was to dismiss this malicious developer.

But now comes the real solution: merge requests (MR), also known as pull requests, and code reviews. No user is able to make changes on the master branch all by themselves anymore. Before merging changes into the master branch, a user

---

[4] 97 Things Every Programmer Should Know. Henney et al.

[5] Software Engineering at Google, Winters et al.

needs to create a public request and wait for someone else to accept it. Only then can the other developer allow the changes to be merged into the master branch.

Now, there are a few things to consider regarding code reviews. First of all, code reviews are great not only for keeping the code quality up to date but also for improving the programming skills of all developers. They are a great opportunity for knowledge exchange. Developers are obligated to look at each other's code and thereby learn a lot.

Drawbacks

However, there are some downsides as well. They can be severe enough that teams have even stopped using MRs altogether. Most importantly, everyone has to adhere to the rules. There is no way to prevent foul play by developers sabotaging the system in a way that renders the MRs useless or even counterproductive.

The first problem is people accepting merge requests without commenting, possibly without even reviewing the MR. This could be due to a lack of understanding, laziness, time constraints, or simply to do the MR author a favor. It might be more beneficial to avoid using MRs altogether.

The second issue is speed, which is crucial. It is of utmost importance to review MRs as quickly as possible. Prolonged idle times for MRs result in a significant decrease in developers' productivity. Moreover, it is highly frustrating to wait for an MR to be reviewed and not be able to continue working.

Another very serious problem is overly long MRs. It may be impossible to judge the quality of a change with a hundred lines of code. It is advisable to keep the tickets, commits, and MRs small. Enormous MRs are a waste of time as they make it difficult for others to understand the changes being made. If a ticket becomes too lengthy, it is recommended to divide the code into several MRs and ensure that tickets are kept smaller in the future. Though the better solution is to keep the tickets small in the first place.

There is a widespread and fundamental misunderstanding regarding MRs. Don't expect the referee to find bugs; this is absolutely impossible. The referee doesn't have time to think through all these details. The author is responsible for writing error-free code along with good test coverage to prove that it is most certainly free of bugs. MRs are more about the general structure of the code and knowledge exchange. The referee can only check that there is a reasonable amount of test coverage.

Always be polite. Giving feedback in an MR is akin to critiquing someone's code via email. It is a delicate task, so maintain professionalism by focusing your comments on the code itself, not the author. If discussions escalate to yelling in MRs, it may be time to consider leaving the job. From my experience, the situation worsened during the COVID-19 pandemic when many developers had to work from home, and my coworkers and I didn't meet anymore regularly. It requires strong team spirit to handle written feedback in MRs effectively.

One thing I can highly recommend is looking at the code together, kind of a pair reviewing. In theory, the referee is supposed to understand the code all by themselves, or at least that's my understanding of an MR. However, discussing the code with the author turns out to be a really good alternative, especially for long or important MRs. Additionally, it keeps up the human touch. It is much harder to insult someone orally than written. This is a highly important feat.

Conclusions

In case you engage in pair programming, you may skip the code review phase altogether since two developers have already agreed that the code is acceptable. Pair programming also enables your team to share knowledge that would otherwise need to be addressed during the code review. This is one of the reasons why pair programming does not necessitate to double the time. The code review process would consume a significant amount of time, which can be saved through pair programming.

For teams with little experience, I believe it is still important to create merge requests. In my opinion, the benefits outweigh the drawbacks. However, this is only effective if everyone adheres to the rules and provides prompt feedback.

With highly experienced programmers, on the other hand, one can skip the code reviews and engage in high-level discussions about the code instead. This approach is faster and typically just as effective. Highly experienced programmers only need to coordinate the high-level abstractions and do not have to review the low-level details. I hope your team reaches this stage quickly as it can significantly enhance productivity.

I generally recommend conducting code reviews. However, if code reviews become burdensome, which can easily happen, you have to reconsider your approach to work and perhaps explore alternative methods to disseminate information about your code. Just remember that sharing knowledge is crucial, albeit quite costly.

Agile

> *All architectures become iterative because of unknown unknowns. Agile just recognizes this and does it sooner.*
> —Mark Richards

Agile is the de facto industry standard when it comes to planning and executing software projects. But it has not always been this way. So how did we get here, and what does Agile actually mean?

Problems of Waterfall

Until the early 2000s, most software development teams followed the waterfall model. Every project involved analysis, design, and implementation phases. While this approach seemed logical and was widely adopted, planning software in a top-down manner proved ineffective. It was not possible to anticipate every detail of the complex process, and evolving requirements exacerbated the situation. In short, most waterfall projects ended in disaster.

The primary issue with the waterfall model was the absence of feedback. The entire project was a massive workload, making it impossible to provide a realistic time estimate for completion. Numerous projects failed dramatically because, at the deadline, a substantial portion of the workload remained unfinished, and no one had alerted the management in advance.

The main issue, however, was that people had the wrong mindset. They assumed that one could plan software development like building a house. The common belief was that one could create a plan at the beginning and then assemble a team of developers to carry it out. This approach, however, usually didn't work out. There is this severe misunderstanding that an architect could plan a house and leave the construction of the house to the workers. This is simply not true. The architect must visit the construction site regularly to address emerging issues. And in software engineering, it's even worse because every project is unique, requiring even more improvisation. Moreover, another significant problem was that the team was operating in waterfall mode, which hindered their ability to adapt to changing requirements or address issues that arose during the implementation process.

Agile Was Born

When planning a project, there are three simple truths:[6]

1. It is rarely possible to gather all the requirements at the beginning of a project.
2. Users will change their minds.
3. There will always be more to do than time and money will allow.

These three truths are the reasons why the waterfall approach was never going to work. Instead, a more adaptive approach was needed – a more ... agile one.

In 2001, a group of software engineers met for two days in the Rocky Mountains to enhance the planning of software projects. The outcome was the Agile Manifesto,[7,8] a concise guideline on how software development should be approached. The key principle is to prioritize working on the most crucial task first (the manifesto

---

[6] www.zuehlke.com

[7] https://agilemanifesto.org/

[8] Clean Agile. Robert C. Martin.

is articulated in a broader manner, but this is its core). Subsequently, the process involves iteration. It is advised not to begin with minor details that could potentially be deemed irrelevant later on.

Another part of the Agile Manifesto is the Bill of Rights.[9] Both developers and customers have their own rights. This serves as a constitution for software development. Like any legal document, it involves making trade-offs. However, it is definitely worth a read.

Work Planning

The product owner has a set of requirements that the code should fulfill. This workload is broken down into small tickets. I would like to emphasize the word small. Each ticket should be manageable by one person during one sprint, preferably even smaller.

Every task is estimated based on the amount of work it will require. The task size is measured in story points, which is an arbitrary unit used to assign a relative size to tasks. However, story points are intentionally kept vague to signify that they are rough estimates. Typically, in projects, a story point represents either half a day or one day of work.

The ticket size is estimated during the sprint planning meeting, where the next sprint is planned. Each ticket's number of story points is estimated by the team. Typically, each developer provides a hidden estimation, and the average becomes the number of story points assigned to the ticket. If there is a significant difference in the estimations, the team needs to discuss the reasons behind it. It could be due to a missed difficulty or that most developers underestimated the task. Unfortunately, this ticket estimation process does not always work effectively. It requires thorough planning so that all developers understand the ticket requirements. Otherwise, the estimations can be significantly inaccurate, especially when the ticket is not well-defined. In such cases, the ticket may need to be divided into smaller tickets.

For these reasons, there are attempts to work without any estimations of ticket size. The approach is to cut the tickets as small as possible and count the number of tickets instead.[10] This method, known as story-based velocity, has the advantage that you don't have to do the notoriously imprecise estimation of the ticket size. Breaking down the tickets into as small chunks as possible is recommended.

Tickets all have inherent business value as they must directly and measurably impact the user. This implies that each ticket represents a comprehensive segment across the software stack, spanning from the database, through the back-end code, and up to the GUI. All components must be addressed within a single ticket. Therefore, you either possess the necessary expertise to work on every layer of the

---

[9] https://www.informit.com/articles/article.aspx?p=2990402&seqNum=3

[10] https://youtu.be/go_pLBt8PP8

software stack independently, or you collaborate with a team member to engage in pair programming to bridge any knowledge gaps.

At the same time, one can write functional tests for every ticket: "... if the user clicks x, then the window closes." This test also serves as the acceptance criterion for the ticket. The ticket is considered accepted if the functional test passes.

The acceptance criteria of a ticket have to be SMART:[11]

- Specific: Use examples with values.
- Measurable: You have to be able to test it.
- Achievable: It should not depend on third parties.
- Relevant: It should be important to the user.
- Time-bound: It should be done in a reasonable timeframe.

Quality Assurance

In waterfall projects, Quality Assurance (QA) teams used to manually search for bugs in the existing software. However, this approach no longer aligns with the agile workflow. In the current scenario, QA should be responsible for writing functional tests for each ticket. Ideally, these tests should be created before developers complete their work on the respective ticket. This practice is akin to Test-Driven Development (TDD) and is known as Behavior-Driven Development (BDD).

Finishing the functional tests before the developers complete the actual ticket is a challenging task. One way to mitigate this issue is by working ahead. The QA team can strive to be half a sprint ahead. However, this is not easy as the sprint planning has not been completed yet. On the other hand, the project manager should have a good understanding of what will follow in the next sprint.

Sprints

In Agile, the entire project is divided into pieces lasting one to four weeks, known as sprints. Each sprint involves sprint planning, time for implementing features, and a sprint presentation meeting at the end to discuss the sprint's outcomes. This framework provides regular feedback on the project's progress, enabling the project manager to assess the current progress and estimate roughly how long it will take to reach the next milestone. This progress can also serve as a monitoring tool to evaluate the development team's performance.

The first meeting of a sprint is the planning. It involves the entire team discussing the tickets and deciding which ones to include in the sprint. The sprint planning for a two-week sprint may take half a day.

---

[11] Zühlke, www.zuehlke.com

A chapter of the meeting involves the planning game (p. 261), where the story points for each ticket are estimated. This is necessary to plan the scope of the next sprint.

Next is the daily meeting. This meeting is not mandatory and it's very short. It is kind of replacing the coffee machine gossip. Everyone very briefly says what they are doing at the moment and if there are any blockers. There are no discussions in this meeting. Discussions are held afterward. The daily meeting may seem like a waste of time to the developers. But it is really important for the PM and PO to keep up with the work being done by the team.

Toward the end of the sprint, the software developers present their work in the sprint presentation meeting. The purpose of this meeting is for all stakeholders to understand the current status of the software. Hopefully, the developers are proud to showcase their completed work.

The last meeting is the retrospective. Here, the team meets to discuss anything that could improve the productivity of the development process. This includes issues such as why the ticket size was estimated incorrectly, blockers that were not resolved for too long, unresolved MRs, etc.

Becoming Agile

What I tried to explain in this chapter so far was supposed to be something like a manual on how to become Agile. The real effort, however, lies ahead of you. There is no Agile manual. It is more like a meta-framework. It defines rules how you can define your own rules. You can extend this framework in many possible directions, whether it makes sense or not.

The most important point from Agile is that you have to figure out by yourself what works best. And be honest with yourself. It may be more convenient to work alone for several weeks and hand in a pile of work in the end than spending some time in meetings every two weeks. You don't know how your colleagues are doing. You lack knowledge of how you are progressing. And not only you but also your PM would like to know how things are going. This is a pretty important aspect of Agile: you gain a lot of information about the progress of the project that will help you to further plan the rest of the work.

Furthermore, there are some things that are absolutely mandatory when working agile. You are not planning the whole software all at once in the beginning. Instead, you have to be able to adapt. Your code has to be flexible. What most people don't understand is that they would have to remain flexible even in waterfall mode, as planning everything from scratch isn't effective.

In order to be flexible, you have to be able to adapt your code. You have to change its structure. You have to refactor. This is a challenging task, and you're probably afraid that you may break something. But it's inevitable. You have to be able to change your code; that's your job. Instead, you have to mitigate your fear of breaking the code. The only way to do so is through automated tests. Loads of them. Practically every single line of your code should be covered by a test. This is the only way Agile can truly excel.

Drawbacks of Agile

Agile is an empirical approach to improve processes. The continuous feedback loop in the process is supposed to enhance the entire software development process. However, it is not simple. It always involves balancing different interests, and often the success of Agile depends on subtle nuances. A friend of mine used Kanban, a method where all tasks are written on paper with quite some success. However, using a digital version did not yield the same results for him. The effectiveness of Kanban relied on numerous small details that were not replicated in the digital version. For instance, it was much easier to notice issues on paper, such as when a task was too lengthy. In contrast, in the digital version, one could easily minimize the task description, concealing the problem.

Another very common problem is the number of meetings. While there is a need to coordinate the work done by team members and keep the marketing team informed about progress, excessive meetings can slow down the team and be counterproductive. Therefore, it is important to constantly assess the effectiveness of each meeting.

Finally, Agile does not solve the problem of inaccurate estimations of the total workload. Although these estimations are less imprecise than they used to be with waterfall, the issue remains that nobody truly knows the exact amount of work required. Estimating the total workload remains an extremely challenging task. While you may have a backlog with tickets and possibly even some vague estimations of their sizes, the total amount of work remaining is still quite uncertain. The actual workload only becomes clear as time progresses.

Requirements Engineering

The most difficult part of requirements gathering is not the act of recording what the user wants, it is the exploratory development activity of helping users figure out what they want.
—Steve McConnell

Written by Felix Gähler

Requirements engineering (RE) is the process of determining what should be implemented. As we have learned in our four rules of software engineering, code should only be implemented if it is truly beneficial for our customers.

It may be surprising why this chapter is even needed. Isn't it obvious what you have to implement? Unfortunately, no. Many times it is highly unclear what you have to implement. You could quickly waste a few hundred thousand dollars if the development team spends a few months developing a feature that isn't used in the end. It is, therefore, crucial to always be aware of what and why you are developing.

Figure 10-1 The different stakeholders and their importance

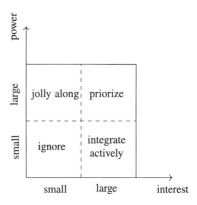

Stakeholders

As is often the case, a significant portion of your work involves interacting with other people. You must discern who holds genuine importance and who simply perceives themselves as important. Additionally, you need to navigate the various personalities within the team and adjust your approach accordingly. This involves understanding company politics. If you are not at ease with this aspect, it may be preferable to remain in software development rather than transitioning to requirements engineering.

Stakeholders are all individuals with an interest in the system. If I forget to consult a stakeholder, they will not be content in the end. Therefore, I compile a stakeholder list, where I assess the level of their interest and power. A stakeholder with significant power must be satisfied, even if their interest is minimal. Stakeholders with high interest but low power should be actively engaged as they are often the primary users. Stakeholders with both high interest and power should be given priority. Those with low interest and low power can be disregarded, even if they are making the most noise.

Goals, Context, and Scope

First, you have to ask yourself what goals you want to achieve with the new system. It is important to define the goals as completely and consistently as possible. They should also be weighted according to their importance. It is worth investing some time in a precise goal description, which is coordinated with the stakeholders.

You always have to be aware of what exactly belongs to the new system and what does not (system boundary or scope). This also includes determining what actually belongs to the system and what is predetermined from the outside. Items within the scope can also be modified during the project.

The scope and context can be represented in a use case diagram. This diagram illustrates how actors influence components of the system.

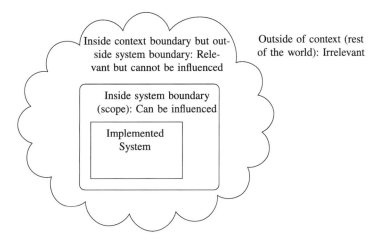

Figure 10-2 Context, scope, and system

In the scope and context, there is initially a gray area. The smaller this area is, the lower the risk of the project. It is therefore worthwhile to determine the context and especially the scope as precisely as possible and to update it regularly in the case of iterative approaches.

Goals, context, and scope form the framework within which the requirements can now be determined.

Requirements Elicitation

Just as writing good code, describing a requirement in a ticket is equally challenging. It should be concise yet clear and well received by developers. Not everything that appears logical to the author of a ticket may be logical for the developer tasked with its implementation.

It's best to include a few examples in the ticket, which can also serve as test cases. These examples should encompass both the "happy case" and boundary conditions, as well as special cases. The latter is often overlooked. For instance, in a bank transfer, it is crucial to prevent the transfer of a negative amount.

The requirements should be formulated as neutrally as possible. They should describe the *what* and not the *how*. The author of the feature should ideally have no knowledge of the technical details of the code. Additionally, developers often have better ideas on how to implement something than external individuals.

It is crucial to involve stakeholders in the requirements elicitation process. This task is challenging, time-consuming, and labor-intensive. I strive to gather as much information as possible and to effectively engage with the stakeholders.

If you think it would be easy to find the requirements for a new system, you are mistaken. The users, both external and internal to the company, are not eager to spend hours discussing the pros and cons of the software with you. They have work to do. Events like company outings and social gatherings can be beneficial.

Sometimes, surveys and interviews can provide more insight. The key is to be a good listener, so that people feel comfortable sharing their concerns with you and trust you.

Furthermore, you must also inform yourself independently about the topic, not solely relying on the users for information. It is crucial to consider not just what the software is capable of, but, more importantly, what the customers desire. Often, one's perspective is too limited. For instance, Nokia resisted developing a smartphone in the early 2000s, despite an engineer's suggestion. Nokia failed to see the potential market for a keyboard-less phone.

The most important sources are

- The stakeholders: Clients, customers, users, managers, operators, developers, architects, testers
- Documents: Laws, norms, standards, concepts, specialist articles, error reports
- Existing systems: Old systems, predecessor systems, surrounding systems, competitor systems

When determining the requirements, there are three different factors:

- The basic factors are often overlooked as they are considered self-evident. However, they must not be forgotten.
- The performance factors are the focus of the users and are usually discussed.
- The enthusiasm factors are those that a user desires, even if they are not aware of it. If you identify these features, you have done an excellent job.

The best way to identify all the fundamental factors, performance factors, and enthusiasm factors is to integrate various survey techniques. Conduct interviews to explore performance factors and utilize creative methods like workshops or brainstorming sessions for enthusiasm factors. Field observation is ideal for identifying basic factors, which interviewees may consider self-evident and thus may not mention at all.

For example, in a hotel, the availability of toilet paper is not mentioned, as it is considered self-evident. However, it can be a problem if it is missing when you are sitting on the toilet!

Documentation of the Requirements

It is best to document the requirements continuously during interviews, workshops, etc. The same or very similar requirements are mentioned repeatedly. Therefore, it makes sense to record the requirements in a consistent format to easily identify duplicates.

I document the requirements in natural language. This approach allows nontechnical readers, suppliers, customers, and managers to be addressed. Stakeholders do not need to learn a tool first; they can work without training.

With the assistance of a glossary, I can define terms utilized in the requirements. This practice helps prevent misunderstandings. For example, the abbreviation

"ABC" can have different meanings in different contexts. It may mean "abstract base class," but also "American Broadcasting Company." The glossary clarifies the meaning of the term in the context of the requirements.

I also document the requirements using formal models. These models help identify gaps and contradictions and streamline the development of solution models. A model is akin to a map, offering a simplified representation of reality that highlights only the pertinent aspects. Each model presents this representation from a specific viewpoint. Hence, it is beneficial to create multiple models that depict reality from various perspectives. Examples of formal models are use case models and class diagrams.

Prioritization of Requirements

You should begin with the most crucial tickets since it is unlikely that you will be able to implement all of them. The requirements should be prioritized (in consultation with the stakeholders). It is common for each stakeholder to want to see "their" requirement at the top of the list. To address this conflict objectively, there are prioritization models like WSJF (Weighted Shortest Job First). This model optimizes economic benefits by comparing the costs of delay and implementation effort. The challenge lies in accurately estimating these costs and benefits.

Quality Assurance of the Requirements

It is much easier and more cost-effective to fix a bug in the requirements phase than in the testing phase or during production (p. 109). Hence, it is advisable to scrutinize the requirements before their implementation. Common errors include inaccurate, incomplete, conflicting, or unrealistic requirements.

A simple and effective method is the review. A moderator invites stakeholders as reviewers, goes through the requirements with them, and creates a list of findings with weighting. Based on the findings, the requirements are then corrected accordingly.

The reviewed and accepted requirements form the baseline for development.

Administration of Requirements

In a small project, the requirements can easily be managed in a text document. Nevertheless, it is beneficial to assign a unique ID to each requirement for reference purposes. This ID can also be utilized for documenting the code.

Requirements have other attributes in addition to ID and description. The most important ones include

- Source of the requirement: This is important for queries.
- Priority of the requirement
- Status of the requirement: Has it been implemented, tested, and accepted?
- Verification tests are used to check whether the requirement is implemented correctly.

It is also important to manage changes systematically. If a requirement changes during the project, I document precisely what was changed and when. The altered requirement must undergo review again and be accepted. Subsequently, the question arises as to where in the already implemented software the change will have an impact.

In security-relevant systems, traceability is a must. This includes tracing back from the functional test to the source of the requirement.

Tools for Requirements Management

For a one-person project, requirements can easily be handled in a text document. But as soon as several people work on a project, it is better to have a tool for managing and tracking the requirements, ordering them by priority, assigning them to a developer, adding specifications and test cases, and tracking the status until completed.

An easy-to-use example of such a tool is Nulab.[12] On this website, the first step is to register the projects and team members. Then the requirements and other backlog items, for example, bugs, can be entered and tracked. The items can be assigned to a team member and given a status like "in progress" or "resolved."

An example of a powerful tool for big projects is Atlassian Jira.[13] With this tool, large numbers of requirements can be grouped and managed in the context of the development methodology used, for example, Scrum. Add-ons can be installed that support coordination of several teams and track dependencies between teams. It helps prioritize the requirements based on estimated cost and benefit. It also allows for documenting test cases, test automation, and tracking of detected errors.

DevOps

Development and Operations, short DevOps, is the combination of Continuous Integration (CI) and Continuous Delivery (CD). In short, it is automating everything from the build, tests, to the release. But in order to understand more precisely behind DevOps, we have to take a look at how software development teams used to work in the early 2000s. What kind of problems they had that DevOps promises to solve.

The Early 2000s

In the early 2000s, working with code was tedious. Not only were Integrated Development Environments (IDEs) lacking a lot of functionality that we take for granted nowadays, also building a project was usually a tedious task. Many projects were lacking a one-click build, and instead the developers had to go through a series

---

[12] https://nulab.com

[13] https://jira.atlassian.com/

of steps in order to build the executable. Then they used SVN as a version control tool because there was nothing better available back then. They could just merge their code on to trunk (something similar to the main branch in git), possibly even without a merge request. And no one knew whether the code was really working. Code could go into production without anyone ever checking that it was working out! You could have even merged a commit that broke the build!

Most teams were not writing tests for their code. It just wasn't fashion back then. Only with the advent of Extreme Programming (XP)[14] and with the Agile Manifesto in 2001,[15] testing started taking up. This was certainly a milestone for the software development, but it added another problem to it. So far, you had to do a build, which was already quite tedious. Now you also had to build and run the tests. It sounds easy, but once you consider that you don't just have one kind of test, but several different ones, it becomes apparent that doing all the builds by hand wouldn't scale anymore. You have unit tests, integration tests, functional tests, performance tests, etc. The only way to keep up with all this new work is automating it. Continuous Integration was born. Not only the build and the formatting of the code was automated. Everything was automated. Code could only be merged if all the invariants were met:

- The code is formatted according to specification.
- The static code analysis passes.
- The build passes.
- Building all the tests works.
- All the tests pass.

Even though there are companies that don't care about the formatting anymore, they just let the formatter run for every merge request on the server. Locally the developers can use whatever format they like. This takes some effort to set up the CI/CD pipeline, but it saves work for the developers.

Then there is also the task of creating an executable. It used to take many manual steps as well, which was again slow and error-prone. Now this is part of the Continuous Delivery.

We have the development (Dev) and the IT operations (Ops) bundled all together; these steps form DevOps. DevOps is automating everything that has to do with building, testing, and releasing of the new software.

Getting a Project

Furthermore, getting started to work with an existing project was frequently a pain. There were so many things that could have gone wrong. "Where do I get the source code from?" "What libraries do I have to install?" "Why does the build not work?" "Ah, I have to use that specific version of this library?"

---

[14] Extreme Programming Explained: Embrace Change. Kent Beck.

[15] http://agilemanifesto.org/

It was a pain. And in many companies, it still is. There is a simple rule about getting started: it has to work with one command. Getting the repository has to be one command, setting up all the libraries has to be one command, building it has to be one command, and running the executable has to be one command as well. If it's any more than one command per step, you have to write a script that does the work for you.

Benefits of DevOps

DevOps has several benefits; among them are[16]

- Speed: Teams that use DevOps have a significantly faster development cycle. Building, testing, and releasing software become much faster.
- Collaboration: DevOps improves collaboration between team members, for example, due to merge requests. This makes teams more efficient.
- Rapid deployment: DevOps allows for rapid deployment. This has become more and more important in the last years.
- Reliability: DevOps improves the reliability of the software. It is easier to find bugs and fix them. Also, the software is more stable as it is tested more thoroughly.

All together it can be said that DevOps is a real game changer and should be used in every software project, despite the initial cost of setting up the CI/CD pipeline.

Mental Health

I didn't really think about this topic until I watched just another random YouTube video about this topic. It's not exactly the topic I wanted to write about in this book to begin with, but as I look at the other chapters around here, it probably makes sense to write about it as well – because mental health is a huge problem in software engineering. Trust me, I've been there as well. Of course, there are also physical problems because we sit too much. But probably more prevalent are mental health issues.

First of all, we have to agree to the fact that we are not machines. We are humans. Our brain is just one of our organs, and it can be damaged. And the most common cause of brain damage is excessive amounts of adrenaline and cortisone, two stress-related hormones. These hormones are great as they allowed us to suppress pain and gain powers to fight off wild animals. But when exposed to them for a long time, they seriously damage our bodies and brains. And this frequently happens in software engineering. We are constantly under pressure to deliver and do not have

---

[16] https://www.atlassian.com/devops

sufficient time to calm down again. In the long term, this is a serious issue as it causes burnout and depression.

One thing you certainly have to be aware of is your working hours. Working more does not make you more productive. You might work overtime before an important deadline, and your adrenaline boost may help you with it. But this is no sustainable working model. You'll need some time to calm down again. Working less might in fact make you more productive. I usually work only 80% (= 33 hours a week in Switzerland) because of this reason. Of course, I'm in this lucky position that I can afford to work less. Though some companies like Microsoft already experimented with a four-day workweek as well.[17] Furthermore, it is important that you don't respond to emails and phone calls in your free time.[18]

There are several signs when you are at the brink of a burnout, and you should take them seriously. The easiest issue to spot is sleeping problems. This can be caused by too much adrenaline and makes you feel awake all the time. However, your body and brain need some rest again to recover. In case you have serious sleeping problems, you should definitely visit a doctor and take a step down at work. Usually, you can keep up this state with too much adrenaline for quite a long time. But once you get back to a normal level of adrenaline, you break down. Your body and brain are exhausted, and you can't do anything anymore. You'll have to recover for several months before you can get back to work.

Another reason is bad mood and mobbing at the workplace. This should be addressed by your boss right away. And if they don't fix it, it's time you look for another job. You probably can't fix this on your own, and you're only risking your mental health by staying any longer. Even if you like your job, it's not worth it. And chances are that you'll find another job that you like as well. I recommend talking to some of your friends about your problems. Probably they can pinpoint some of your problems and help you solve them.

On the other hand, there are also plenty of things that can make you feel better – most notably if you have a good mood in your team. This is something that cannot be overstated. People who like working with their coworkers are less likely to suffer from mental problems and won't quit their job easily. Already the old Romans figured out that a good moral and motivation was very important for their legions, and a sense of humor was one of the criteria to be accepted into their legions.

Furthermore, a rewarding work is also very important to keep your spirits high, for example, if you frequently finish your tickets in time, and you are praised for it by your boss. On the other side, it is very depressing if your tickets are too big to be finished and you are constantly behind your schedule. This is a common issue in Agile development. Your work is only rewarding if your team is setting up realistic goals about how fast they can work.

---

[17] https://4dayweek.io/case-study/microsoft
[18] https://youtu.be/C4GOekfDrOQ

Hiring and Getting Hired

That's the moment you've all been looking forward to your whole life – your first real job, the initial position as a software engineer. But how do you get there? What is the process behind getting hired? Or rather, what should the process of getting hired look like?[19]

Hiring

Let's be honest. Unfortunately, many job application processes suck. There's no sugarcoating it. The root of the issue is simple. The application process is overseen by a manager who values numbers. They believe that having five years of professional Java development experience is a sufficient qualification. However, there are numerous developers with over ten years of experience who struggle to produce quality code. They have not taken the initiative to enhance their skills and continue to produce subpar code they were creating a decade ago. On the other hand, an individual who has worked for three different companies for one year each has likely made significant improvements in their programming skills during that time.

Instead of using bulleted lists of requirements, a company should describe in complete sentences what they are doing and specify the type of candidate they are seeking.

Similarly, for the interviews, it's about getting to know each other personally. This is a challenging task, but there's no way around it. That's why many companies hire psychologists to support the HR processes. Therefore, ask personal questions, such as what did you do at your previous job? What were the challenges you faced? How did you get along with your previous colleagues? There are hundreds of such questions, and you won't find answers to any of them on the CV nor the letter of motivation.

Avoid wasting time by asking standard Java questions like "how can I create a memory leak?" And if you ask technical questions, the Java version used should be up to date. There's no point in asking questions on outdated Java versions. And certainly don't ask them LeetCode questions. I don't understand why LeetCode became popular to begin with. I heard that in the United States, LeetCode is so common that there are now entire books about how to solve it. I think this is a complete waste of time.

Instead, you could do some pair programming during the interview. Let the applicant bring their own laptop and give them Internet access. They should be working in an environment they're used to. It's not about testing their knowledge on the latest IDE or testing framework. It's about finding out whether they're smart and sharing the same coding values as you do. It's about having fruitful discussions on the code being written, simulating a real pair programming scenario that may

---

[19] The Software Craftsman. Sandro Mancuso.

occur if the applicant is hired. This way, you probably figure out as well whether the applicant is smart, and at the same time you do something useful.

Search for applicants with that extra edge. Look for developers who are actively involved in open source projects (or writing a book :-) during their free time. There's hardly any better sign that someone is a very motivated and possibly also a skilled programmer. Join one of these software development groups, possibly sponsor an event. This is a great opportunity to network with software professionals and potentially recruit them without the need for a lengthy application process.

Keep recruiting all the time. If you hire someone under pressure, you may end up with a candidate who is not fully capable of handling the job.

Getting Hired

Getting hired does not require as much expertise as hiring someone, mainly because you are the one being invited and mostly following the hiring process. However, it is essential to remember that you are an equal participant during the application procedure. If you disagree with something, you have the option to withdraw from the recruiting process at any time.

As mentioned earlier, the purpose is to get to know each other. Therefore, feel free to ask questions. In fact, it is encouraged that you ask questions. If you're unsure about what to ask, consider inquiring about the developer's current projects and the challenges they are encountering. This can serve as a good starting point.

You shouldn't take the application process too seriously. Just be yourself. They ask for three years of experience? Well, that's what they wish for. But in reality, two years are usually enough if your application is otherwise convincing.

Make yourself visible through your application. Include any open source projects, blog posts, and conferences you have participated in. This will also serve as a strong starting point for the interview. It shows your motivation, which is a key factor in the hiring process.

Summary

Software engineering is so much more than just about writing code. You'll have to collaborate with other team members, do code reviews, and take care of your health. Go out to the real world and explore the endless possibilities and challenges of software engineering.

Glossary

I learned quite some things reading books and watching YouTube videos, even though not as much as I did when thinking about and discussing code at work. The selection of books may be somewhat biased by the algorithms used by Amazon and YouTube. There are probably plenty of other good books and videos out there, I just didn't know about them. It is also very well possible that I forgot to mention some books that I read or YouTube channels that I watched. There were simply too many. I'm also sorry that I didn't cite more books and videos. But it was really hard to keep track of where all the information came from.

Here are the books that I read for writing this book:

***The Pragmatic Programmer*, 2nd edition (Thomas, Hunt) Addison-Wesley Professional, 2019**
***Clean Code* (Robert C. Martin) Pearson, 2008**
***Code Complete* 2 (Steve McConnell) Microsoft Press, 2004**
***Clean Agile* (Robert C. Martin) Pearson, 2019**
***The Art of Readable Code* (Boswell, Foucher) O'Reilly, 2011**
***Software Engineering at Google: Lessons Learned from Programming Over Time* (Winters et al.) O'Reilly, 2020**
***97 Things Every Programmer Should Know* (Kevlin Henney et al.) O'Reilly, 2010**
***Design Patterns* (Gamma et al.) Prentice Hall, 1994**
***Domain-Driven Design* (Eric Evans) Pearson International, 2003**
***Effective C++* (Scott Meyers) Addison-Wesley Professional, 2005**
***Effective Modern C++* (Scott Meyers) O'Reilly, 2014**
***Working Effectively with Legacy Code* (Michael Feathers) Addison-Wesley, 2013**
***Refactoring*, 2nd edition (Martin Fowler) Pearson International, 2018**
***BBV Cheat Sheet* (Urs Enzler)** https://en.bbv.ch/publikationen-category/cheat-sheet-en/
Google Style Guide https://google.github.io/styleguide/

And several YouTube channels:

- @alexhyettdev
- @ArjanCodes

- @ThePrimeTimeagen
- @CodeOpinion
- @derekbanas
- @TechWithTim
- @ContinuousDelivery,

Index

A
Abstract base classes (ABC), 71–72, 85, 145–146, 160–161, 163, 267–268
Abstraction, 21, 147–148
Abstract syntax tree (AST), 183–184
Acceptance tests, 98, 262
Accessor methods, 79–80
Aggregation, 197–200
Agile
  becoming, 263–264
  de facto industry, 259
  drawbacks, 264
  quality assurance, 262
  sprints, 262–263
  truths, 260–261
  waterfall problems, 260
  work planning, 261–262
AI code generation, 13, 157
Amazon Web Services (AWS), 201
Anticorruption layer, 194
Application-level code, 23
Application programmable interface (API)
  bugs, 177
  DI, 134
  interfaces, 27–28
  levels of abstraction, 23
  testing, 98
Artificial intelligence, 8
The Art of Readable Code (book), 32, 189
Assertions, 125–126
Automated tests, 95, 125, 210

B
Behavior-driven development (BDD), 262
Beyoncé Rule, 110
Black magic code, 170
Booleans, 43
  binary system, 44
  DI, 45
  if statements, 44–45
  logic, 7–8
  for loops, 46–47
  match case statements, 45–46
Boost library, 158
Boy Scout rule, 208
Breaking up dependencies, 172
Break statement, 60
Brittle tests, 82, 121–122, 149
Bugs
  cost, 176
  feature, 176
  fixing, 178
  refactoring, 205
  reports, 176–177
  tracking down, 177–178
  worst-case scenario, 175
Bus factor, 254–255

C
C++
  classes, 163
  const, 163
  description, 161
  hiding complexity, 170
  low-level languages, 163–164
  passing function arguments, 162
  smart pointers, 162
  structs, 163
  vectors, 161–162
Circular dependency, 172–173
Class diagram, 190
Classes, 43
  abstract base, 71–72
  C++, 163
  constructors and destructors, 76–77
  coupling and cohesion, 81–82
  data class, 66, 68
  delegating, 69, 198

278   Index

drawbacks, 84–85
functions *vs.* methods, 75–76
getter and setter methods, 77–80
implementation, 72
inheritance, 72–74 (*see also* Inheritance)
OO programming, 65
private/public, 66–67
pure method, 68–69
recommendations, 74–75
refactoring, 213–215
special, 71
static expression, 83
structs, 66
types, 82–83
unit tests, 102–103
worker, 70–71
Clean Code (book), 48
Code duplication, 6, 16
Code interfaces, 26
Code review, 257–259
  drawbacks, 258–259
Cohesion, 6, 81–82, 144, 147, 185, 212
Collisions, 32, 35
Command line, 224
Comma-separated values (CSV), 247
Commented-out code, 241
Comments
  bad, 238–241
  commented-out code, 241
  AI code generation, 245
  docstring, 243
  documentation, 237
  magic numbers, 244–245
  replacing code, 242
  requirements, 242–243
  TODO, 241–242
  writing, 244
Communication, 256
Compile-time constants, 52, 55–56
Complexity
  black magic code, 170
  of code, 167–168
  estimation, 168–169
  precision and accuracy, 169
  single-line, 169–170
Complicated code, 10–11
Composition, 87, 89–90
Conduct interviews, 267
Constructors, 19, 71, 75, 76–77, 217
Context map, 194
Continue statement, 60
Continuous delivery (CD), 269
Continuous integration (CI), 107, 113, 194, 250–251, 269–270

AI code generation
  comments, 245
  data files, 250
  functions, 61–62
  interfaces, 31
  naming, 37–38
  refactoring, 220–222
  unit tests, 104
Correlation, 165
Coupling, 147, 174
  and cohesion, 81–82
  and inheritance, 83
  ISP, 144
  software architecture, 185
  temporal, 154–156
Custom exceptions, 179
Custom file formats, 250
Cyclic dependency, 171

D

Databases (DBs), 249–250
Database-syntax-free zone, 202
Data classes, 66, 68
  getter and setter methods, 78–79
Data files
  AI code generation, 250
  CSV, 247
  custom file formats, 250
  databases, 249–250
  formats, 246
  HDF5, 248–249
  JSON and Co, 247–248
Data types
  Booleans, 44–47
  description, 39–40
  enums, 42–44
  filtering lists, 41–42
  lists, 40–41
  strings, 47–49
DDD, *see* Domain-driven design (DDD)
Debugger, 7, 79, 99, 177
Debugging, 177
Decorator pattern, 187
Decoupling, 174
Delegating class, 69, 74, 84, 198
  getter and setter methods, 80
Dependencies
  breaking up, 172
  circular, 172–173
  early days, 171
  example, 173
  graph, 171–172

Index

Dependency injection (DI), 8, 44–45, 98, 102, 104, 121
    API, 134
    definition, 134
    drawback, 136
    functions, 137
    I/O, time and random numbers, 136–137
    legacy code, 224
    polymorphic code, 136
    refactoring, 216
    solution, 135
    testing, 135, 149
    third-party library, 201
Dependency injector, 216–218
Dependency inversion principle (DIP), 145–146
Dependent tests, 120–121
Descriptive and Maintainable Procedures (DAMP), 114
Design for flexibility, 148
Design for testability, 149
Designing interfaces, 184
Design patterns
    definition, 185
    end of, 187
    factory, 185–186
Destructors, 19, 71, 75, 76–77
Developer-client relationship, 194
Development and Operations (DevOps)
    benefits, 271
    definition, 269
    early 2000s, 269–270
    getting project, 270–271
Diamond problem, 87
Dictionaries, 15, 50
Directed acyclic graph, 171
Distributed system, 177
Divide and conquer algorithms, 146–147
Division by zero exception, 179
Docstring, 243
Domain-driven design (DDD), 6, 23
    anticorruption layer, 194
    boundaries, 193
    bounded context, 193
    building blocks
        aggregates, 197–200
        entities, 195
        services, 197
        value object, 196–197
    conformist, 194–195
    context map, 194
    definition, 188
    developer-client relationship, 194
    documentation, 190–191
    domain levels, 191–192
    domain model, 189–190
    DSL, 192
    implementation, 191
    separate ways, 194
    shared kernel, 194
    ubiquitous language, 188–189
    UML diagrams, 189–190
    unified model, 193
Domain model, 23, 168, 189–190
Domain-specific language (DSL), 192
Do not repeat yourself (DRY) principle, 6, 250
    copy-pasted code/conceptual duplication, 14
    dictionaries, 15
    exceptions, 15
    polymorphism, 14–15
    procedural violation, 99
    social security number, 14
Double-entry bookkeeping, 112–113

E

Emergence, 18
Encapsulation, 102
End-to-end (E2E) tests, 98
Enterprise-wide codebase, 193
Entities, 195
Entropy, 164, 204
Enums, 42–44, 144
Exceptions, 122–123
    catching and re-raising, 180
    and goto, 180–181
    invalid state, 178–179
    logical errors, 178
    try-except blocks, 180
    wrapping, 179–180
Explorative tests, 107, 108
Extract function, 219–220
Extreme programming (XP), 270

F

Factory pattern, 185–186
Faking, 133–134
Fast Fourier Transform (FFT), 147
Filtering lists, 41–42
Final keyword, 88
"Fizz Buzz" game, 9
Flaky tests, 121
For loops, 46–47
Formal models, 268
Fourier Transform, 148, 236
Friend classes, 90

Functionality, 28, 144
Functional programming, 151–154, 174, 196
Functional tests, 6, 23–24, 98, 100, 105–106, 110, 124–125
Functions
  arguments, 10, 116, 211–212
  break and continue, 60
  AI code generation, 61–62
  definition, 57
  DI, 137
  levels of indentation, 58–60
  vs. methods, 75–76
  number of arguments, 60–61
  one line of code, 58
  output arguments, 62
  return values, 63

G
get() function, 162
Getter methods
  data classes, 78–79
  definition, 77–78
  delegating classes, 80
  worker classes, 79–80
Getting hired, 274
Gherkin approach, 192
Global variables, 55, 65, 87, 174, 227–228
Goto statement, 180–181
Graphical programming, 190
Graphical user interface (GUI), 23–24, 105–106

H
HDF5, 248–249
Helper functions, 118–119
High-level design
  DDD (*see* Domain-driven design (DDD))
  design patterns, 185–187
  software architecture, 183–185
  third-party software, 200–202
Hiring, 273–274
Humble Object, 101, 105
Hyrum's law, 208

I
Image processing algorithms, 123
Immutable variables, 52–53, 56
Implementation class, 72

Implementation inheritance
  definition, 85
  drawbacks
    error-prone, 86
    obscure code, 87
    overriden base class functions, 87–88
    tight coupling, 86
Independent testers, 108
Infrastructure code, 22–23
Inheritance, 174
  abstract base classes, 73
  advantages, 88–89
  and composition, 89–90
  conclusions, 90
  coupling and, 83
  description, 85
  implementation, 72–73, 85–88
  interface, 85
  issues, 73
  multiple, 87
  non-abstract base classes, 73
  override keyword, 74
  types, 85
Inherited variables, 56–57
Integers, 43
Integrated Development Environments (IDEs), 43, 269
Integration tests, 104, 108–110, 124–125
Interface inheritance, 85, 163
Interfaces, 71
  adding functionality, 28
  APIs, 27–28
  code, 26
  AI code generation, 31
  definition, 25
  designing, 184
  example, 26–27
  orthogonality, 29–31
  partial, 184
  payment method, 142
  real-world example, 25–26
  semantic versioning, 28–29
Interface segregation principle (ISP), 88, 143–145
isclose function, 114

J
JavaScript Object Notation (JSON), 247–248

K
Keyword arguments, 10

L

LeetCode, 273
Legacy code
  area of change, 229
  description, 222
  enabling point, 224, 229
  issues, 223
  micro level, 223
  no interfaces, 226
  nomenclature, 223
  no tests, 226
  pinch points, 225
  problems
    classes can't be instantiated, 227
    extremely long functions, 226–227
    global variables, 227–228
    missing enabling points, 227
    missing sensing points, 227
  refactoring untested code, 225
  seams, 224–225
  sensing point, 224, 229
  sprout method, 230–231
  testing, 228
  without tests, 229–230
  wrap function, 231–232
  writing tests, 229
Levels of abstraction, 34, 82
  API, 23
  application level, 23
  circular dependencies, 173
  code example, 24
  concept, 17
  delegation class, 74
  dependencies, 21–22
  domain level, 23
  extract function, 219
  functions, 58
  GUI and functional tests, 23–24, 106
  infrastructure code, 22–23
  layers, 21
  programming example, 19–21
  properties, 21–22
  real-world example, 17–18
  in software project, 21
  third-party libraries, 22
Levels of indentation, 58–60
Linus Torvalds' rule, 59
Linux kernel, 75, 153, 169, 180
Liskov substitution principle, 142–143
Lists, 40–41
Logging, 245–246

M

Magic numbers, 7, 34, 244–245
Match case statements, 45–46
Member variables, 54, 84
Memory allocation problem, 19
Memory management, 71, 77, 197
Mental health, 271–272
Merge requests (MRs), 107, 255, 257–259
Merge sort, 147
Microservices, 174
Mini-globals, *see* Member variables
Mocking, 132–133
Multi-paradigm programming languages, 151
Multiple inheritance, 87, 163
Mutable variables, 53, 56

N

Namespace, 83
Naming
  antipatterns
    generic names, 37
    useless words, 37
  AI code generation, 37–38
  functions, 36–37
  importance of, 32–34
  things, 34–36
Natural language, 49–50
Not automatable tests, 123
Number of arguments, 60–61

O

Object-oriented (OO) programming, 54, 63, 65, 90, 151, 152, 167, 187, 190
Obsolescence, 149
One-line functions, 58
Open-closed principle (OCP), 140–142, 213–214
Orthogonality, 25
  adapter, 31
  advantages, 31
  concept, 29
  downstream and upstream person's coordinate system, 30
  water taps, 29–30
Output arguments, 62
Overengineering, 166–167
Override keyword, 74, 86
Overriden base class functions, 87–88

P

Parameterized constructor, *see* Dependency injector
Partial interfaces, 184
Performance-critical code, 63
Performance optimization
  energy consumption, 237
  large-scale simulations, 235
  manual, 237
  test-code-refactor work cycles, 236
  v-table, 236
Performance tests, 106–107
Physical laws of code
  correlation, 165
  entropy, 164
  overengineering, 166–167
  quality, 165–166
Pointers, 51
Polymorphism, 14–15, 44, 46
The Pragmatic Programmer (book), 29
Primitive obsession, 39–40
Private method, 66–67, 102, 110
Problematic tests
  brittle, 121–122
  dependent, 120–121
  flaky, 121
Procedural programming, 151–153
Product manager (PM), 105
Programming languages
  AI code generator, 157
  C++, 161–164
  code examples, 158
  complexity, 167–170
  description, 157
  dynamic typing, 157
  existing, 158
  Python, 159–161
Programming paradigms, 151–152
Project manager (PM), 254
Project owner (PO), 254
Protocols, 160–161
Public method, 66–67, 102, 110
Pull requests, *see* Merge requests (MRs)
Pure functions, 153–154
Pure method class, 68–69
Pytest, 96
Python
  abstract base classes and protocols, 160–161
  data class, 66
  elements, 63
  helper function, 24
  pointers, 51
  slots, 160
  testing library, 96
  type hints, 159

Q

Quality assurance (QA), 94, 262, 268
Quality of test code, 114
Quality spectrum, 165–166
Quantum mechanics, 18

R

RAII, *see* Resource Acquisition Is Initialization (RAII)
Random numbers, 122
Recursion, 154
Refactoring, 4, 73, 93, 112, 130–131
  breaking classes, 211
  bugs, 205
  changing legacy code, 222–232
  circle of doom, 207–208
  AI code generation, 220–222
  definition, 203
  dependency injector, 216–218
  dynamic, 207
  extract function, 219–220
  fundamentals, 203–205
  large-scale, 206
  levels, 206
  methods, 211–212
  minor scale, 205
  problems, 210–211
  process, 209
  recommendations, 208–209
  renaming, 215
  safety net, 204–205
  scratch, 218–219
  splitting classes, 213–215
  structuring variables, 212–213
  TDD, 205
  techniques, 210
Refactoring (book), 210
Requirements engineering (RE)
  administration, 268–269
  definition, 264
  documentation, 267–268
  elicitation, 266–267
  goals, context and scope, 265–266
  prioritization, 268
  quality assurance, 268
  stakeholders, 265
  tools, 269
Resource Acquisition Is Initialization (RAII), 20, 197

Return values, 63
Reusability, 148
Rule of zero C + +, 76–77
Runtime constant, 52
Runtime polymorphism, 85

S

Safety-critical systems, 176
Scope of variables, 12–13
Scratch refactoring, 218–219
Seams, 224–225
Self-code documenting, 58
Self-explanatory code, 8
Semantic versioning, 28–29
Set_node function, 61
Setter methods, 77–80. *See also* Getter methods
Setting up project, 250–251
Setup functions, 116–118
Shared kernel, 194
Single-argument function, 114–115
Single-line complexity, 169–170
Single responsibility principle (SRP), 1, 6, 7, 9, 35, 65, 114
  advantages
    bug fixing, 17
    easy testing, 16
    less bugs, 16–17
    naming, 16
    no duplication, 16
    understanding, 15
  aggregates, 199
  assertions, 125
  comments, 238
  definition, 13, 140
  drawbacks, 17
  DRY principle, 14–15
  functions, 61
  lists, 40
  unit tests, 100
Singletons, 57
Software architecture
  AST, 183–184
  coupling, 185
  definition, 183–184
  designing interfaces, 184
  end of architecture, 184
  separate libraries, 185
Software development process, 264
Software engineer, 254
  coding activities, 2
  description, 1–2
  rules

    cleaning up code, 4
    writing code with purpose, 4–5
    writing correct code, 3–4
    writing readable code, 2–3
  tasks, 255
  tests, 123
Software engineering. *See also* Software engineer
  coupling, 174
  entropy, 164
  interfaces, 25–31
  issues, good code, 5–8
  levels of abstraction, 17–24
  naming, 32–38
  principles
    abstraction, 147–148
    anticipate obsolescence, 149
    cohesion, 147
    coupling, 147
    design for flexibility, 148
    design for testability, 149
    divide and conquer, 146–147
    pay now/pay more later, 149–150
    reusability, 148
  rules, 2–5, 129
  speed and quality, 166
  SRP, 13–17
  testing, 94, 108
  understandable code, 8–13
Software testing, 96–97
SOLID principles
  DIP, 145–146
  ISP, 143–145
  Liskov substitution principle, 142–143
  OCP, 140–142
  rules, 139–140
  SRP, 140
Sorting algorithm, 53, 148
Spaghetti code, 9, 55
Special classes, 71
Specific, Measurable, Achievable, Relevant, Time-bound (SMART), 262
Sprints, 262–263
Sprout method, 230–231
Square function, 99
SRP, *see* Single responsibility principle (SRP)
Stakeholders, 265
Static expression, 83
Static variables, 54
Story-based velocity, 261
Strategy design pattern, *see* Dependency injection (DI)
Stringly typed objects, 47–49

Strings, 43
  description, 47
  stringly typed objects, 47–49
Structs, 66, 163
Structured objects, 115–116
Switch statement, 45
Syntax errors, 175

T
Team structure, 254
Teamwork
  bus factor, 254–255
  communication, 256
  customers, 257
  description, 253–254
  developers, 255
  structure, 254
Teardown functions, 116–118
Temporal coupling, 36–37, 154–156
Test-driven development (TDD), 26, 76, 93, 122, 149, 262
  definition, 126
  example, 128–131
  implementation, 127–128
  importance, 128
  refactoring, 205
  steps, 127–128
  YAGNI, 126–127
Testing
  assertions, 125–126
  cost of fixing bug, 109
  description, 93–94
  development team, 108
  double-entry bookkeeping, 112–113
  example, 95–96
  exceptions and, 122–123
  existing code, 125
  fakes, mocks and DI, 131–137
  features, 95
  fixing, 97
  helper functions, 118–119
  independent tester, 108
  infrastructure, 98
  not automatable, 123
  number of cases, 114–116
  problematic, 120–122
  properties, 110–112
  pyramid, 109–110
  quality of code, 114
  random numbers, 122
  recommendations, 113–114
  running, 107–108
  setup and teardown, 116–118

software structure, 96–97
stages, 116
TDD (*see* Test-driven development (TDD))
thoughts, 112
types
  explorative tests, 107
  functional tests, 105–106, 124–125
  integration tests, 104, 124–125
  performance tests, 106–107
  unit tests, 98–104, 123–124
writing, 108–109
Third-party libraries, 7, 22, 158, 177, 185, 201–202
Ticket estimation process, 261
Tight coupling, 81–82
TODO comments, 241–242
Transistors, 18
Trees, 51
Try-catch block, 180
Try-except block, 180

U
Ubiquitous language, 188–190, 192, 215
UML diagrams, 187, 189–190
Understandable code
  AI code generation, 13
  assigning variables inside conditions, 11–12
  complicated code, 10–11
  human perspective, 8–9
  scope of variables, 12–13
  spaghetti code, 9
  structuring function arguments, 10
Unified model, 193
Unit tests, 6, 48–49, 76, 93, 107, 109
  classes, 102–103
  AI code generation, 104
  example, 99–100
  execution time, 100
  function call, 124
  production code, 111
  properties, 98–99
  running, 124
  setup and teardown function, 117
  setup phase, 124
  small-scale level, 123–124
  testing files, 100–102

V
Value objects, 196–197
Variables
  comparison, 55–57

compile-time constants, 52
description, 51–52
global, 55
immutable, 52–53
member, 54
mutable, 53
refactoring, 212–213
runtime constant, 52
static, 54
Vector class, 20, 111

W
Waterfall problems, 260
Waterfall refactoring, 207
Weighted Shortest Job First (WSJF), 268
Worker class, 70–71
coupling and cohesion, 81–82
getter and setter methods, 79–80

Working Effectively with Legacy Code (book), 33, 86
Working in teams, *see* Teamwork
Worst-case scenario, 82, 175, 176
Wrap function, 101, 231–232
Wrapping exceptions, 179–180
Writing tests, 23–24, 55, 76, 84, 105, 108–109, 112, 113, 125, 227

Y
You Aren't Gonna Need It (YAGNI), 7, 126–127, 166, 184
Yo-yo problem, 88

Z
Zero arguments, 60

Printed in the United States
by Baker & Taylor Publisher Services